"The Christian tradition has long valued learning the *ars moriendi* (the art of dying), not because the faith is unduly negative or pessimistic but because it has understood the inseparable connection between one's future death and one's present life. In our contemporary Western world, we do all we can to ignore and downplay death—but living in this denial is hurting us in ways we don't even realize. Todd Billings offers us the great gift of a contemporary *ars moriendi*, providing a textured narrative that weaves together personal stories and wise theological reflection. With Todd's help we can learn to live in the shadow of death in a way that is painfully realistic, honestly liberating, and ultimately hopeful."

—**Kelly M. Kapic**, author of *Embodied Hope: A Theological Meditation on Pain and Suffering*

"Todd Billings is one of my favorite theologians. *The End of the Christian Life* highlights many of the reasons why. He writes out of a depth of personal experience and the depths of the Christian tradition. In this remarkable book Billings calls us out of the frantic avoidance of death that characterizes our culture and into the Christian practice of remembering our death. In so doing he charts the path of true flourishing and shows how we might find God amid our mortality, finitude, and limitations. Billings writes not only with the mind of a brilliant theologian but also with a pastoral heart, so his work is also practical and accessible. Here you will find a fellow traveler—and fellow mortal—whose deep love of God, commitment to the church, and profound wisdom are evident on every page."

—**Tish Harrison Warren**, priest in the Anglican Church of North America; author of *Liturgy of the Ordinary: Sacred Practices in Everyday Life*

"Wow! I needed this book more than I knew. Our culture is running from death, yet *The End of the Christian Life* is a treasure trove overflowing with theological riches and poetic reflections on the power of embracing our mortality before God. Billings is a trustworthy guide on a journey through the biblical ' ¦ pit of the grave in Sheol to the presen¦ ¦ ath to resurrection. This is a vital book ¦ iden- tity as a small yet beloved child ¦ ¦ —in the face of death."

—**Joshua Ryan Butler**, pastor of Redemption Tempe; author of *The Pursuing God* and *The Skeletons in God's Closet*

# THE END
## OF THE
# CHRISTIAN
# LIFE

How Embracing Our Mortality
Frees Us to Truly Live

# J. Todd Billings

**Brazos** Press
*a division of Baker Publishing Group*
Grand Rapids, Michigan

Published by Brazos Press
a division of Baker Publishing Group
PO Box 6287, Grand Rapids, MI 49516–6287
www.brazospress.com

Printed in the United States of America

Library of Congress Cataloging-in-Publication Data
Names: Billings, J. Todd, author.
Title: The end of the Christian life : how embracing our mortality frees us to truly live / J. Todd
  Billings.
Description: Grand Rapids, Michigan : Brazos Press, a division of Baker Publishing Group,
  2020. | Includes index.
Identifiers: LCCN 2020007100 | ISBN 9781587434204 (paperback) | ISBN 9781587435119
  (casebound)
Subjects: LCSH: Death—Religious aspects—Christianity. | Death—Biblical teaching. |
  Resurrection—Biblical teaching. | Hope—Religious aspects—Christianity. | Christian life—
  Reformed authors.
Classification: LCC BT825 .B4735 2020 | DDC 236/.1—dc23
LC record available at https://lccn.loc.gov/2020007100

20  21  22  23  24  25  26       7  6  5  4  3  2  1

In keeping with biblical principles of creation stewardship, Baker Publishing Group advocates the responsible use of our natural resources. As a member of the Green Press Initiative, our company uses recycled paper when possible. The text paper of this book is composed in part of post-consumer waste.

*To Tom and Nancy Billings*

# Contents

Introduction   9

1. Welcome to Sheol: *A Guided Tour of Life in the Pit*   21

2. Two Views of Mortality: *Is Death an Enemy or a Friend?*   49

3. Mortals in Denial: *Living as Dying Creatures*   72

4. Interplanetary Exploration: *The Strange New World of Modern Medicine*   95

5. The Way of Prosperity and the Christian Way   121

6. The Fracturing of Our Stories, and Life after Death   148

7. Hoping for the End as Mortals   177

Conclusion   213
Acknowledgments   221
Notes   223
Scripture Index   235
Subject Index   237

# Introduction

To desire eternal life with all the passion of the spirit.
To keep death daily before one's eyes.

—The Rule of St. Benedict[1]

We are all dying. This seems obvious enough, at least in the abstract. Yet in our day even this abstraction is denied by some. A Silicon Valley research foundation called SENS pursues the ambitious mission to "prevent and reverse age-related ill-health."[2] "I think it's reasonable to suppose that one could oscillate between being biologically 20 and biologically 25 indefinitely," says Chief Science Officer Aubrey de Grey. He claims that some of us living now will live one thousand years. But he also clarifies, "What I'm after is not living to 1,000. I'm after letting people avoid death for as long as they want to."[3] For de Grey, death must be approached not as the intractable end but as a tool to be taken out of the toolbox when it's convenient. Should we live each day with an awareness of death, a mortal end that shapes each season of our life? For de Grey, such an awareness seems antithetical to full human flourishing.

Imagine this in your own life. If you knew you could live to be one thousand, with your body oscillating between the biological ages of twenty and twenty-five, when would you start to think about death?

Perhaps the first 990 years would be full of safety and pleasure, like Disneyland without the high prices. If you no longer had to fear death because of aging, you would likely consider a life of hundreds of years to be what you deserve. However, even apart from the question of how much wealth and resources you would need, this vision of flourishing, upon reflection, is illusory. What about violence, virus pandemics, car accidents, and natural disasters? Would not the fear of these ways to die be magnified? Is it even possible to live as if there is no end in sight?

Although de Grey's mission of enabling a millennium-long life is far from mainstream in the medical community, it crystallizes a vision of human flourishing that many of us assume in our day-to-day lives—namely, that death doesn't apply to us, nor does it apply to those we love. And because it doesn't apply to us, we think we can live in a world "sanitized" from the reality of death, leaving it as a topic for Hollywood dramas and the news media.

However, if someone close to you has died unexpectedly or has faced a terminal diagnosis, you may have begun the process of being shaken out of this illusion. The hard fact of dying, or of living in a disease-afflicted body, punctures and deflates our hopes for the life we thought we had—perhaps the life we thought we deserved. It breaks us open. As a result, we might want to close the wound and try to return to a death-denying life, sanitized from regular reflection upon our mortal limits and our end.

For Christians, however, coming to terms with this open wound actually teaches us how to properly live and hope as creatures. Only those who *know* they are dying can properly trust in God's promise of eternal life. Christians throughout the ages have recognized this self-deceptive tendency to deny one's mortality in day-to-day life. "*Memento mori*," they said. "Remember death." In the sixth century, Benedict of Nursia gave monastic Christians the imperative quoted at the beginning of this introduction: "Keep death daily before one's eyes." Over a millennium later, New England pastor Jonathan Edwards made a regular practice of intentionally reflecting on his mortality, writing that he was resolved "to think much on all occasions of [his] own dying, and of the common circumstances which attend death."[4]

I used to think that such resolutions were for morbid people—those who eagerly awaited the newest zombie flick or Stephen King novel. But then I was diagnosed with terminal cancer.[5] In my own journey of treatment and coming to know others in the cancer community, I've realized that the process of embracing my mortality is a God-given means for discipleship and witness in the world. As strange as it seems, coming to terms with our limits as dying creatures is a life-giving path. Benedict was right: whether young or old, each of us needs a daily recovery of what it means to exist in the world as transient creatures who live and die before an eternal horizon. For Benedict, reflecting on our mortality goes hand in hand with desiring eternal life "with all the passion of the spirit."

The strange thesis of this book is that whether you are nineteen or ninety-nine, whether you are healthy or sick, or whether the future looks bright or bleak, true hope does not involve closing over the wound of death. Instead, even the wound can remind us of who we are: beloved yet small and mortal children of God, bearing witness to the Lord of creation who will set things right on the final day. Our lives are like a speck of dust in comparison to the eternal God, and we cannot be the true heroes of the world. But we can live lives of service, loving God and neighbor, in a way that does not allow the fear of death to master us.

A myriad of cultural forces tell us that we must marginalize death in our daily lives to truly flourish. But Christians should know better. As the apostle Paul says, God's good creation has been "groaning in labor pains until now" (Rom. 8:22). There is no point in denying it. In fact, Paul says that those who are in Christ and "have the first fruits of the Spirit . . . groan inwardly while we wait for adoption, the redemption of our bodies" (Rom. 8:23). In other words, when we groan with the rest of creation and as adopted children awaiting the final redemption, we join the Spirit's work. Aching and groaning is the heartbeat of our prayer, as the Spirit "intercedes" for us "with sighs too deep for words" (Rom. 8:26). Praying and living as *mortals*—accepting that we are dependent creatures fully loved by God—is an act of witness to a world that tells us to live as though our lives will never end.

Unfortunately, the church in the modern West often follows a different path. Like the culture around us, we can insulate ourselves from the groans of creation by moving our churches and homes away from neighborhoods that struggle with poverty and high crime rates. We can drown out the groans of others by keeping our eyes on the prize of rising attendance numbers among demographics that can support the church's financial future. On a personal level, we can live as though God is simply cheering us on as we add to our résumés and perform as the stars in the glorious movies of our lives. We can participate in society's practice of putting the sick and the elderly in isolated institutions, sending their groans out of earshot and thus out of the sphere of our concern. We can attend a single-generation church made up mostly of younger people and thus come to see death and dying as something of an enigma, the unfortunate lifestyle choice of an older generation.

Insulating ourselves from creation's groaning removes us from reality. When we block out the groans of others, we find ourselves unprepared when the time comes for our own groaning. We lack language for grief as we stand near the graves of our loved ones. We wonder why we didn't live differently, why we didn't understand that life is indeed short. This way of being not only denies the reality that all of us are groaning creatures of dust. More profoundly, it also masks our deepest Christian hope. It chooses death-sanitized pleasure over joy in the midst of beauty and tears. But the path of Christian discipleship involves honest and regular reminders of both our mortal limits and those of our loved ones and neighbors. The path of Christian discipleship involves moving *toward* the wound of mortality, not *away from* it. Paradoxically, this is a life-giving path, a path of freedom and love. Pushing away the reality of death is actually a form of slavery to the temporal, one that makes us cling to mortal life as though it will last forever or fulfill our ultimate needs.

The story of David and Karin Eubank has recently helped me see what overcoming this slavery can look like. After serving in the US Army for nearly a decade, David left to attend Fuller Theological Seminary, where he hoped to discern God's call for what was next. David wanted "the freedom to go where God was leading." Then he met and married Karin, and together they started Free Burma Rangers, a humanitarian aid organization helping those in war-torn areas (starting with Burma). They now live in Iraq with their three children.

Their work was out of the spotlight until some journalists saw David rescue a young girl amid the rapid gunfire of ISIS in Mosul, Iraq. The journalists were shocked—did he not fear death from gunfire? And did he not fear exposing his family to ISIS? But when he saw the trapped girl, Eubank's thought was, "If I die doing this, my wife and kids would understand." Karin expressed to the *Los Angeles Times* their rationale for bringing their kids to Iraq, with a keen awareness of the way their family receives love even as they seek to give love in the midst of conflict. "It's not like we thought 25 years ago, 'Let's take our kids to a war zone with ISIS.' But in Burma the people we worked with poured love into us, and this is more than what I can give my kids on my own," she said.[6]

David and Karin Eubank do not seek death. Indeed, they fear death to some extent. But the fear of death does not *master* them. They know that they cannot make wars cease or solve the global refugee crisis. Still, in crisis situations they give and receive love deeply and sacrificially— even joyfully.

Whether we, like the Eubanks, are in close proximity to the drama of war or far from it, we can easily become slaves to fear rather than to love. Even when we don't consciously reflect directly on our mortality, the fear of death can drive the tunnel-visioned pursuit of our self-chosen goals—for our own (and our family's) safety, for security, for the legacy we hope to leave. We trust in our own efforts to enable a flourishing life here and now rather than trusting a Savior to take on a problem that we are impotent to solve: decay and death. Yet if we are disciples of the incarnate Lord, we belong to the one who has broken the ultimate power of death. "Whether we live or whether we die, we are the Lord's," Paul testifies (Rom. 14:8). The fear and denial of death no longer need to be the driving forces of our lives.

In this book I explore how recovering a sense of our mortality can be an exercise the Spirit uses to help us cultivate authentic resurrection hope. I write as a patient with terminal cancer, as a follower of Christ, and as a theologian on pilgrimage.

For me, a reframing of death began in 2012 when I was diagnosed with an incurable cancer. I was thirty-nine, and our kids were one and three years old. Since that time, I have undergone intensive chemotherapy and a stem cell transplant, and I continue on a lower dose of chemotherapy. Each day as I worked on this book, I dealt with physical pain and heavy fatigue, both of which will likely continue for the rest of my life. At times, I share snapshots in the book from my experience as a cancer patient. Throughout, its content is shaded by this experience.

This book, however, is not a memoir. In my 2015 book, *Rejoicing in Lament*, I presented a memoir-like story of my cancer diagnosis and early treatment.[7] Interwoven with this story was a biblical and theological exploration of how my individual cancer story fits into the much more profound drama of the Triune God acting in a world gone awry. This book is not a sequel to that one, at least not in a straightforward sense. Rather, it presents the reflections of a traveler to a different culture. I live in the same town and work at the same school that I did before I was diagnosed with cancer. But what I thought was familiar has become strange. I've stepped onto a path of rediscovery. With new eyes, I've come to see what I had missed before: how life is lived among the dying. In the cancer community, the tasks of parenting, aging, exercising, and praying all take on a different cast. Since joining this community, I've developed friendships, both with the living and with some who have since died. I've also immersed myself in a range of scholarly literature that is helping me make sense of what dying means in our current cultural moment, especially for cancer patients.

I also write as a Christian—not just in my beliefs but also in my communal identity. Those who don't share my Christian faith are invited to listen in; we will explore topics relevant to all mortals. Many of us feel the "cross-pressures" of living in what philosopher Charles Taylor calls "a secular age." Our culture pulls us in different directions. We are torn, at ease with neither a simplistic atheism nor a fundamentalist religion that stiff-arms challenging questions. In our day, many atheists are haunted by the possibility of faith, and many believers are haunted by persistent doubt.[8] For both believers and unbelievers "the sense can easily arise that we are missing something, cut off from something, that we are living behind a screen."[9]

While I write as a committed Christian, like many others I feel the cross-pressures of identity as I approach death. With the church, I trust God's promise that death will not have the final word. But I do so with an awareness that we could be wrong. I also realize that many others follow different paths. In facing death, mortals face a mystery we cannot master. My approach to the cross-pressures and this humbling mystery is not to set my Christian convictions on the shelf but to live into them, trusting that truth is possessed first and foremost by God. My ultimate hope is that I belong to the one who is the Truth, Jesus Christ, not that I am the owner of truth. I approach with curiosity the many religious and nonreligious options our culture puts before us as we encounter dying and death. But ultimately, I seek to cultivate trust in God's promises— which are so astonishing that I could never have come up with them myself—even as I wrestle with hard and unanswered questions.

Thus, even in the midst of cross-pressures, I derive life from Scripture and from the rich witness of the Christian tradition. As I wrote this book I was repeatedly amazed by Scripture's capacity to nourish our lives as mortal creatures. The Spirit's word through Scripture is so much deeper and wider than the stereotypical story of Christians "praying the sinner's prayer" and then trying to stay in God's good graces until they finally reach heaven. In fact, readers may be surprised that in this book I rarely speak about heaven except in the final chapters. The reason for this is biblical: in the Lord's Prayer, we pray for God's kingdom and will to come "on earth, as it is in heaven." But what does that mean? Theologically speaking, heaven is where God dwells in fullness. Scripture tells us that God intends creation to be a place where he dwells in fullness, so that things "on earth" really are like things "in heaven." Thus, while I seek to bear witness to the mystery and glory of heaven in this work, because of our own often unhelpful and preconceived notions (such as delicate baby angels sitting on clouds) I only gradually move toward speaking of heaven.

Instead, I invite the reader into the biblical story of how God creates the cosmos as a sanctuary in which to dwell with his creation, which is disrupted by the alienation of sin. In that context, we join the psalmist in crying out from "the Pit" ("Sheol"), longing for the temple—the place, in the midst of a fallen world, where God has promised to dwell in beauty and holiness. Praying with the psalmist trains our hearts to hope in the ultimate temple dwelling place (Jesus Christ) and the new creation in the age to come, when Christ returns to judge, restore, and dwell with his people. In this textured biblical context, then, we long for heaven and continue to pray for God's kingdom to come "on earth, as it is in heaven." We pray and ache for the final day, when all knees are bent before the crucified and resurrected Lord, Jesus Christ, and God dwells in full fellowship with his creation.

In addition to being shaped by Scripture, my approach emerges from the mundane yet joyful realities of living as an active member of the church and participating in its worship and service. I gather with my congregation to receive the Word in sermon and sacrament. I pray for others and receive prayer. I visit the sick, just as I am visited while sick. Beyond my personal experiences of life within the church, I also had the opportunity to probe the meaning of resurrection hope throughout the course of a year by leading a series of three colloquies on death and dying in congregational life with other pastors. I heard about their visits to the dying, both young and old. I heard about their funerals for parishioners and for those alienated from the church. I heard stories of courage and stories of capitulation in the face of death's woes. All of these experiences inform this book.

Ultimately, I write as an act of pilgrimage. I cannot possibly master the realities about which I speak in this book—the mysteries of death and new life, of God and his gospel among crumbling mortals. Biographers of Abraham Lincoln try to read every speech he delivered and every letter he wrote, and even then they do not *master* Lincoln and his life. But if a biography's subject matter focuses on the "who, what, and where" of Lincoln's life, its writer can eventually come to a series of likely explanations for his convictions. In speaking of God, I speak of One whom I cannot comprehend. As Augustine of Hippo stated boldly in the fourth century, "If you have been able to comprehend it, you have comprehended something else instead of God."[10] I cannot see the realities of which this book speaks as God sees them, for I see now "in a mirror, dimly," as the apostle Paul says, anticipating the day "we will see face to face" (1 Cor. 13:12). Even as I anticipate that glorious day in the future, mysteries remain. I'm merely a creature with mundane, mortal concerns—like what to do about that dent in the car, how to get my daughter out of bed in time for school, how to teach third graders about Jonah in Sunday school.

Thus, all of my theological reflection happens on the road of discipleship, the path of pilgrimage. I'm reminded of a wonderful sixteenth-century Protestant theologian named Franciscus Junius, who taught that all Christian theology occurs in union with Christ for the purpose of deepening our communion with God in Christ. Our knowledge of God is real, but it is partial. We know God in Christ in a way that is sufficient for our earthly pilgrimage, but it "is incomplete if it should be compared with that heavenly theology for which we hope." In the age to come, we will have face-to-face knowledge when we receive the "glorious vision of God" in Christ.[11]

To state it differently, I'm writing imperfect theology that invites the curious, the confused, and those seeking authentic hope amid death into deeper fellowship with Christ. Readers may notice that I do not present an abstract theological claim and then "prove" it. Rather, I intertwine the experiential and sociological conundrums with biblical and theological reflection, entering into a very old practice suggested by the Book of Common Prayer: the prayerful attempt to "read, mark, learn, and inwardly digest" Scripture so that "we may embrace and ever hold fast the blessed hope of everlasting life."[12] In this process of "eating" Scripture, I receive its testimony about Sheol, the temple, and other biblical motifs as exquisite nourishment that cannot be reduced to mere information; this is food for a knowledge-soaked communion with God in Christ. The sweet and bitter words of Scripture strengthen us on the pilgrimage to the holy city where God will dwell with his people in the age to come.

I've felt a sense of urgency throughout the process of writing this book. More than once I've prayed that I would live long enough to complete it. For whether one is a pastor or church member, whether a funeral director or plumber or teacher, all of us bear the weight of slavery to the fear of death. In our age of medical and technological marvels, we are especially tempted by counterfeit versions of resurrection hope. We seek to extend life and defer death, whatever the cost. We seek the promise of prosperity in the present moment, of "your best life now," with no groaning necessary.[13] But if we take Christian discipleship seriously, we need to move—as individuals, families, and congregations—more deeply into authentic resurrection hope.

What is that resurrection hope? It is the hope in Christ's judgment and renewal of the whole cosmos on the final day—a thrilling, earthly, embodied, and glorious hope in the deliverer from sin and the source of loving communion. In the book's overall arc, I begin by exposing the much-suppressed truth about our mortality, unveiling the idolatrous hopes that drive us on a daily level; and then, with increasing intensity in the final chapters, I move toward exploring the authentic hope in the beautiful, Christ-centered, God-disclosing promise of the resurrection. If you ache as you begin this book, you will likely ache at the end as well. Yet I pray that this book places these aches and groans within a growing awareness of our identity as God's beloved children, bound to the hope of new creation in Christ.

Indeed, for the apostle Paul, even this groaning has a hopeful tone. After speaking of how we "groan inwardly" while awaiting the resurrection, he goes on to say that "in hope we were saved. Now hope that is seen is not hope. For who hopes for what is seen? But if we hope for what we do not see, we wait for it with patience" (Rom. 8:23–25). We wait in hope, eagerly yet patiently. The "patience" of Paul here is not passivity but is closer to the sense of the English word "long-suffering." We cannot bring in God's kingdom ourselves. Our present bodies are decaying. We have not, and cannot, fully experience the resurrection now. And yet our daily lives—our habits, our priorities, our willingness to take risks—are shaped by a durable hope for what is to come. We're called to long-suffering amid the trials we face, because we know—in hope—that *we* are not the ultimate solution to the world's ills. We are free to act in love and gratitude, even when our efforts seem futile. For the God of Israel, who entered into covenant with Abraham, Moses, and David, has brought Gentiles into "the riches of the glory of this mystery, which is Christ in you, the hope of glory" (Col. 1:27). Christ is in us. We belong to Christ. We are children of God in Christ. And yet this reality always looks forward—to the "hope of glory," the glorious hope of sharing in his resurrection, of sharing in the perfect communion that the Son has with the Father through the Spirit. In our eager patience, we look to the hope of the restoration of the cosmos in and through Christ.

In this way, this book welcomes you into a journey of ache and joy, of despair and hope. Embrace your mortality and lift up your hearts to the true hope of glory. We have a foretaste of that glory now. But an appetizer is not a banquet. The great feast is still to come.

Until then, we travel on pilgrimage. We walk and stumble, not only in the sunlight, but in the shadows. We learn to delight and lament and love along the way until we reach the city that "has no need of sun or moon to shine on it, for the glory of God is its light" (Rev. 21:23).

# One

## Welcome to Sheol

### A Guided Tour of Life in the Pit

Dead means dead. No one is half dead or a little bit dead, except for the occasional zombie staggering forward in postapocalyptic television shows. Like the idea of being "a little bit pregnant" or "sort of an identical twin," halfway dead isn't a possibility. Until the heart stops and the brain shuts down and the doctor in the ICU pronounces death, we are alive. If my flesh shows no signs of animation and my body exudes the smell of decay, you can be pretty sure that I'm dead. There are only two options: either I've departed or I'm still here—either I'm deceased or I'm alive—just as the bright fluorescent lights in my office are either on or off.

At least that's what I used to think.

### Traveling to Sheol: Life in the Pit

The shadow of death covers the faces of the living—it's something I've noticed since entering the world of cancer patients. Even though my heart still beats and my blood still pumps, I've somehow made my way to Sheol. Along with a cluster of related terms in the Old Testament, the Hebrew word *sheol* describes a deep, miry pit, far away from light. Sheol is a place of darkness, a prison for those who are silenced, cut off from life.

On days where I feel bright and shadows seem distant, I stop short at the word "Sheol" in praying the Psalms. "You have delivered my soul from the depths of Sheol," the psalmist says, after crying out to the Lord as one who is "poor and needy" (Ps. 86:1, 13). When should I identify with the psalmist's cry? Am I in Sheol when I feel abandoned and cut off? Or will I go to Sheol after my heart is silenced and my breathing ceases? It's not always clear.

At times, the psalmists imply that Sheol is the land of the dead, the biologically deceased. In the desperate prayer of Psalm 88, the psalmist laments, "For my soul is full of troubles, / and my life draws near to Sheol," and goes on to plead, "Are your wonders known in the darkness, / or your saving help in the land of forgetfulness?" (vv. 3, 12). Here we face the fear of death along with the anguish of slipping into the darkness. This particular use of Sheol is similar to how ancient Mesopotamians and Egyptians imagined the underworld: as the place of the dead, who are cut off from the living, unable to return. In their vocabulary, the place of the dead was for all whose hearts have stopped beating, whose limbs have stiffened from rigor mortis. For example, ancient Egyptian hieroglyphics gave instructions for how the dead were to navigate the underworld, this place of the dead. At death, the spirit leaves the body, but a spirit needs to recognize its body in order to rejoin it and continue on in the underworld. Thus, elite Egyptians mummified their dead fathers and mothers and cats and birds, and they inscribed hieroglyphics with the passwords and spells necessary to reach different parts of the underworld.

Anyone who has lost a father or mother, a daughter or son, a brother or sister knows that the Egyptians—and the psalmist in Psalm 88—were right in their basic conviction that the dead are gone and that their absence is a wound that remains. The dead are mute and cut off from us. Even believers in the coming resurrection experience this stinging absence of the dead. As an elderly man in my church moaned in a whisper, a year after losing his wife of five decades, "I just miss her! I know I should think that she's in a better place. But I want her *here*!" His body shook, and tears rolled down his face. He was hunched over in embarrassment, judging himself for not having enough faith to believe that his loss was only gain, and not also a wound.

However, the Israelites had a peculiar angle on the notion of Sheol as the place of the dead. Unlike the Egyptians and Mesopotamians, they repeatedly suggested that the biological dead are not the sole inhabitants of Sheol. Somehow I missed that when I was in Old Testament class at seminary—and its significance didn't really hit me until I was a cancer patient, praying psalms that speak from the standpoint of Sheol. For example, in Psalm 107 the psalmist recalls the experience of Israel in exile, as "prisoners in misery and in irons," and declares,

> Then they cried to the LORD in their trouble,
>   and he saved them from their distress;
> he sent out his word and healed them,
>   and delivered them from destruction [Sheol]. (Ps. 107:19–20)

The Israelites in exile cried out to the Lord, and they were delivered from Sheol. Sheol is not "hell" in the Christian sense of the term, nor is it simply a place for the dead in general, in this instance. Here Sheol is the Pit, the place of the living and the dead who are silenced and cut off, crying out to the Lord for deliverance.

If this picture from the Psalms seems overly subtle, we might look to the prophet Jonah, who presents a more visceral image of living, breathing existence in Sheol. In the opening lines of the book, Jonah flees. The Lord has given him the audacious commission to warn the pagan Ninevites of their wickedness. A journey into a bustling city in what is modern-day Iraq is not on Jonah's agenda, so he runs. But he does not just flee the city—he flees, as the book repeatedly claims, "from the presence of the LORD" (1:3).

In chapter 2, Jonah apparently receives what he had wished for: he is far from the Lord. But this place is one of darkness; it is "the belly of the fish." He cries out,

> I called to the LORD out of my distress,
>     and he answered me;
> out of the belly of Sheol I cried,
>     and you heard my voice. (2:2)

Thus, the belly of the fish is the belly of Sheol: dark, sticky, ensnaring. Jonah continues his prayer by following a psalm-like pattern in his appeal to God:

> You cast me into the deep,
>     into the heart of the seas,
>     and the flood surrounded me;
> all your waves and your billows
>     passed over me.
> Then I said, "I am driven away
>     from your sight;
> how shall I look again
>     upon your holy temple?" (2:3–4)

Jonah is in not only a dark place, but a chaotic place of seas and floods and waves and billows. Jonah had wanted to flee from the Lord. He thought he knew what was best. Yet here he is with all of the bitterness of an unwise wish fulfilled—stuck in the belly of Sheol, far from the Lord's sight. From this dark place, Jonah cries out that he needs deliverance. He wants to look again upon the Lord's holy temple.

Much hangs on these two simple words, "holy temple." In his longing to see the Lord's holy temple again, Jonah is not simply praying for his suffering to cease. He is boldly aching to enter into the presence of the holy

Lord, the King of the universe. The temple was the place where God dwelt with his people, just as the tabernacle had been in the Hebrew people's wilderness wandering, and just as the garden of Eden had been at the dawn of creation. Jonah aches for the dwelling place of God—for Eden, for the tabernacle, for the temple. The righteous Lord is a consuming fire; the temple, therefore, is holy ground. As one who fled from the Lord, Jonah should be wary of entering the temple. But he aches for it anyway.

Notably, Jonah's prayer is not "Leave me alone, God—you got me into this mess!" Instead, as Jonah cries out to escape the belly of this claustrophobic, hazardous fish, he wants to move toward the frightening—and yet healing—place of the Lord's presence, the temple:

> As my life was ebbing away,
>   I remembered the LORD;
> and my prayer came to you,
>   into your holy temple. (2:7)

From the pit of Sheol, Jonah repents. He turns from his rebellious path and aches for the Lord's presence. Without even mentioning Nineveh, Jonah prays for the "one thing" that the psalmist desires in Psalm 27:4: "to behold the beauty of the LORD, / and to inquire in his temple." Jonah longs for the Lord's temple, the Lord's holy and beautiful home. Sheol is far from that. For Jonah, as for the psalmist, the most fundamental polarity is not between biological life and biological death but between the Lord's presence and the Lord's apparent absence. Sheol—the place of perceived abandonment, the Pit, light-years away from the Lord's presence—is the opposite of the temple, where the Lord has promised to dwell. The Lord dwells in light and life; those in Sheol dwell in darkness and estrangement in the Pit.[1]

Today, doctors, social workers, and advertising campaigns advise cancer patients to embrace spirituality in the face of biological death. As far as I can tell, "spirituality" in this context refers to a set of prayers or religious practices customized for each person; it's a means to our own preferred end, whether that's becoming calm, finding peace, or discovering meaning. It's a bit like getting to choose our favorite shovel to dig ourselves out of the pit of Sheol, where our lives are increasingly cut off from the living—even seemingly cut off from God. We are told that if we focus on each day and on what is in our control, we will make our way out of Sheol and perhaps achieve "a good death."

Sheol in the book of Jonah could hardly be more different. Jonah is stranded in Sheol, and living day by day won't help. Self-help platitudes are useless. Jonah's instincts for self-preservation were strong—he had good reason to avoid the dangerous mission to Nineveh. But now he's trapped in the fish's belly. He cries out for deliverance:

> I went down to the land
>> whose bars closed upon me forever;
> yet you brought up my life from the Pit,
>> O LORD my God. (2:6)

No shovel or scalpel—and certainly no self-empowerment plan—will deliver Jonah. Only the Lord can release him from this snare. Rather than praying for his life to be prolonged, he prays to return to the Lord's presence—which inevitably involves the nasty task of bringing the Lord's word to the vile Ninevites. Being in the Sheol of the fish is bad, but moving toward the temple is no holiday, either. Approaching the temple requires repentance and the holiness of being set apart for God's purposes. Speaking of the temple, the psalmist asks,

> Who shall ascend the hill of the LORD?
>> And who shall stand in his holy place?
> Those who have clean hands and pure hearts,
>> who do not lift up their souls to what is false,
>> and do not swear deceitfully. (Ps. 24:3–4)

The temple, for all that it requires, is nonetheless a beating heart, while Sheol is a heart that is limp and silent. In the words of Jewish scholar Jon Levenson, "To move from Sheol to the Temple is to move from death to life. To long to gaze upon the Temple is to long for life itself." This movement, the deliverance from death to life, is dependent on God. "Were it not for God's just and gracious rescue," Levenson writes, those who are helpless to rescue themselves "would have been destroyed. Those delivered from death to live in the Temple depend on their relationship with their God for their very lives."[2] Indeed, apart from God's rescue, Jonah is utterly helpless in moving toward life. The bars of Sheol block the way, the Pit is too deep, and self-help is no help at all.

## Praying from the Pit

If we follow Jonah and the psalmists rather than the Egyptians, then people all over, regardless of physical location, are living in Sheol. From Boston to Bangalore, from Madison to Mosul, from the wide-open Kansas wheat fields of my youth to the precisely calibrated environs of the International Space Station—Sheol's geography is expansive. The pit of Sheol does not necessarily involve biological death. Sex trafficking or prison or loneliness or shame can just as readily bring people to the Pit.

Israel's psalms have an earthy particularity, but they apply to a broad range of circumstances—such that Israel, Jesus himself, and the church could pray them. When the psalmists call to the Lord for deliverance from the Pit, their cries are often full of loneliness and fear.

> I lie awake;
>> I am like a lonely bird on the housetop.
> All day long my enemies taunt me;
>> those who deride me use my name for a curse.
> For I eat ashes like bread,
>> and mingle tears with my drink. (Ps. 102:7–9)

The threat of biological death may not be imminent, but it is frequently close by. We can only speculate about the original circumstances of the Psalms: sometimes war and violence seem to have been at hand, and in other cases, illness. The psalmists, in addition to crying out to see the Lord in his temple, often cry for deliverance from the pit of premature death. "O my God," they say, "do not take me away / at the midpoint of my life, / you whose years endure / throughout all generations" (Ps. 102:24).

I sometimes picture Sheol as a large, sun-blocking canopy; beneath its shade are clusters of smaller tents. Anyone who has lived in places of bondage and silencing, where it feels as if God is utterly absent, has lived under the shadow of Sheol in a particular tent. A person who feels cut off after losing a parent or child or sibling or close friend occupies a tent—a part of themselves having been severed, just as the departed is cut off and segregated from the living. In an adjoining tent, cancer patients like me also dwell in Sheol, sharply attuned to a sense of our imminent biological decline and death. We dwell there together with six-year-olds and ninety-six-year-olds whose lives slip away in spite of reported progress in "the war against cancer"; as they die, we feel the same acids burning away our own biological lives and our own dreams for the future. Many other tents are spread out across the forlorn landscape of Sheol—tents filled with refugees driven from their homes, or women and men living with shame after abuse, and countless others hailing from dark places of loss and fear and loneliness. How many tents are in Sheol? I suspect the number is legion.

In fact, it may seem arrogant to speak about myself as a cancer patient in "the Pit" while millions of families are being displaced around the world as refugees, often facing imprisonment, persecution, and even death for no just cause. Others live in fear of even walking their sidewalks because of the violence and alienation in their midst. A student of mine grew up in a rough urban neighborhood on the West Coast. "Sheol has always been our residence," he told me. "By nineteen years old, I had already been shot and stabbed multiple times." Dozens of his friends and acquaintances have been murdered. In a cultural context animated by gangs and reprisals, where the reality of death is all around and undeniable, the primary temptation may not be to deny one's mortality; rather, it could be to fall into despair in the darkness of Sheol.

Is it wrong for readers from more privileged backgrounds and cultures, like my own, to claim to inhabit the pit of Sheol? I've enjoyed astonishing blessings: I've lived for more than four decades in peaceful environments; I have access to medical care; I enjoy the blessings of a caring family and church. Indeed, there's no genuine room for self-pity, for each breath is a gift from the Creator. There was no guarantee that I would be born in anything other than a war zone, or that I would take in even a single breath outside the womb.

Each person's suffering has its own character, though, and a brush with death can transport any of us to Sheol in short order. When Facebook vice president and billionaire Sheryl Sandberg faced the sudden death of her husband while they were on vacation, she found herself in the Pit. Her wealth, her social capital, her career—none of it could protect her. "Time slowed way, way down. Day after day my kids' cries and screams filled the air. . . . My own cries and screams—mostly inside my head but some out loud—filled the rest of the available space. I was in 'the void': a vast emptiness that fills your heart and lungs and restricts your ability to think or even breathe."[3] The affliction of sickness, the bondage of addiction, the death of someone close, the experience of oppression—any of these can bring us down to the Pit. And the Psalms meet us there, in that lowest of places.

The Psalms teach us to pray and cry out in a way that expresses our deepest miseries. We are not in a contest to determine whose experience of Sheol goes the deepest, whose anguish is the greatest. God offers to meet all of us through the cries of lament in the Psalms, in these prayers from the Pit.

Moreover, even though Sheol is, by definition, a place where we feel abandoned by God—distant from God's presence—there is a remarkable consolation at this very point: Jesus Christ. As the truly innocent sufferer, he came to join us in Sheol when he expressed Psalm 22's cry of abandonment on the cross: "My God, my God, why have you forsaken me?" (Ps. 22:1; see Matt. 27:46; Mark 15:34). Christ felt forsaken, abandoned, and cut off—even by the God who creates and calls us. According to the Heidelberg Catechism, this aspect of his suffering can bring us comfort: Christ pioneers this forsaken path "to assure me during attacks of deepest dread and temptation that Christ my Lord, by suffering unspeakable anguish, pain, and terror of soul, on the cross but also earlier, has delivered me from hellish anguish and torment."[4]

Jesus Christ himself experienced the alienation that mortals who are far from the temple feel. Yet as the Gospel of John tells us, the eternal Word of God "became flesh and lived among us"—literally, in Greek, "tabernacled among us" (John 1:14). In becoming incarnate in our suffering flesh, God tabernacled and dwelt among us. Indeed, John's Gospel portrays Christ not only as the portable temple (the tabernacle) but also as the temple itself, in his own person (John 2:18–22). Thus, in a breathtaking paradox, on Christ's cross the temple himself experienced the alienation of being far from the temple. The light of the world entered into darkness. The life-giving presence of God descended to the deep pit of Sheol. This is a blinding mystery, one that we will return to again in this book. But at this point, one morsel of consolation should be enough to cleanse our palates, to ready us for the right kind of food: if we live parts of our lives in the shadows of Sheol, at least we have some very good company.

Indeed, I suspect that no mortal lives for long without visiting Sheol for a time. And those of us who look forward to the day of resurrection will suffocate our hope if we treat the cavernous pit of Sheol as if it were merely a tiny crack in the pavement in a life of ease.

## Living among the Dying

For many generations, and around the world, humans have known life in the pit of darkness. Knowing the sight and smell and sound of the Pit can give us a realistic sense of what it means to live as mortal creatures. Yet most who occupy the middle and upper classes in the Western world have attempted to purge their lives of any hint of death, pushing dying away from daily life in a way that would have seemed bizarre in earlier eras.

For example, what we now call the "living room" was in earlier generations referred to as the "parlor"—a place for shared family life together. This was the same space in which children nursed their parents or grandparents through the process of dying. In this way, family members lived and died in the same room, in the parlor. Today we know the "parlor" as a space exclusive to funeral homes; the "funeral parlor" is the awkward place for viewing the dead, "outfitted to look like the family parlors" with "overstuffed furniture, fern stands, knickknacks, draperies, and the dead."[5]

In the 1940s, most Americans died in their own homes. By the 1980s, just 17 percent died in their homes.[6] For many in earlier times, caring for the dying was part of the job description of being a child, and it took place in the family parlor. Today, in contrast, we've sequestered the dying in sanitized hospitals and nursing homes, and we've done our best to shield our children from the harsh realities of death. It's all part of a state of mind in which we think, *If I can rid myself of the odor of death, maybe I can live as if death is not intertwined with my everyday life, my every moment of living.* As a cancer patient living in this death-sequestering environment, that state of mind is a luxury that I used to have, but it has slipped away.

I thought of this as I held the collar of our thirteen-year-old dog, Max, while sitting on the floor in our parlor (or living room). When Max developed chronic pain that we couldn't control and he started bumping into walls and doors, our vet diagnosed him with dementia. My wife, Rachel, and I decided that we needed to find a way to make space for his death in our home, with our two children, ages four and five at the time.

Max was a furry, red-and-white Welsh corgi, one of the friendliest creatures on planet Earth. At our first meeting, I remember him cheerfully leaping onto the couch so that he could cuddle between our laps as we petted his warm, thick coat. Now I held his collar and rubbed his shedding coat softly as he lay on the wood floor. Our vet, who makes house calls for interventions like this one, was with us and had moved to eye level with Max, as he does with all his canine patients. "You're a good dog, Max," he said gently. "You may feel a little sting, Max, but it won't be too bad," he said, as if Max were curious. After receiving the shot, Max fell into a deep sleep. Another shot, and it was done. Max's chest breathed in and out a few more times. And then I felt him go limp. "I know you're a Christian. Can I pray right now?" The vet offered a blessing, a benediction.

Yet the drama was just beginning. The vet left, and I continued to rub Max's back. Ten minutes later, the grandparents came in with Neti, our daughter, and Nathaniel, our son. The kids walked over to me, calmly at first. For weeks we had been warning them that Max was very, very old and that he would die soon. Earlier that day, Nathaniel had searched the house until he found Max and proclaimed his relief. Apparently, in his four-year-old mind, to die was to disappear.

Max had not disappeared. Yet he was dead, cut off from us. With tears in my eyes, I told them, "Max has died."

"He's dead?!" Nathaniel cried in terror.

"Yes."

Grandpa went to help Rachel with the grave-digging in the backyard as I held the two wailing children in my arms. We petted the fur on Max's back, on his side, above his short, stubby legs. But he was limp. He would no longer wake up and lie awkwardly on our laps, no longer chase a thrown treat; his brown eyes would never sparkle again. We cried out loudly and wept. For Nathaniel, the boundary between grief and anger was thin, and he started to throw toys across the room. Through the tears, I said prayers that I had prepared in advance.

We can hope in God. But deaths are sad. They are real. That's what our family's counselor had suggested that Rachel and I tell the children. Chances are that I will not live long enough to see either Neti or

Nathaniel graduate from high school. Max's death might have been our only chance before my death to really help the kids understand what death is. When Grandpa came in wearing his dusty boots and lifted Max's body, the kids and I were still wailing.

In the days that followed, Max's death spurred many questions. "Where is Max now?" "Is Max in heaven?" I skirted the "dog in heaven" question, simply saying, "God will take care of Max. Max's body was hurting, and Max was confused. He isn't hurting anymore." Over the course of a few weeks, the questions became less frequent, and the meaning of death seemed to sink in, ever so slightly. Death is often played for laughs in children's cartoons: a character's eyes cross, he falls over, and a flower sprouts up. But a cartoon death is a far cry from reality, as my kids gradually came to realize. They were living among the dying.

Two years earlier, our neighbor friend Oliver had died of cancer at the age of six. Oliver was a cheerful boy who liked to play with LEGOs and teach my daughter math—and had learned to conceal his pain with a straight face. Oliver said that he and I had a special bond. We were both cancer patients, and we had both had a stem cell transplant; thus, we knew what it was like to live for a season without an immune system. Oliver improved for a while, but then the cancer hit back hard. The last time my kids and I saw him alive, his dad was carrying him to pursue an ice cream truck, which was broadcasting its music to invite the neighborhood kids to purchase a treat. Oliver used to run after the truck himself, but the cancer had hollowed out his strength. He looked up at us, his body thin and his skin tight on his bones. He was nearly limp, almost like Max in Grandpa's arms. Neti and Nathaniel continued playing in the backyard, but neither really comprehended what was happening.

On the two-year anniversary of Oliver's death, we gathered with other neighbors and collected LEGO sets in his honor. Nathaniel asked, "When will we see Oliver again?" Oliver is like Max, we told him. Oliver has died. He is not coming back, but God is taking care of him. "Do you think that God has given him toys in heaven, because he liked to play with toys?" Our son was worried that Oliver would be bored if there were no toys in heaven. Rachel said she was sure that Oliver was not bored, that it's not boring to be with God. I'm not sure whether the question about toys got answered.

For better or for worse, our children have begun to see the shadow of the Pit. We can, and should, hope in God. Nevertheless, the dead are silenced, cut off, taken away from us. They will not return.

Our family is still coming to terms with dying being a part of life. Perhaps Rachel and I were overly dramatic in our liturgy for Max's death—like a daughter who is called to the parlor to kiss her deceased mother's cheek before the burial. Our ritual, however, has made dying and death just a bit less abstract, so that fears can be discussed and prayers offered. "I am scared of being dead!" Nathaniel declared about eighteen months after Max died. "You don't have to be scared of being dead. You *won't be there* when you're dead," Neti responded with stunning insight. (While I promise that I had not forced her to read Ludwig Wittgenstein at age six, her comment reflects the philosopher's observation that "death is not an event in life: we do not live to experience death.")[7] Later, Nathaniel again earnestly asked, "Will God protect you when you are dead?" I paused to take in the question. Slowly I said, "Yes, God will protect you when you are dead."

We wail with tears and grief and anger when the dead are taken from us, cut off, silenced. But *we* are the ones wailing, not the deceased. It's almost as if *we* are the ones who have gone to Sheol, not them.

## Sheol and the Limits of Control

Those among the living who fall into the Pit face a puzzle: *How did I get here? Can I get out?* Being in Sheol involves feeling trapped, as we've seen. But can we exercise *control* in the place of the dead? Perhaps we can climb out; or perhaps the harder we try, the deeper we sink, as if we're in quicksand. When we fall into the Pit, should we fight and push to escape? Or is that a pathological instinct for creatures like us?

As intelligent and passionate creatures, our clinging to control is fundamental to who we are. In many ways, this is both natural and right. Unlike other animals who are guided by instinct shortly after birth, human babies are helpless, requiring a long period of growth and development. And that growth involves a growth in control. While I wouldn't have expected my newborn son to clean the table or load the dishwasher, I'm doing him no favors if I fail to give him such chores when he's seven years old. Being able to dress yourself, tie your shoes, and control your body when you are angry helps build confidence.

Indeed, theologically speaking, we're wired to exercise certain kinds of control. In the book of Genesis, immediately after the declaration that humans are created in the image of God, the Lord commissions them to "have dominion over the fish of the sea, and over the birds of the air, and over the cattle, and over all the wild animals of the earth, and over every creeping thing that creeps upon the earth" (Gen. 1:26). On the one hand, this "dominion" or "rule" should not lead to the exploitation of the natural world. Instead, as representatives of the true King, humans are to rule in a way that mirrors the extraordinary creativity and care of the Lord of creation, who made the platypus and the amoeba and the Milky Way galaxy.[8] Nevertheless, this rule clearly does involve work—the active exercise of mind and muscle, of individual and group.

Ultimately, human work involves exercising some control over one's environment, but in a way that is not paralyzed by the fear of fatalism. Since the 1950s, some psychologists have turned this into a general axiom. Charles Duhigg, in *Smarter Faster Better*, summarizes the idea: humans thrive with an "internal locus of control" causing them to "feel in charge of their own destiny and attribute success or failure to their own efforts." This "internal locus" is connected to the achievement of a wide range of goals. "People with an internal locus of control tend to earn more money, have more friends, stay married longer, and report greater professional success and satisfaction." In contrast, people with an "external locus of control" perceive that their "lives are primarily influenced by events outside their control."[9] They do not become empowered to work harder and pursue their goals when control is perceived as external to themselves.

Duhigg's advocacy of internal control strikes me as prudent and even wise in many circumstances. But in light of the biblical depiction of Sheol, we may be permitted to wonder: Is the psalmist who is stuck in the Pit left with anything besides an "external locus of control"? Should Duhigg's practical advice to "find a choice, almost any choice, that allows you to exert control" be turned into a general principle?[10] If so, I sense that Duhigg's geography would not include the deep pit of Sheol.

And yet, perhaps Duhigg's account simply suggests that humans are hardwired for action. When we're in the Pit, we're still creatures equipped to act, even if things go haywire. When our ancestors, calmly walking along, saw a bear lunging in their direction, the limbic portion of their brains activated a series of immediate and intense physical reactions: increased heart rate, slowed digestion, and blood flow to muscles to jolt the human body into action, responding to the acute danger. Thankfully, danger is perceived not only as an idea but also as a tangible and immediate threat, so that the body and mind both leap into action. With the aid of her limbic system, a mother surges into the street to pull her toddler from oncoming traffic. With the limbic system, a child runs away from a house that has burst into flames.

I suspect that it was his limbic system that sprang into action when King David was fleeing from a militant mob led by his son Absalom. After being warned of the danger, David told his officials, "Get up! Let us flee, or there will be no escape for us from Absalom. Hurry, or he will soon overtake us, and bring disaster down upon us, and attack the city with the edge of the sword" (2 Sam. 15:14). Get up! Flee! Escape! David sought control by springing into action. Psalm 3, described as "A Psalm of David, when he fled from his son Absalom," reflects the same limbic, fight-or-flight response:

Rise up, O LORD!
Deliver me, O my God!
For you strike all my enemies on the cheek;
    you break the teeth of the wicked. (v. 7)

For readers breathing calmly in a secure environment, this language
seems stark, perhaps even extreme. We can analytically wonder how
the psalmist could pray that God "strike" his enemies and "break the
teeth of the wicked." But, as prayed by one fleeing a murderous sword
and fighting for survival, Psalm 3 is truly the prayer of a body in fear.

We can and should cry out for deliverance. We can and should dash
toward the toddler, run from the abuser, flee from the burning home.
We are wired for action, for seeking and embracing a certain kind of
control. But in Sheol, things are different. In the pit of Sheol, we're
stranded. As Psalm 40 says with regard to Sheol, we are stuck in "a
desolate pit" and "a miry bog"—in one particularly graphic translation,
"in slimy mud" (v. 2). We try to jump and run and swing, but we're in
a hole, and sludge cements our feet to the bottom. Ensnared in the Pit,
we feel fear. We may even slide into hot anger and sharp grief.

I suspect that fear, anger, and grief are all in play in Psalm 137:

By the rivers of Babylon—
    there we sat down and there we wept
    when we remembered Zion. (v. 1)

For a people invaded and conquered and exiled, the idea of an internal
locus of control seems like a cruel illusion. Indeed, speaking about
internal control to those who feel oppressed and powerless today may
sound nonsensical. The psalmist here speaks for his people as captives
and prisoners:

For there our captors
    asked us for songs,

> and our tormentors asked for mirth, saying,
>> "Sing us one of the songs of Zion!" (v. 3)

The Babylonian captors mock both the people and their God, who promised to dwell in the temple in Zion, in Jerusalem, the promised city of the promised people. Even though a quickened heartbeat and short, shallow breaths cannot provide deliverance from this pit, the psalmist brings this angry, grieving energy before God:

> Remember, O LORD, against the Edomites
>> the day of Jerusalem's fall,
> how they said, "Tear it down! Tear it down!
>> Down to its foundations!"
> O daughter Babylon, you devastator!
>> Happy shall they be who pay you back
>> what you have done to us!
> Happy shall they be who take your little ones
>> and dash them against the rock! (vv. 7–9)

Like Psalm 3, this is the prayer of a body in fear. But it's also the prayer of people who are dislocated, cut off from their inheritance, disgraced before others, feeling abandoned by God. God has promised to dwell in the temple, to be present with his people in Jerusalem. But the Israelites drink their own tears in exile, and Jerusalem lies in ruins. Far from the temple, this people's prayer arises from Sheol. Fear mixes with grief and anger to form words that may strike us as both bizarre and disturbing. I am grateful, though, that the Psalms include prayers from Sheol. These are the prayers of bodies taut with anger, minds veering out of control, stuck in fear and grief that they cannot master, flailing and slipping in the slimy bog.

"No one ever told me that grief felt so like fear," C. S. Lewis wrote after the death of his wife, Joy Davidman. He told himself that he was not fearful, but his body acted otherwise, kicking into action. "I am not afraid, but the sensation is like being afraid. The same fluttering in the stomach, the same restlessness, the yawning. I keep on swallowing."[11]

Although she did not consciously realize it at the time, writer Joan Didion had the same reaction after the sudden death of her husband: "Tightness in the throat. Choking, need for sighing."[12] And "if I thought of food, I learned that night, I would throw up."[13] As if she were running from a bear, Didion's digestion dramatically slowed, her heart started racing, and her breathing became shallow. Didion's body seemed to have a mind of its own. Grieving ended up being more than thinking of her husband, or missing him, or wishing he could be with her when she woke up in the morning to share a meal together, to make a decision together. Grief and fear and anger blended together in her, and the results were nothing less than bodily.

Didion pored over the medical literature about grief after her husband's death, discovering that much modern advice emerged from a culture deeply uncomfortable with grief. In a 1965 book by Geoffrey Gorer, *Death, Grief, and Mourning*, she found a chronicle of how death and grieving had become an anomaly. While, in the past, death had been "omnipresent," Gorer wrote, beginning in 1930 most Western countries began to "treat mourning as self-indulgence, and to give social admiration to the bereaved who hide their grief so fully that no one would guess anything had happened."[14] This corresponded with the development of vaccines and the increasing power of modern medicine. But it also generated a new ethic—an "ethical duty to enjoy oneself" and an "imperative to do nothing which might diminish the enjoyment of others."[15]

Didion was in Sheol, in the Pit, but a thousand little signals from her friends told her to shove down her grief and act as if the sun were shining brightly. Didion's body contracted with fear and grief, but those around her wanted her to master her grief, both for her own sake and for theirs. Yet her body felt the pain and grief, even if she tried to think her way out of it. She found odd solace in the chapter on funerals in Emily Post's 1922 book on etiquette: "Persons under the shock of genuine affliction are not only upset mentally but are all unbalanced physically. . . . Their disturbed circulation makes them cold, their distress makes them unstrung, sleepless. Persons they normally like, they often turn from."[16]

Post describes the bodies of persons in deep grief—bodies that do not want to eat, that turn away from loved ones, that find no comfort in daily joys. Post is talking about what it's like to be in Sheol, the Pit. This isn't just the fight-or-flight response of "Rise up, O LORD!" (Ps. 3:7), but the aching grief of those who sat down and wept (Ps. 137:1). Psalm 88 describes this experience:

> I am counted among those who go down to the Pit;
>     I am like those who have no help,
> like those forsaken among the dead,
>     like the slain that lie in the grave,
> like those whom you remember no more,
>     for they are cut off from your hand. (Ps. 88:4–5)

We want control. But Sheol leaves us trapped, even if energized for action. Given the choice, I wonder whether I might prefer to be chased by a bear than be stuck in the pit of Sheol. I'm not sure. At least in fleeing the bear, the body's response is direct and aimed at preserving life. When the body is grieving in the Pit, the heat of choice seems to fall into cold darkness. But whether we flee with our legs lunging forward or we are frozen in grief with a throat that cannot eat or drink, the result in Sheol is the same: we cannot escape, and our efforts to exercise control may well make us sink deeper into the quicksand.

## The Sheol That Consumes

Strangely, in the Old Testament, Sheol not only holds tightly to the feet of those in the Pit, Sheol also consumes. The prophet Isaiah speaks of Israel going into exile, in hunger and thirst, and notes that "Sheol has enlarged its appetite / and opened its mouth beyond measure" (Isa.

5:14). The exiles still "go down" to Sheol, but Sheol actively takes them into the Pit. Sheol is "never satisfied" (Prov. 27:20) but swallows those who are alive (1:12).

Thus, living in the Pit is more like having a chronic illness than an acute one. Friends bring a loaf of bread or flowers to the hospital for someone with an acute illness. A year later, all is forgotten, perhaps even by the one who was ill. But a chronic illness continues for months and years after all the hospital visits, after the flowers have wilted and the bread has turned blue and green with mold. When I was hospitalized for pneumonia several years before my cancer diagnosis, the pain was searing, the fear palpable as I gasped for breath with my fluid-filled lungs. But a few weeks later, my body and psyche were more or less intact. For a short time my plans had been disrupted, but eventually my daily life and overall hopes for my future moved forward.

For those in the Pit, in contrast, the world has been shattered, and the pieces can't be put back together again. Cherished hopes for the future have been attacked and taken away. The attacker, Sheol, has swallowed the living.

Patients with incurable cancer know this experience well: the cancer attacks, triggering the body's fight-or-flight mechanisms. Breaths become shallow, bodies tighten, and we're ready to leap away from the approaching bear. Except that there is no bear. Death appears in the peripheral vision; the mind perceives, based in part on its knowledge of others who have been swallowed, that death's appetite is insatiable. But where to run? Our fearful attempts to flee Sheol, the Pit, only leave our feet more firmly stuck in the "slimy mud." The walls of this tomb-like hole are high and steep.

Throwing a rope, even a flimsy rope, to someone in the hole may sound merciful. For those not in the Pit, it's better than doing nothing. But this is an outsider's perspective. In the words of Christian Wiman, reflecting on his terminal cancer diagnosis, "Life is short, we say, in one way or another, but in truth, because we cannot imagine our own death until it is thrust upon us, we live in a land where only other people die."[17]

The cancer patient in Sheol is desperate, gasping—trying to find breath, to secure safety. We may grasp at the rope, even if it is guaranteed to snap, if only to have a few moments of feeling that we are in control.

There is no medical cure for my cancer, and it is terminal. No one knows what causes my form of cancer. Perhaps that's why I frequently receive so many ardent recommendations for "cancer soups," for special diets, for scores of "alternative" cancer treatments that rage against the machine of the medical establishment. On one level, I don't quite understand why a multimillion-dollar industry exists for the sake of selling cancer cures that have no medical evidence in their favor. But I do understand why patients like me take them: we're desperate. We'd rather hope in something that falsely claims to be a cure than give up the light of hope altogether—and admit that we're just stuck in this pit.

I recall one young cancer patient, Amy, pulling me aside to tell me about her most recent "alternative medicine" treatments, including a very stringent anticancer diet. A young mother working full-time, Amy was already financially strapped, her money flowing like an undammed river to the insurance company. She struggled to keep up at work as she withstood the side effects of treatment. But her eyes brightened and her voice became hushed with excitement. She had read the online testimonials about this special diet—yes, this could be a game changer. "This is something that I can do about this cancer!" she said. She wasn't going to wait around to die.

When I caught up with Amy about a year later, her shoulders were hunched over and she looked weary, but her blue eyes still had a spark of energy. "My cancer levels rose again, so I'm on chemo again," she said. "I think the cancer returned because I only stayed on the diet for three months. After I started to eat a regular diet again—*boom*—the cancer came back in a few months." Amy felt guilty for abandoning her diet but seemed reassured by the fact that she could return to it. "Next time, next time, I tell you—I'm staying on that diet!"

I expressed support for Amy and gently tried to move the subject away from her self-blame for the cancer's return. No oncologist on the planet would say that her failure to stay on the diet brought back the cancer. But if I burst her balloon, what hope would she have left? Would Amy be able to carry on if she faced the reality that her cancer's ebb and flow was completely outside her control?

Perhaps this is the most disturbing part of life in the Pit. We are silenced, in the darkness, swallowed up. There is no bear to flee, no attacker to fight. It's useless to give such a person sugarcoated advice or predictions. "Oh, it probably won't end up too badly." ("I wonder if you said that to my three friends who have died this year from this cancer," the patient thinks.) "I just saw a news update, and I think they've already found a cure with one patient in Canada." ("Why don't my oncologists think so?") "If you put your mind to it, I know you can pull through this." ("Pull through what, exactly?")

And yet we strive for control. Our bodies, even through the fatigue and pain of treatment, surge with nervous energy attempting to "fix" our situation, to deliver us from the Pit. My own cancer started to show itself through a compromised immune system. Pneumonia put me in the hospital; then bronchitis dragged me down; then a cold led to bronchitis again, and to pneumonia again. "Wash your hands very regularly," my doctor said the summer before my cancer diagnosis. "That's really all that you can do." After a pause, I asked, "How do I know if I'm washing my hands too much?" "Well, just wash them after using the bathroom, after physical contact like shaking hands, before eating, and situations like that."

I used to rely on thoughtless habits for cleanliness. I wouldn't consciously think, *Now I'm going to wash my hands*, or ask myself, *Did I wash my hands?* I washed my hands when most other people did: when my unconscious triggers indicated that I should. But now—now, I felt like I had to fully satisfy an inner "cleanliness supervisor" and an inner "cleanliness tester" and, before long, an inner "cleanliness worrier." *Did I wash my hands? Did I wash them long enough? Those commercials say to wash your hands for a really long time—did I wash that long? Did I just shake hands and then touch my beard, my mouth?*

*I can't remember. Should I wash my face now? Maybe I should wash my hands again.* These inner regulators moved my limbic system into action, energizing me to fight the enemy.

After my diagnosis the doctors warned me that my immune system would become even more compromised by the chemotherapy. "Take hand sanitizer with you wherever you go," the oncology nurses said. "If you must shake hands, always sanitize afterward." Now my inner cleanliness supervisor, tester, and worrier were all on full alert. And just like Amy and her obsession with the cancer diet—which made it seem as if cancer was an enemy that was totally under her control—I became obsessed with my hands and their cleanliness and what I could and couldn't remember about washing and cleaning them. Even though my cancer swallowed me up, like Sheol does—in complete disregard of my habits of hygiene, height, weight, race, and economic status—my body acted as if I still had a fight on my hands. Fight. Fight. Fight. Because to feel powerless, to feel helpless—that would be too much.

The same cultural forces that told Joan Didion that mourning after the death of her husband was "self-indulgence" also tell cancer patients to deny that they are in the Pit. Cancer centers in my area, competing for patients, post inspirational billboards to promote this exact idea. Each shows a photo of a confident adult with protruding chin and penetrating eyes looking into the middle distance. They each talk to "cancer" the same way an NBA player might trash-talk an unfortunate opponent. "Dear cancer, you're going to wish you had never messed with me." Such billboards imply that if you feel impotent, powerless in the face of a disease that will kill you, then you've given up the cause. Don't indulge in mourning, in helplessness. Start the fight against cancer. Join the war. Become a soldier and perhaps a martyr for the great battle against the enemy disease.

But what would happen if Amy—or I or Joan Didion or any of us—stopped fighting? What would happen if we awakened to the fact that we are in the Pit, admitting that our enemy is not down here with us? What if we gave the limbic system a rest, releasing our clenched fists even as we continue in the darkness? What if we were to open our eyes and breathe deeply in the Pit itself? When we're all out of choices, this may be all that is left for us.

## What Cannot Be Mended

Some people visit the woods or the beach to help them breathe deeply. In these places, they may experience the opposite of "fight or flight" in the body—slowing breath, loosening muscles, the parasympathetic nervous system helping the body and mind to be calm. I do enjoy the woods—the beach, not so much, especially if it's crowded. But somehow, for me, a good cemetery seems to work wonders for my agitated mind and tightened body.

Of course, "a good cemetery" may sound like nonsense. But the ones with trees and gravestones that rise up high above the ground, bearing simple dedications to mothers, sons, fathers, and daughters—those are my favorite. They seem to put the doctor's prognosis and the daily pain and fatigue into some perspective.

At a local cemetery on a recent morning, I was taking in the musty scent beneath the weeping pines shading the ground with their long, drooping branches. I could hear the highway in the distance, but louder were the insistent calls of cardinals and the squawks of crows. The soil seemed soft as I walked across the grass, reading the headstones.

Born in the nineteenth century, the dead in these graves bear names such as Jacob, Irma, Florence, Herman, Rita, Ida, Mayme. I try to fit families together, almost like a jigsaw puzzle. Sometimes the last name is a clue. Usually, beside the birth and death dates there is only a single word: "Mother." "Father." "Husband." Others have no family role affixed to their gravestones, though they were certainly sons or daughters.

The dates themselves are often puzzling: "Margaret" with the single date June 8, 1948. Why only one date? It must be both the birth and the death date. She lived for only a day. "Gerald," also with a single date, this time only a year: 1948. He must have died within the year. Then "Florence." I did the math in my head. Florence lived twenty-four years.

So many stories. At the time, the loss of a nine-month-old child must have swallowed the world of the mother, the father, the family. But the catastrophe seems distant now. That child's headstone is joined by so many other small headstones for children who lived two weeks, two years, eight years. As I gazed at other stones, I could glimpse other stories: mothers burying sons, husbands burying wives. The shaking of worlds, the swallowing up of the living into Sheol. Yet the earth-shattering can seem so trivial to someone living only seventy years later. The leaders of nations continue to govern and fight and have scandals. The oceans and woods continue to shelter plants and strange creatures, large and small. The shattering of worlds seems so insignificant. And those in Sheol realize that many others have been there before.

As I stand in the graveyard, it's not just the mysterious stories of tragedy that intrigue. It's the long marriages, the long lives, the wealthy who leave behind large headstones—they must have made a great impact, right? But I have no idea who they are now, and few among the living do. Strikingly, when Ecclesiastes famously proclaims that human endeavors are "vanity," it's not mainly talking about the activities of idleness or wasted time. Some who have a brush with death take up a cause and try to make the most of each day, realizing the shortness of life. But the point in Ecclesiastes is nearly the opposite: "Then I considered all that my hands had done and the toil I had spent in doing it, and again, all was vanity and a chasing after wind, and there was nothing to be gained under the sun" (Eccles. 2:11). As psychologist Jonathan Haidt observes, "The author of Ecclesiastes wasn't just battling the fear of meaninglessness; he was battling the disappointment of success."[18] Our greatest accomplishments turn out to be very small. And despite the self-congratulatory way in which we tend to view such accomplishments, they're actually vanity, dust, blown away by the wind. Our gargantuan struggles turn out to be tiny. The most self-empowered among us will be forgotten, in all but the barest details, within a hundred years. How much do I really know about my great-great-grandparents?

It turns out that opening our eyes to the reality of the Pit can be a great relief. Yes, there is value to an internal "locus of control." Yes, there is value to medical care. But among the dead, we see that we cannot deliver ourselves—that burden is not on our shoulders. Whether you are empowered or imprisoned, whether you receive medical help or not, whether our lives are extended or not, in the Pit we face a reality before which we are utterly impotent: death. Even if we see this in the Pit, we can't necessarily get our hearts and minds around it. In the words of Harvard surgeon Atul Gawande, "There's no escaping the tragedy of life, which is that we are all aging from the day we are born. One may even come to understand and accept this fact. My dead and dying parents don't haunt my dreams anymore. But that's not the same as saying one knows how to cope with what cannot be mended."[19] The reality that we are dying from the day that we are born is one that cannot be mended. We can see that in the Pit.

Only the captives seek deliverance. Only the wounded long for their cuts to be mended. Only those who have tasted the food of dust and the drink of tears ache for bread and water. Only those who know the pit of Sheol pine for the temple. "My soul longs, indeed it faints / for the courts of the LORD," the psalmist cries (84:2). And only those who open their eyes in the place of darkness can see well enough to crave the resurrection light.

## Discussion Questions

- What are the spaces of Sheol in your life? In daily life, in what ways do you tend to act as if you can deliver yourself from Sheol?
- The psalmist declares that "if I make my bed in Sheol, / you [the Lord] are there" (Ps. 139:8). And Christ experienced human

darkness on the cross as he joined the psalmist in crying, "My God, my God, why have you forsaken me?" How do these scriptural testimonies stretch our understanding of God's presence with us in the Pit? How have you experienced God's presence or absence in the Pit?

- My family experienced the reality of death as my children said goodbye to our family pet. How might practices like this prepare us and our children to "face the shadow of the Pit" in other areas of our lives?

- Who in your life is facing a season in Sheol? What would it mean to move toward them right now and walk with them in lament and hope?

# *Two*

## Two Views of Mortality

### Is Death an Enemy or a Friend?

Sometimes death strikes down the living abruptly through a heart attack, a suicide, a car accident, a drowning. Loved ones can be left feeling stranded, breathless, and unprepared. In contrast, many forms of cancer operate in slow motion. Dying is protracted. Even if the process takes only weeks, patients and their loved ones observe and anticipate each step along the way. My own cancer hollows the inside of my bones, so that they become "like Swiss cheese," one doctor quipped with a slight smile. Vital organs become compromised, failing one by one. If this process of deterioration does not stop the heart and breathing, the side effects of the chemotherapy and ongoing treatment will do the job soon enough. Although I could be hit by a car tomorrow, terminal cancer patients like me tend to assume that we can foresee our upcoming demise, like the witches in Hamlet who prophesy his fate. We just don't know *when* it will come. But when the cancer comes back to carry me down the road of death, the doctors will do what they can to fight this injury, this violation, this offense.

This way of talking about cancer simply intensifies the views I absorbed about death as a young person growing up in a Christian community. Death was a violation, a horror. It was supposed to happen only to a very old person. And even then death was an indignity, a foe. As a Christian, I reminded myself, the apostle Paul was on my side, referring to death as "the last enemy to be destroyed" (1 Cor. 15:26)—although that obviously had not happened yet. As I learned more about the Bible, I found more evidence to bolster my case that death was fundamentally unnatural: the garden of Eden, framed in Genesis as a place where God dwells, appears to be free from the sting of human death. Indeed, Eden, with the tree of life and guarded by the cherubim, is a type of garden-temple (later reflected in the tree-shaped menorah and cherubim symbols in Israel's temple). Furthermore, in the Holiness Code of the Old Testament (Lev. 17–26), those who touched a corpse were considered ritually unclean and could not enter the temple until they underwent purification. In the New Testament, the apostle Paul claims that "just as sin came into the world through one man, and death came through sin, . . . death spread to all because all have sinned" (Rom. 5:12). Death occurred as a consequence of sin, so it obviously was not a good thing. In most of the Christian books that I read after my cancer diagnosis, death was portrayed as an enemy, a punishment, a departure from God's intention. And I found this convincing, since I, for one, didn't want to die.

And yet gradually I discovered a different Christian story about death as well. I discovered it not only as I read Scripture and books of theology, but also as I went to funerals and as I've come to know those who have lived many years and feel ready to embrace death. They have a sense of completion, like Job, who died "old and full of days" (Job 42:17). Some of these see dying as a challenge, the last lap in a race. Others embrace dying as a welcome release from wearisome burdens. For both groups, it is quite possible to live too long—to insist upon breath at all costs when the body is caving in on itself. Little by little, they have taught me that if our present earthly life were to simply go on forever, it would be a curse. In Genesis, Adam and Eve are banished from the garden after their cardinal disobedience, with a particular consequence: the man "must not be allowed to reach out his hand and take also from the tree of life and eat, and live forever" (Gen. 3:22 NIV).

Over dinner one day, my wife, Rachel (an Old Testament scholar), suggested that this banishment from the tree of life and immortality could be a form of divine mercy. Perhaps such banishment has its own grace built within it. How? Because for sinful humans to live forever would be a terrible burden, not a gift. J. R. R. Tolkien, referring to characters in his book *The Silmarillion*, wrote that "the doom of the Elves is to be immortal." They are gifted, yet also caught in a cycle: "to love the beauty of the world, to bring it to full flower with their gifts of delicacy and perfection, to last while it lasts, never leaving it even when 'slain,' but returning." In contrast, humans are freed from bondage to the "circles of the world" through mortality. Human mortality is both a source of "grief" and "an envy to the immortal Elves."[1] In Christian terms, to live as a fallen creature without a terminus could, in fact, be a banishment to Sheol, a place of darkness cut off from the graces of creaturely limits.

In my book *Rejoicing in Lament*, I championed the view of death as an enemy as I reflected on my own experience as someone diagnosed with incurable cancer. But as I discussed the book with a group of men and women in their eighties and nineties at a retirement center, I began to wonder whether I had missed something.

This group of forty had met weekly in smaller groups for a couple of months to read each chapter aloud and share their thoughts with one another. On the evening of our discussion, I addressed questions that the groups had written down. One question arose again and again, in various forms: Why did I speak about death as an enemy, when many of them were *looking forward* to death? In fact, wasn't death a reward? They understood why death was an adversary for their kids or grandkids. Moreover, they didn't want me to die, especially since I have young children. But for them? Their bodies were wearing out, deteriorating, falling apart. Their biggest fear was that they would live too long, debilitated by decay but kept afloat by medical technology. Most of their peers, their friends, had already died. Death would come as a welcome, even overdue, friend.

So which view is correct: death as an enemy, or death as a relief, a mercy? This has been a friendly debate between Rachel and me over the dinner table since the time that we started dating, and it has continued into our married days: Is death portrayed as "natural" in Scripture, or is it fundamentally "unnatural," deeply contrary to God's intention for creation? Is death always a foe, or is it sometimes a friend? Our discussion gets very complicated very quickly. Usually it ends with rolling eyes and some laughter.

We can't fully assess these views from the outside—as if death didn't apply to us—but only as mortals. Death lies before all of us, out of our immediate reach. We can speculate, but we cannot actually *know* whether it will be feared or welcomed in our final moments. In the meantime, we live expecting our death to be either "friend" or "foe," and the process of dying to be one of edification or of injury.

Which view is truly authentic for frail human beings? Which view is faithful to the testimony of Scripture? I've come to think that a provisional answer to these questions may be "both." Jesus, the pioneer of our faith, takes on death as a challenge, an opportunity for service and witness; yet he also enters into the depths of Sheol, wounded and abandoned, as he weeps in Gethsemane and dies on a cross outside the temple and outside Jerusalem's walls. Somehow, both views about death are embodied and culminate in Jesus Christ. And I sense that both views will apply to those who find life in Christ as well.

## Death as Pedagogy: Walter and Irenaeus

"What did she die of?" That was my boyhood question to adults when they mentioned they were going to a funeral. The usual response was spoken quietly but firmly to this and any follow-up questions: "She died of old age." By the time I reached adolescent contrariety, I would protest, "Old age is not a disease! You can't die of old age!" I started to press for specifics. "How did she die? What was her illness?" But after hearing one speculation after another about why a ninety-five-year-old patient's heart stopped beating, I ended up thinking to myself, "She died of old age." A natural end, not a puzzle to be solved. Death in old age is natural, with blessings of its own. This end seems a bit like that of Abraham, who "breathed his last and died in a good old age, an old man and full of years" (Gen. 25:8).

Walter, a friend from church, died of old age. Old age was not his disease, of course, but his life arc was ending—an arc of over ninety years, from birth to childhood to adolescence to marriage, parenting, and eventually grandparenting. He had skin in the game in each season of that arc. Even dying was something he did with a certain confidence, as if it were a calling.

I could quickly identify Walter in any crowd—whether he was at church, in a coffee shop, or slowly striding down the sidewalk near his retirement home. He walked with a shiny silver cane and a slight hunch, bringing him to just over five feet in height. His eyeglasses were supposedly "transitional"—changing from clear to dark, adjusting to the indoor or the outdoor light—but they always seemed to be as black as night. Yet Walter never hid behind them. He usually sported a light-colored jacket, a white shirt, slacks, and a wide, black tie. His attire lent a dignity to Walter that was reinforced by his dramatic, expressive voice, which sounded like that of an NPR announcer. Wherever I met him, he would greet me by name, give a firm handshake, and introduce himself to anyone else in the vicinity, whether he could see them clearly or not. When asked how he was, he would always speak about some blessing of the day and a grandchild providing cheer, as if his voice were singing a buoyant song. Then, in a low voice, he would report that he was saddened by his wife Edith's progressing dementia. But he would rarely linger in his melancholy.

Walter would ask me about teaching, about the seminary where I work, about the ministry of young pastors today. Usually these questions were congenial, but sometimes I felt a sting. This man more than twice my age would find his way into any and every Sunday school class I taught, and he seemed to enjoy challenging my theological ideas in stark terms. Yet as I got to know Walter, I sensed that he offered these challenges affectionately. He tutored at-risk middle schoolers until the week before he died, and he mentored any seminary interns who were willing to meet with him. Walter had retired from his pastoral work decades before. He was going to die soon, and he knew it; he spoke of it in casual conversation. He didn't speak of it with dread, but with an inevitability that he refused to fight. Until death took him, he was going to get out in the sun, care for his wife, love his grandchildren, mentor middle schoolers and seminary students, and occasionally put a burr under the saddle of young professors. He enjoyed all of those things.

By contrast, when I spent time with Edward, an older family friend, I would hear his complaints—anger at how people had treated him and about how foolish and corrupt teachers, leaders, and young people are today. Edward occasionally spoke about how he had "shown" those who thought he was just a parochial pastor's kid. His own dad was long dead, and those whom he was "showing" were either dead or out of contact with him. Edward's bitter drama continued only for him; the audience and the other actors had already left the theater.

Walter, on the other hand, seemed to radiate a sense of gratitude; he was "full of years," like Abraham, and blessed by God. He felt the ache and burn of daily pain, he had lost much of his vision, and he was becoming less and less mobile. He helped feed, bathe, and care for the love of his life, Edith, who no longer recognized him most days. But he didn't really expect or want to be young anymore. He would die soon, and he seemed to embrace that arc. And his response was gratitude.

Anglican theologian Ephraim Radner points out that it is increasingly difficult for us to embrace each stage of our life as a gift, as a testimony to God's faithfulness. "One reason that adults [today] cannot stick with things—marriages, their children, their jobs, the generations of their flesh and community, their ecclesial commitments—is because we have failed to learn the patience that comes with recognizing our lives as given, in an order, in time, in their places."[2] Perhaps that's why a friend was both grieving and radiant after Walter's funeral. "It's sad, but it is also so encouraging," she said through her tears. As little clumps of dust given the breath of life, we have the concrete, creaturely task of receiving the joys and griefs that we are given, loving our neighbor in our home and down the street and living in a way that leads not to resentment but to praise. When I embrace earthly mortality throughout life rather than living as if I had no limits, no terminus, I can "engage these realities of my life as a *creature* whose experiences turn me toward my creatureliness in God's hands."[3]

The second-century bishop Irenaeus painted a portrait of Jesus, and secondarily of Adam, that fits in significant ways with this embrace of the creaturely stages of life. For Irenaeus, the embodied arc of growth, adulthood, and dying is a creaturely good. This was a crucial claim for the early church leader, for many in his day followed the teaching of Gnostics who insisted that the vulnerability of flesh being born, maturing, and decaying was an embarrassing scandal. The Gnostics declared that God must be distanced from that whole carnal process. The Gnostic God would never take on mortal flesh in an incarnation. Irenaeus, by contrast, celebrated the bodily, creaturely life as good, in all its stages of growth and decline. Indeed, he even spoke about Jesus as experiencing old age. Jesus "was an old man for old men, that He might be a perfect Master for all, not merely as respects the setting forth of the truth, but also as regards age."[4] Although Irenaeus seems to have given Jesus a couple of more decades than the historical record can countenance, his point about the embodied, creaturely life is salient. In childhood, adolescence, adulthood, and even old age, the human person lives a life that the Lord calls "good." Walter would have agreed. He embraced life with limits—even the sharp-edged limit of dying and death.

As unnerving as it sounds to our culture, so vigilant to stave off death at all costs, Irenaeus claimed that dying itself can be part of a divine pedagogy for coming to know the mercy of the Lord. Irenaeus came to this conclusion while commenting on the story of creation. Adam and Eve were created as good and yet not fully refined and perfected creatures. They were inexperienced infants, not fully mature adults. This was not a mistake on God's part but an act of mercy. A mother could try to feed an infant a three-course meal prepared for a hungry teenager, but that would not be appropriate for the infant. In the same way, "it was possible for God Himself to have made man perfect from the first, but man could not receive this [perfection], being as yet an infant."[5] God does not force-feed his children but nurtures them on the path of growth like a good parent. Part of God's intention for creaturely growth is that one comes to love family and community, food and festivity, work and play—and yet, as a mortal, learns to let go of all those things for God's sake.

Thus, for Irenaeus, dying presents us with an opportunity, a choice: either trust in God as the source of life, or try to have life on our own terms (similar to Adam and Eve's sin in the garden). The act of dying becomes an opportunity for growth, a lesson taught by the divine parent. Embracing the mortal course of our lives is a step in our maturation as creatures who trust in the living God. Walter's daily care for Edith, even as she seemed to become less like herself each day, was tender. Walter's mentoring of at-risk children filled him with passion. And yet even these good deeds would need to slip out of his fingers. God was asking Walter to give up his life of service as the arc of his mortality took its course, coming to rest only in the One who is life's source.

As Irenaeus would see it, Walter was not walking a self-congratulatory road. His path of growth displays the depth of human vulnerability— the utter human need for the incarnate Lord Jesus, who shows his loving strength through weakness. As the risen Christ proclaims to the apostle Paul, "My grace is sufficient for you, for power is made perfect in weakness" (2 Cor. 12:9). Christ shows us that true humanity does not lord it over others but takes "the form of a slave," as Paul's letter to the Philippians testifies:

> Being found in human form,
>> he humbled himself
>> and became obedient to the point of death—
>> even death on a cross. (Phil. 2:7–8)

As Irenaeus expresses it, God's power is displayed through the Word made flesh, who is "capable of being tempted, dishonoured, crucified, and of suffering death."[6] Jesus reveals the form of the fully matured human by loving when he is hated, choosing obedience when he is tempted, and enduring suffering and death as a creature before the face of God. Jesus is made completely and perfectly mature only through taking on mortal suffering and death. As Hebrews declares, "He learned obedience through what he suffered; and having been made perfect, he became the source of eternal salvation for all who obey him" (Heb. 5:8–9). Christ took on the pedagogy of dying and death, disclosing true humanity to us. And rising from the dead, he brought true humanity into the glory of heaven.

Irenaeus says that once we have come to taste the sweetness of trusting the Lord on the path of suffering and dying pioneered by Christ, we develop the taste buds and stomachs to feed "from the breast of His flesh, and having, by such a course of milk-nourishment, become accustomed to eat and drink the Word of God, may be able also to contain in ourselves the Bread of immortality, which is the Spirit of the Father."[7] In Irenaeus's vision, although death entered the world through sin, the biological fact of human mortality has been taken up into the mercy of God, giving us a path to trust in God's Word even at our life's end.

Walter sensed that mercy. More than once he smiled and quipped to me that he didn't want to live forever. He embraced his dying as part of the arc of human life, each day an opportunity to walk on the path of fellowship with God that Christ pioneered and the Spirit upholds. The path of dying did not make him slip into Sheol but prepared him for the temple of the Lord.

As with Walter, sometimes the season of dying seems fitting for one who has lived a life "full of years." Irenaeus's theological reflection helps us to see how dying can be a gift, an instrument of the Triune God. But one might wonder: Did Irenaeus develop his view of dying because he enjoyed a long, privileged life of security?

When we look at his life, that is clearly not the case. Irenaeus was no stranger to suffering, early dying, and unseemly deaths. In his day, Christians were persecuted by the state. Irenaeus recalls that, as a child, he sat and listened to a bishop named Polycarp. He remembers vividly his experiences with this elder Christian. According to a letter Irenaeus wrote as an adult, "I can speak even of the place in which the blessed Polycarp sat and disputed, how he came in and went out, the character of his life, the appearance of his body, the discourses which he made to the people." Polycarp shared his faith as one who had received the message of Jesus from "the eyewitnesses of the Word of Life." Polycarp's presence and words touched Irenaeus deeply: "I listened eagerly even then to these things through the mercy of God which was given me, and made notes of them, not on paper, but in my heart, and ever by the grace of God do I truly ruminate on them." At some point during Irenaeus's growth from a boy into a man, however, Polycarp was bound, burned, and stabbed for his faith.[8] Irenaeus later became the bishop of Lyon, an office made vacant by the martyrdom of the previous bishop. Irenaeus undertook this shepherding role amid the especially violent persecution of Christians by the Roman emperor Marcus Aurelius in 177. For Irenaeus, the martyrs died not in defeat but as athletes who were undergoing their final training. These martyrs freely chose to identify with Christ in suffering and death. They chose the path of weakness and lowliness as the true path of the Christian life. They chose courageous witness rather than fearful cowering in the face of death.

Although it first struck me as strange, I've come to embrace the Irenaean view of death as deeply illuminating. I've also come to see how it reflects biblical convictions about creaturehood, finitude, and the incarnation of Christ. The elderly residents of the retirement home I spoke at usually embraced a quite Irenaean perspective on their own mortality: they were content to welcome death as the final season of their mortal lives, dying "full of years" in gratitude to the Creator. But even as they embraced the limits of their mortality, they still knew that dying can be an indignity and death can be a terror. When talking about how death cut down their children or grandchildren by disease or violence, splintering a young family into pieces, they spoke of the raw wound of death. The Irenaean view, on its own, can seem incomplete, even offensive. For death can come as an enemy and can sting as an affliction.

## Death as Irrational: Augustine and Melissa

If, in the second century, Irenaeus is the theologian of dying as a creaturely good, Augustine of Hippo, in the fourth century, is the theologian of death as an irrational horror. In his early writings Augustine described death as concordant with the natural order of things. "When things pass away and others succeed them," he wrote, "there is a specific beauty in the temporal order, so that those things which die or cease to be what they were, do not defile the measure, form or order of the created universe."[9] Human beings die as creatures, fitting into the wondrous order that any biologist or ecologist would recognize. Sometimes this is how children's stories approach death as well. As I snuggle beside my son on a couch with a children's book, we encounter the character "Freddie the Leaf." Freddie loves the sunshine and the wind in summer. But when the decay of autumn comes, Freddie learns that it's his job to fall from the tree, enter the ground, and become fertilizer for new growth after the winter cold. Likewise, the book suggests, human creatures die as part of the ordered cycle of life.

Augustine's theology, however, developed and changed from this "cycle of life" approach as he entered into debates with the British-born theologian and teacher Pelagius. These debates sharpened Augustine's convictions about creation, God's grace, and the staggering implications of human sin. Eventually, Augustine repudiated his earlier view in the strongest possible terms. Death is not a created good, Augustine says, for "God did not create any death for man in his nature, but it was imposed as a just punishment for sin."[10] For Augustine, death is not a step in the divine pedagogy by which humans grow. Death is not good for anyone. It tears apart soul and body, which are conjoined and interwoven in a living being. This is not the last lap in the training of an athlete. Death, in Augustine's view, is a catastrophe, inherently violent and fundamentally unnatural.

Augustine's view reminds me of the memorial service that was held for my friend Melissa. It was a warm Saturday afternoon as the sanctuary filled to overflowing for this mother of two young children. While the service claimed to be a celebration of her "homecoming," the pastor's opening greeting recognized our grief and confusion and anger. We had gathered for a "victory celebration" for Melissa, we were told. Yet we were right to be angry at her death, the pastor told us, for in our anger we acknowledged that something was wrong. We were angry because death is an enemy, an intruder, in this universe. Death was not part of God's original plan. So be angry with Satan, the pastor told us; be angry with sin.

After a couple of songs, Melissa's brother Ryan approached the front of the sanctuary. He spoke of how Melissa had loved to memorize Scripture and to hear the stories of the missionaries their family hosted. Ryan shared how his sister felt called to attend a Christian college and seminary and then to go overseas as a missionary. She married a classmate who shared her missionary calling to live sacrificially in witness and mercy. Over the course of a few years, they had two daughters. Then, after years of preparation and discernment about where they should serve, they moved to Mexico. But without warning, after just two years on the mission field, Melissa became ill and suddenly died. "I never in my wildest dreams imagined that she would get sick and pass so suddenly," Ryan said. Ryan was not naive; he knew the mission field could be dangerous. There could be opposition, persecution, and even imprisonment, such as the apostle Paul faced. But for Ryan and for many of us in the crowded sanctuary, an underlying question animated our shock: How could Melissa's heart just stop beating so abruptly? How could an unexpected disease cause oceans of hope to dry up so quickly? Persecution is one thing; a quick and senseless illness is another. Melissa's life seemed to be gaining momentum, not slowing down. Five minutes in her presence would bring a smile to my face, generating hope for how God would use her in the future. Couldn't God have found someone else to "take home" that day? Whose side is God on, anyway?

In that sanctuary, I heard how Melissa's death would be for God's glory. That seemed both right and terribly problematic. What could it possibly mean that Melissa's death was for God's glory? Job properly testifies that "in [the Lord's] hand is the life of every living thing / and the breath of every human being" (Job 12:10). Every halting breath is a gift, and the Lord of life is necessarily the Lord of death. And yet Job gives this testimony in the midst of debates about suffering with his friends, teetering between thanksgiving and searing lament. Job also opines that the Lord "destroys both the blameless and the wicked. / When disaster brings sudden death, / he mocks at the calamity of the innocent" (Job 9:22–23). Shouldn't we have hoped for something better than this "disaster" bringing "sudden death"? Why did Melissa's death look more like a slip into the pit of Sheol than an ascent on the road to Zion?

For nearly an hour and a half, we both laughed and cried as Melissa's friends and coworkers told stories about her. We stood up between the stories and tried to sing songs of praise. It was hard to sing, but we were right to do so. God is always worthy of praise. Early in the book of Job, after the sudden loss of his children and his wealth, Job declares,

> Naked I came from my mother's womb,
>   and naked I will depart.
> The Lord gave and the Lord has taken away;
>   may the name of the Lord be praised. (Job 1:21 NIV)

But even as I sensed that it was right to praise God, I also wondered if the band could play something other than upbeat, sunny songs. Did these cheery love songs to Jesus recognize our nakedness? Two young girls had just lost their mom. A young husband had lost his wife. All of us had lost a friend; we lost dreams that we didn't know we had for her. But in the service we didn't join the psalmist or Job in lament. We had not, as a community, learned how to sing praise in a minor key.

Years later, Melissa's death still stung. Whether or not I would have used the pastor's words about anger at death, they seemed to disclose something of the genuine horror of the moment at the memorial service. The pastor's comments reflected the German theologian Helmut Thielicke's stark claim that death is "the expression of a catastrophe which runs on a collision course with man's original destination or, in other words, directly *opposite* of his intrinsic nature."[11] This is the Augustinian story about death, and it's not surprising that Melissa's funeral evoked this theme as well.

Perhaps, as Irenaeus claims, Melissa's sudden death was part of her—or *our*—education in the glory of God. But Augustine offers us a needed word as well, a crucial reminder that death is both irrational and horrible. We can't find a reason for a death like this; in fact, according to Augustine, we can't even fully define what the catastrophe of death really is. "But as it is, death is a reality; and so troublesome a reality that it cannot be explained by any verbal formula, nor got rid of by any rational argument."[12] Death broke into Melissa's family, into our friendships, into our unfolding story. It did so as an absence, a sundering, an enigma.

Indeed, for Augustine, death has no rational explanation, and hence it leaves us in silence—in a way that parallels the mystery of sin itself. For instance, in his classic example illustrating the nature of sin in his *Confessions*, Augustine recounts how he stole pears from his neighbors as a boy. Was there a logical justification for his action? No, Augustine says. "We took away an enormous quantity of pears," Augustine recalls, "not to eat them ourselves, but simply to throw them to the pigs." Probing the question a bit more, Augustine says, "Perhaps we ate some of them, but our real pleasure consisted in doing something that was forbidden."[13] And just as Augustine's theft was fundamentally irrational, so Adam and Eve's sin in the garden was fundamentally irrational and mysterious.

Likewise, Augustine suggests, death stalks creatures simply to tear them apart, not to help fertilize the soil and push the cycle of life into its next beautiful season. "The death of the body was not inflicted on us by the law of our nature, since God did not create any death for man in his nature, but it was imposed as a just punishment for sin."[14] Death is not a created good but a consequence of mistrust, of turning toward the self rather than God, of disobedience to the divine command.

And what good could we make of Melissa's death? A young family torn apart. A mission of mercy and witness upended. A person with a joyful presence, gone from the world. Job's lament seemed to unearth the nonsense of attempting to explain why this should happen. "Your hands fashioned and made me, / and now you turn and destroy me," Job says, both testifying to the Lord's work and questioning the Lord about it from the Pit. "Remember that you fashioned me like clay; / and will you turn me to dust again?" (Job 10:8–9). Melissa may be in a "better place," but that's not where we want her. We want her here. Her girls need her here. Death is a crushing blow to the here and now that we desire. "If he tears down, no one can rebuild; / if he shuts someone in, no one can open up" (Job 12:14). Why this tearing down, O Lord, when her body seemed so strong, with so much life and potential and future? Why would the hands that fashioned Melissa turn her into dust again right now, with a husband and young daughters and a vocation in global mission just underway?

Perhaps these unanswered questions point to our need for a pioneer, a priest who knows our weaknesses, a Savior who has been to Sheol. Precisely because death and many of the sufferings we face are not good in any intrinsic sense, we can have our hearts awakened by the innocent one who "offered up prayers and supplications, with loud cries and tears, to the one who was able to save him from death, and he was heard because of his reverent submission" (Heb. 5:7). Christ offered up prayers, and they were heard; though he died on a cross as one who was apparently cursed, he was actually entering into the holy of holies, the most sacred part of the temple. "He entered once for all into the Holy Place, not with the blood of goats and calves, but with his own blood, thus obtaining eternal redemption" (Heb. 9:12). Christ did not marry, have children or grandchildren, or enter into old age. He had no earthly inheritance as he faced death. His heart stopped beating and his breath stopped heaving outside of the temple, in Sheol. As he took on this disgraceful, untimely death, he bore the shame of *our own* deaths, which also appear to be outside of the temple, far from the Lord's promise.

For Augustine, this astonishing mystery is precisely what God takes on in the incarnation and the cross of Christ. Christ does not simply live and then die a natural death. Christ, "the reflection of God's glory and the exact imprint of God's very being" (Heb. 1:3), freely chooses obedience that stoops to the point of death to show God's love to helpless sinners. "He deigned to be crucified, became obedient even to the death of the cross. He who was about to take away all death, chose the lowest and worst kind of death. . . . It was indeed the worst of deaths, but it was chosen by the Lord."[15] Christ acts as both the priest whose sacrifice is perfect and the pioneer whose journey into Sheol proves the psalmist right in saying,

> If I make my bed in Sheol, you are there.
> ................................................
> If I say, "Surely the darkness shall cover me,
>     and the light around me become night,"
> even the darkness is not dark to you;
>     the night is as bright as the day,
>     for darkness is as light to you. (Ps. 139:8, 11–12)

The darkness, of course, is still dark to us. But since Christ embodied the temple in his person—and yet absorbed the black hole of Sheol in his dying and rising—we know the darkness is not all there is.

I wonder, though, whether we sometimes miss this work of Christ by pitching our praise only in major keys rather than in minor ones as well. Christ, the light of the world, died in terrible darkness. In the words of Job, the Lord

> has walled up my way so that I cannot pass,
>     and he has set darkness upon my paths.
> He has stripped my glory from me,
>     and taken the crown from my head. (Job 19:7–9)

I believe the speaker at Melissa's memorial service was right to say that her death will serve God's glory, but maybe that glory involves a stripping of earthly glory, a participation in Christ's dark death. Indeed, Christians are marked by the sign of the cross, a doubly violent horror—both in the crucifixion itself and in the miscarriage of justice that led to it. In Augustine's view, this leads to a transfiguration of glory as a mark of the Christian. "He was to have that very cross as His sign; that very cross, a trophy, as it were, over the vanquished devil, He was to put on the brow of believers, so that the apostle said, 'God forbid that I should glory, save in the cross of our Lord Jesus Christ' [Gal. 6:14]."[16]

We mortals do not just need some bodywork to fix the dings and dents caused by sin. We need a love that seeks us out in the Pit, even while we are hostile, while we are enemies of God and his purposes. We need the cross—a sign in the darkness of God's radiant, friend-making love. In Augustine's words, "he came into the world as a lover of his enemies," and "he found absolutely all of us his enemies, he didn't find anyone a friend. It was for enemies that he shed his blood, but by his blood that he converted his enemies. With his blood he wiped out his enemies' sins; by wiping out their sins, he made friends out of enemies."[17]

Melissa's life, and certainly her death, was marked by the sign of the cross. Maybe, just maybe, the darkness of Melissa's death testifies to the astonishing brightness of Christ's love, which makes friends with us in our darkness. I can't figure out how Melissa's death fits into any human plan for good. I can't see how it was "for the best," as we sometimes tell ourselves. But even though I don't know the reasons why, or how her death could be for God's glory, I do trust that Melissa belonged to Jesus in life and in death. Because Jesus died in darkness, Melissa's death in darkness is mysteriously a death in the temple, in Christ as the dwelling place of God, in the one in whom "there is no darkness at all" (1 John 1:5). The crucified and risen Lord holds Melissa's death in his hands; and this same Lord Jesus can use it, if he wishes, as a witness to his own friend-making love.

## Which Death? Which Story?

You may be wondering, Which will be the story of my own death? Will it be more like the story of Walter or of Melissa? Will I die "full of years" at the end of a long life? Will my dying be the final stretch in the race of discipleship? Or will my death be a sudden and inscrutable horror to my friends and family?

Mortals can be certain of one thing on this point: we don't know. Even patients with a terminal diagnosis like me don't know. Death is always out before us, beyond our reach. As soon as we *could* know which story is ours, it will be too late. "You won't be there when you're dead," in the words of my daughter. Our earthly life will be over. We can talk about what medical interventions we want if we end up in the hospital or hospice, but our heart could unexpectedly stop beating, and it all would come to nothing. When I asked my father about the death of his grandpa at the age of sixty, he said, "Probably a heart attack, but we don't really know. He was just working on the farm, and he died one day." The improved technologies utilized in postmortems today may give us more probable answers about why a sudden death occurs. But they can't prevent the accident or the unforeseen malady that takes away our breath and stills our heart.

Given this uncertainty, it makes sense to pursue growth throughout each stage of life with Irenaeus, but also to recognize with Augustine that death itself is an enigma, a reality always beyond our grasp, a foe that cannot be fully domesticated or befriended. The Lord's work is expansive enough to encompass both the Irenaean and the Augustinian sides of death. In Christ, God has taken on our mortal, creaturely life and pioneered a true humanity that displays mature power through humble obedience. And we also see that in Christ's cross and resurrection, God plunges the darkness of the Pit into his vast universe of light, forgiving the enemy and giving new life to those whose feet are stuck in the miry bog.

In all likelihood, our own deaths will not fit exclusively into one theological view of death or the other. They will have a bit of both. Indeed, even in the stories of Walter and Melissa we see fragments of both views held together. Walter lived a long life, "full of years," and his dying was an opportunity for service and witness. Yet he also experienced the irrational horror of death as dementia pulled his wife, Edith, more and more away from him, away from their shared past, away from the present moment. "Old age can be very frightening," a character in a P. D. James novel confesses, revealing that he is losing his memory. "My son died young, and at the time, it seemed to be the most terrible thing that could happen to anyone in the world—to him, as well as to me. But perhaps he was one of the fortunate ones."[18] This may be part of Walter's story with Edith as well.

Melissa's death was a horror, and many at her funeral spoke of her unlived years and what could or should have been for her and her young family. Yet we also heard about how, weeks before her unexpected death, she had completed a writing project to share her faith with her daughters. Perhaps even as a young mother she had started to embrace her mortal limits and come to terms with her eventual death. Whether we face death at fifteen or fifty or ninety, we are likely to have both Irenaean and Augustinian elements woven into our dying.

In what ways can these two types and theologies of death be reconciled? As in the cases of Walter and Melissa, living and dying involve both joy and sorrow. And both Irenaeus and Augustine testify to the God of creation, who takes on death and its consequences in the dying and rising of Jesus Christ. Yet, held together, the two types of dying can seem like oil and water—like a strange recipe in which the two main ingredients just won't mix. Yes, our living and dying will probably reflect aspects from both Walter's and Melissa's stories, both Irenaeus's and Augustine's visions. But the combination won't make for a bland soup. No, the contrasts will remain: sweet and sour together, soft and sharp. For us and our loved ones, our own dying will likely be both an offense and a gift, an affliction and a consolation, a catastrophe and a strange work of providence.

Thus, to be attentive to the tastes and smells of God's gifts in living and dying, we need to embrace two apparently contrary realities. On the one hand, dying is a dimension of the gift of life, an opportunity for growth, for witness, for service. The dying should receive not just our sympathy and our prayers for healing but also our prayers for courage as they witness and serve, even as they depend on others. The dying are still athletes running the race. God works in his dying creatures, often showing his strength in and through creaturely weakness. Whether we are young or old, the reality of our mortality can goad us to cultivate faith, hope, and love; reminders of our mortality can lead us to seize the day for kindness, for faithfulness to family and friends, for courage in the face of adversity. If we deny and push away our mortality, we miss the gifts that our small and fragile creaturely status gives us, the opportunities that knowledge of our dying opens up for us in daily life.

On the other hand, we also need to embrace the icy truth that death itself is an enigma and a wound. We become slaves to fear when we refuse to speak the word "death" and give only euphemisms in its place: "passing on," "promoted to heaven," moved to "a better place." Yes, these euphemisms testify to something true, but they also treat an open wound like a trophy. The dead are now corpses, deceased, taken from us—for no reason that we can understand. Without acknowledging this Augustinian view of death's inherent violence, we ignore the ways in which the death of a loved one leaves us with branches withered on the vine.

When we honestly name the wounds, the withered branches, the ways in which we are undone, we vaccinate ourselves against the overpowering fear of death. We give death its space, let its wounds breathe without fabricating explanations about how it makes sense or works for the best. Otherwise, the fear of death actually enters our bloodstream. With the Preacher in Ecclesiastes, we admit that "a living dog is better than a dead lion," that the dead will "never again . . . have any share in all that happens under the sun." Accepting this can help us to experience the creaturely joy and wonder of the next verse: "Go, eat your bread with enjoyment, and drink your wine with a merry heart" (Eccles. 9:4, 6–7).

Admit it: we cannot master death or understand its ways. But this Augustinian surrender can be a liberating victory. And this Augustinian insight can point, like the death of Melissa, to the most courageous and liberating death in the cosmos: the death of the one through whom all things were made, the death of Jesus in darkness, the one who is "crowned with glory and honor because of the suffering of death, so that by the grace of God he might taste death for everyone" (Heb. 2:9).

This Augustinian perspective on the fundamentally irrational character of death in darkness can point us to the absolute necessity of a mediator, a redeemer who tasted death on our behalf. If we don't embrace this deeply, we can spend a great deal of anxious energy blaming one person or institution or another, as if they themselves thought up the idea of death. We may perform acrobatic feats of logic to get God off the hook for horrific deaths, to answer those "why" questions for Melissa and so many others. Ironically, such preoccupations tend to inject the fear of death into our lives, distracting us from the larger reality that we are mortal and that God's promise does not nullify our mortality. We don't have answers to all of our "why" questions, but the world is still full of wonder and beauty, and God's promise testifies that death will not have the final word.

> Where were you when I laid the foundation of the earth?
>  Tell me, if you have understanding.
> Who determined its measurements—surely you know!
>  Or who stretched the line upon it?
> On what were its bases sunk,
>  or who laid its cornerstone
> when the morning stars sang together
>  and all the heavenly beings shouted for joy? (Job 38:4–7)

As strange as it seems to say this, the Lord's reply to Job out of the whirlwind is a liberating one: it does not answer Job's questions or cure his fears, but nevertheless enables him to live again—to raise children, to run a farm, to live for many more years and eventually see "his children, and his children's children" (Job 42:16). He does so as one who knew the Pit and the riddle of death, and knew that the riddle could not be solved. He does so as a creature with wounds and scars, but he also, as chapters 38 and 39 go on to emphasize, continues on as a mortal who knows the joy and wonder of the world of bears and lions and ravens and mountain goats and ostriches and eagles that the Lord governs in ways Job did not previously understand. Job trusts in the Lord, the Creator, whose ways he cannot fathom. And, like Abraham, like Walter, he dies not controlled by fear but, as the concluding verse of the book testifies, "old and full of days" (42:17).

Whether our own deaths look more like Walter's or Melissa's, we can trust that even in our dying and our death we've not slipped out of the hands of the Creator and Redeemer, the crucified and risen Lord, who entered into the darkness on our behalf. The darkness is still dark, but it's not given the final word. For in the words of Paul, this Lord, Jesus Christ who was crucified, is "the blessed and only Sovereign, the King of kings and Lord of lords. It is he alone who has immortality and dwells in unapproachable light" (1 Tim. 6:15–16).

## *Discussion Questions*

- In this chapter I suggest that living forever "as a fallen creature without a terminus could, in fact, be a banishment to Sheol, a place of darkness cut off from the graces of creaturely limits." What questions does this raise for you? In what ways do you resonate with this perspective, or not?

- We encounter two Christian views about death in this chapter—one that sees death as a fitting completion to a creaturely life, and one that sees death as fundamentally violent and unnatural. Which view of death do you typically hear? In what situations might we understand death as something that helps us grow?

- Might it be possible for the two views of death explored in this chapter to both be true at the same time? "For us and our loved ones, our own dying will likely be both an offense and a gift, an affliction and a consolation, a catastrophe and a strange work of providence." As you think about your own experiences of losing loved ones, how might you see both aspects in those experiences?

# *Three*

## Mortals in Denial

### Living as Dying Creatures

The heart has four duties to fulfill:
What to love, what to fear,
What to rejoice in, and for what to be sad.

—Bernard of Clairvaux[1]

It was a bright southern California day on Santa Monica Beach, and the ocean waves were almost luminous in the sunlight beneath the long horizon. A seminary intern, I'd left behind the books in my apartment to join my church's youth group on a beach trip. I thought I'd try to be the role model of having fun, riding a boogie board on the waves. That is, until I lost control on a breaking wave and was plunged into the salty tide.

My thinking ceased, or so it seemed. When my head finally made it above the water for a moment, I gasped for breath before being pulled back into the undertow. If I had been a fish returning to the ocean depths, nothing would have been easier: the strong hands of the ocean hold you, carry you, bring you into the deep sea. But even without thought, my body instinctively knew that the deep sea was not where I wanted to go.

When I made it to the surface again, I gasped for oxygen and tried to get my bearings. My boogie board was far out of reach, bouncing on the tide and rolling closer to the beach. A few more dunkings, and then some salty water swept down my throat as my body broke the surface.

Eventually—I don't remember how—I made it back to the beach. I kneeled on the sand and heaved air into my lungs. I hadn't asked anyone to watch me, but another youth group leader saw me and walked in my direction. That's when my thoughts caught up with what my body had experienced all along: fear. "I was fighting for survival," my body told me. I could have rested in the undertow, making my way into the wide ocean, but instead my body sprang into action. The *thought* of fear—that "I could have died here"—came afterward. The body fears death, whether or not I'm thinking of death.

It's an audacious claim, but I think there are good reasons to believe that my experience that afternoon points to something woven deeply into our created selves and our biological wiring. I can't claim that the experience itself is universal; human experience has extraordinary variety simply because different persons in different contexts have different bodies. If one of the middle schoolers in my youth group had been caught in the same undertow, their reaction may have differed. Yet I would wager this: that if taken by surprise, the bodies of my fellow *Homo sapiens* would fight for life, whether or not thoughts came to mind, whether they had viewed the future with hope or with despair before entering the water. Our bodies have a "survival instinct," biologists say, whether or not our thinking decides to catch up with them. The body of an infant knows it, and the bodies of everyone everywhere know it. No school or parent needs to teach this: our bodies fear death.

In the past fifty years, numerous studies in social psychology have sought to provide empirical evidence to support the claim that our fear of death is more basic than our thought. One implication is that the reality of our mortality powerfully affects our thoughts and actions, even when we aren't consciously aware of it. This cheery-sounding school of thought is called "terror management theory." We experience awe and joy, and yet, researchers say, "we are also perpetually troubled by the concurrent realization that all living things, ourselves included, ultimately die, and that death can occur for reasons that can never be anticipated or controlled." Indeed, the "potential for terror is omnipresent" because our daily activities remind us of our connections to the earth, to which we will return. We are defecating, urinating, vomiting, flatulent creatures, even if we are uncomfortable being such creatures. And yet, paradoxically, in day-to-day life, we cannot function as creatures who are constantly aware of this death-fear. If we fully surrendered to our fears as mortal, decaying creatures, then we would be "incapacitated by overwhelming terror."[2]

Whether or not one believes in God or in Scripture's veracity, these scientists demonstrate just how muddy the Sheol-pit is. As mortal creatures, we are caught in the mud, stuck between terror about our dying and the necessity of hoping for the light as we live and love each day.

### Overcoming the Fear of Death?

Sometimes Christians glibly claim that they no longer fear death. I don't think the body agrees. And the Christian faith speaks directly to our predicament of facing death-terror when it claims that we are not pioneers in this death-fear. In the incarnation, God himself has taken on suffering and dying flesh: "In bringing many sons and daughters to glory, it was fitting that God, for whom and through whom everything exists, should make the pioneer of their salvation perfect through what he suffered," the book of Hebrews tells us. "Both the one who makes people holy and those who are made holy are of the same family. So Jesus is not ashamed to call them brothers and sisters" (Heb. 2:10–11 NIV). The result is astonishing: "Since the children have flesh and blood, he too shared in their humanity *so that by his death he might break the power of him who holds the power of death*—that is, the devil—and free those who all their lives were held in slavery by their fear of death" (2:14–15 NIV, emphasis added). On the cross, Jesus breaks the bonds of the devil, which hold us in slavery to death. Said differently, Jesus descends to Sheol, "for just as Jonah was three days and three nights in the belly of the sea monster, so for three days and three nights the Son of Man will be in the heart of the earth" (Matt. 12:40).

If anyone else had descended to Sheol through a cross, it would not have had the same effect, according to this biblical reasoning. Hebrews emphasizes that Christ our "brother" is also the royal Son who is "heir of all things" and "the reflection of God's glory and the exact imprint of God's very being, and he sustains all things by his powerful word" (Heb. 1:2–3). This exalted one "through whom" God made the universe (v. 2), with all its creatures, was rejected and crucified by the creatures themselves. Jesus went to Sheol as his sweat dropped to the ground like drops of blood in the shadowy garden of Gethsemane; he went to Sheol in his cry of dereliction from the cross, "Why have you forsaken me?" (Matt. 27:46; Mark 15:34). His crucifixion occurred far from the blessing of the temple, as one accursed. Unlike Abraham, Isaac, David, and even Job, Jesus did not die after he had become old and "full of days." He died in darkness.

But Hebrews insists that, even in what appears to be a bloody defeat, Jesus somehow disarms the satanic power that threatens to overtake us each moment—the power of slavery to the fear of death. We're still dying, that is clear. The breathing "I" who reads the words on this page will cease to inhale. Whether our dying comes after a life of many years or a life cut short, our dying and death and decay is a certainty. And Christians still fear the illnesses and accidents and people that threaten to steal our lives away. Every cell in our bodies aches to survive. But Hebrews does not say that Christians should no longer *fear* death because of Christ, the God-enfleshed pioneer. No. Our deliverance is from *slavery* to death's fear. Stated differently, the goal for the Christian life is not eliminating the fear of death but removing death from its throne. For as long as the fear of death rules, we cannot fully serve, worship, and bear witness to the true King, Jesus.

## Creatures of the Earth, Children of the Lord

Young children often serve unwittingly as a family's instructors in what it means to be a child of the Creator, a creature of the earth. Children teach us what it means to be enfleshed and mortal, even in our own ambivalence about such things. In potty training, some kids show much more interest in making observations about the shape and size of their output—or painting on the bathroom tiles with it—than in learning to deliver it to the sewer system. Other kids turn potty training into a titanic struggle, thinking that if they *resist* strongly enough, their bodies will stop making this terrible, yucky thing. Usually, for both types of kids, few insults provoke a faster response than a peer calling them "poopy" or a "poophead." Delighted by discovering this holy grail of attention-getting, children cleverly return again and again to that insult, that joke. Poking at this wound of suppressed anxiety can be funny, especially because it contrasts so starkly with the buttoned-up, polite world of adulthood that they find themselves dragged into.

A child who does not poop or urinate cannot grow or function apart from an intervention to address the problem. We share these acts with crows, cattle, cats, and carp. We also share with them our mortal frame. Creatures eat and excrete, develop and die. These things are not curses but part of the sometimes funny, sometimes embarrassing blessing of being earthly creatures.

Despite this, Christians and non-Christians alike have often been embarrassed by the portrait of human life in the Old Testament. "It's so earthy," some say. A fair number of Old Testament passages are avoided by preachers and even by the lectionaries used in liturgical congregations. In the Baptist church of my youth, we would memorize passages of Scripture, and members of the youth group would choose a "life verse"—a passage of Scripture that they aspired to make their own. When my friend Kevin was asked what his life verse was, he would say Leviticus 12:3. Smiling faces became puzzled—no one had memorized that one. Inevitably, someone would reach for a Bible to look it up. Haltingly, a high schooler would read Kevin's life verse as Kevin looked on earnestly: "On the eighth day the flesh of his foreskin shall be circumcised."

This reading from Leviticus had a way of fracturing the ever-ascending expectations for life verses in youth group conversation, breaking up the gathering with nervous giggles, rolling eyes, and reproachful looks. But Kevin's contribution, and our reaction, made one point very clearly: there are significant elements of the Old Testament that we consider to be indiscreet. What covenantal sign did the Lord use to mark his chosen people? A memorized prayer, a philosophical treatise, a badge? No. In Genesis 17, after giving his astonishing promise to Abraham to be in covenant with "you and your offspring," the Lord gives a direct command: "Every male among you shall be circumcised. You shall circumcise the flesh of your foreskins, and it shall be a sign of the covenant between me and you" (Gen. 17:10–11). Upon hearing a passage like this, the youth group boys would squint and move their eyes to the floor, some of us kicking at imaginary dust on the cream-colored tiles. Yet this surgical act was a divine command, a sign of God's mission in the world.

The Lord also gave regulations about the temple, with very specific instructions concerning the bleeding of women during periods and the emission of semen by men. The temple worship that the Lord required of his people involved the earthy tasks of baking bread and slaughtering sheep. The Lord even opened the wombs of Sarah, Rebecca, Rachel, Hannah, and other women for the wondrous yet bloody process of giving birth to children. The Lord did not stand apart from blood and sweat and reproductive organs but incorporated them into his covenant mission, his plan for Israel to be a people who would bless the nations. We are connected to the earth by our bodies—as creatures with a penis and a foreskin, or with a vagina and a womb—and the covenant Lord chooses to make use of our bodies, even (and perhaps especially) the indiscreet parts, in carrying out his redemptive promises to a people whom he has adopted as his own.

When I read various children's Bibles to my kids, such stories are either edited or omitted. But it's nothing new to be embarrassed about the way in which private parts, discharging fluids, and other bodily functions are woven so explicitly into redemption history. In the fourth century, the young Augustine rejected the Christian faith because the Old Testament was just too earthy. For a while, he joined a Gnostic group called the Manichees, who embraced a dualism between God and the material world, a reassuring divide between the highest heaven and the putrid stench of the earth. The God of the Jews, they claimed, was a demon. One Manichee wrote to Augustine to chide the earthy focus of the Old Testament: "'Put forth thy hand over my loins, kill and eat, increase and multiply,' I knew that you always hated such stuff. I knew you were one who loved lofty things, things that shunned the earth, that sought out heaven, that mortified the body, that set the soul alive."[3] When Christians today edit out the bodily indiscretions from the Old Testament, I wonder whether we're animated by a Manichean instinct: that religion means denying that we are of the earth and that we are to move toward lofty thoughts and feelings instead, away from the body and its embarrassing ways of discharging, defecating, and decaying.

Yet at the advent of the new covenant, the first acts of the Lord were physical and earthy. The barren womb of the elderly Elizabeth was filled with a boy who would grow into a prophet, who lived in the wilderness and called for repentance while wearing "clothing of camel's hair with a leather belt around his waist, and his food was locusts and wild honey" (Matt. 3:4). The virgin body of Mary was gifted with a child. In this child, Israel's Lord himself would take on the joys and indignities of creaturely flesh. The Old Testament promise would be embodied in an earthly man, Jesus of Nazareth, the Messiah, the Son of the Most

High. The fulfillment of God's most exalted promises involved the God of the universe taking on fragile, mortal flesh and making it his own.

### Ernest Becker, the Denial of Death, and the Engine of Culture

One of the last century's most profound thinkers about the fragility of our mortal flesh was a social scientist named Ernest Becker. In 1972 he handed off his groundbreaking book on the myriad forms of death-denial to a publisher. Later the same year, he was diagnosed with cancer, which took his life in sixteen months. Two months after his death, his *The Denial of Death* won the Pulitzer Prize.

Becker's tome started out on my pleasure reading stack of books—fiction and nonfiction works that I want to read but can't figure out how they fit with my research and teaching as a theology professor. But before long it became both pleasure reading and professional reading, even something like friendly communion with a fellow traveler. Like me, Becker was aching for words and categories to help express the meaning of mortality for the living. When I felt that same ache, which was often, my mind would usually return to Psalm 39.

> LORD, let me know my end,
>     and what is the measure of my days;
>     let me know how fleeting my life is.
> You have made my days a few handbreadths,
>     and my lifetime is as nothing in your sight.
> Surely everyone stands as a mere breath. (vv. 4–5)

As I helped my kids get ready for school, attended faculty meetings, taught in the classroom, ate dinner with the family, or swam in the pool, I would wonder, *How does all this relate to the fleeting nature of our life as a "mere breath"? How do politics and childhood and painted nails and antiaging creams all relate to our mortality?* Somehow, I sensed that they *were* connected. John Calvin wrote that we tend to deny the reality of our mortal finitude in our day-to-day lives. Small, transient humans are "bound fast to the present state of existence, [and thus they] proceed in the affairs of life as if they were to live two thousand years."[4]

Ernest Becker made the same observation about the human condition. Becker's *The Denial of Death* makes sweeping claims about the power of death-denial in the contemporary psyche. But then he moves beyond generalization, probing concrete examples in painstaking detail. The denial of death, Becker argues, is an engine that is central to human culture itself, an omnipresent aspect of our moment-to-moment lives. And yet much of its power lies in its repression, its hiddenness: "The fear of death cannot be present constantly in one's mental functioning, else the organism [the human] could not function."[5] Still, the hidden fear goes to work. What emerges is "a hyper-anxious animal who constantly invents reasons for anxiety even where there are none."[6]

In bold contrast to Sigmund Freud, who postulated that frustrated sexual desire is the root cause of widespread neurosis, Becker argues that neurosis emerges from a deep discomfort with our dusty connections to the earth. Human bodies, blood, excrement, and copulation all disturb us, for "the fear of death haunts the human animal like nothing else; it is the mainspring of human activity—activity designed largely to avoid the fatality of death, to overcome it by denying in some way that it is the final destiny of man."[7] Like the Manichee who expressed his hatred of the messiness of bodies with their animal functions, Becker thinks that the rest of us are deeply distressed by the same realities. Yet we try to hide this vexation, and in the process we are energized for action in the world, which tries to cover over the wound of our mortality.

Becker was a nonreligious Jew from Massachusetts who served in World War II and saw the horrors of the Holocaust (Shoah) up close, as his unit helped liberate a Nazi concentration camp. Continuing his education, Becker became enamored with Enlightenment ideals of science. He drew upon psychiatry, sociology, and anthropology to pursue his probing questions about the nature of humanity.

However, over the course of his academic career Becker became less infatuated with traditional Enlightenment ideals of science and instead drew more upon the resources of theology and religion. Dietrich Bonhoeffer and Martin Luther King Jr. became models for him and his work. He also found himself enamored with the Danish philosopher and theologian Søren Kierkegaard. As Becker's work matured in the final years before his death, he claimed that the highest, most humane way to live as a mortal creature is to live religiously, positioned and oriented to the Transcendent, who is beyond all human imagining. Thus, turning to psychotherapy or sex as modern replacements for religion is destined to fail. Only life in relation to the Transcendent enables us to live most fully as human creatures.

Becker was attracted to Kierkegaard's searing critique of his nineteenth-century Danish context, which Kierkegaard accused of creating a false sense of health in its denial of creaturely finitude: "To be a 'normal cultural man' is, for Kierkegaard, to be sick—whether one knows it or not."[8] Kierkegaard was convinced that in the Christendom of his day, those who claimed to follow Christ didn't know their sickness, and they were led into sin—acting as if they didn't have mortal limits—because of it. For Kierkegaard, dread, or angst, was neither good nor bad in itself but merely a reality of human creatureliness, our awareness that on our own we simply cannot overcome the foe of death. Deny this, and one lives in self-reliance and sin. Accept this destitute state before God, and the possibility of faith is opened up.

Even though Becker remained unsure of how to speak about God, he sensed that Kierkegaard's countercultural approach to faith, which accepted creaturely limits in the face of the Transcendent, was a promising path to true human flourishing. For when humans don't live in "faith," in this sense, they turn to authoritarian figures (like Hitler) or regimes of power (like the structural racism facing black Americans). Becker's role models, Bonhoeffer and King, displayed faith from the standpoint of finitude as they protested against these forces, which dehumanized both their followers and, more generally, the oppressed.

While Becker embraced certain aspects of the student protest movements of the 1960s, his work pushed back against those who experimented with sexual liberty as a new form of religious fulfillment. Becker's break with Freudianism—on both the academic and the popular levels—became sharp over his career. Popular-level Freudianism is still with us, as seen in the oh-so-predictable Hollywood plot that reaches its climax in a revelation of sexual desire or deviance. As one cultural historian noted a few years ago, popular Freudianism finds widespread expression in "theater, novels, television. A generation ago, [Freud] animated Woody Allen's jokes; more recently, we could find him in *The Sopranos*, and today he is all over *Mad Men*."[9] Growing up in the 1980s and '90s, I watched television shows and movies that delivered dozens of variations on the Freudian theme, but, like Becker, I doubted that "pop" Freudianism could explain the deepest human motivations.

Becker argues that, though Freud was right to look beneath the level of everyday consciousness to account for human action, pointing to sex as the deep, underlying cause of neurosis was misguided. Freud explained away his own anxiety about death as the reflective "instinct" of one who is "primarily a pleasure-seeker of sex" rather than "that of a terrified, death-avoiding animal."[10] For Freud, death was not the fundamental cause of human anxiety or problem for human culture. In the words of Freud's brilliant student and, later, rival psychiatrist Otto Rank, "When [Freud] finally stumbled upon the inescapable death problem, he sought to give a new meaning," speaking of the "death instinct rather than death fear. The fear itself he had meantime disposed of elsewhere, where it was not so threatening." Freud's strategy was to make the general fear of death into "a special sexual fear (castration fear)," then seek "to cure *this* fear through the freeing of sexuality."[11]

Why did Freud make this mistake? Becker argues that Freud turned to sex rather than the fear of death because, unlike Kierkegaard, he was determined to consider faith in God to be a neurosis, a sickness. For Kierkegaard, in the face of death's inevitability, mortals have no path to authentic human living besides faith. In contrast, Freud rejected any semblance of religion because of "his need to rid himself of any suspicion of intellectual dependence on others or spiritual dependence upon a personal God," as one scholar notes.[12] Freud feared faith and a confrontation with the enigma of death. Perhaps modern Hollywood's enduring fixation on sexuality speaks to a similar fear of faith as the sober embrace of our mortality as well. Reducing human motivations to repressed sexual desires, as Freud attempted to do, provides a more immanent, visually stimulating, and marketable account of human life and culture.

## The Paradox of Partialization

If death itself has been pushed to the margins of contemporary Western societies, is it plausible to think that the fear of death—rather than sexual repression—underlies so much human action? In the past half century, researchers have attempted to assess Becker's overarching claim through over 160 studies in eleven countries, with double-sided results. On the one hand, when young and middle-aged people encounter poignant images that make them reflect on their own death, they turn inward and go into survival mode, becoming aggressive toward those who hold different worldviews. They are more likely to cherish their country's flag and to feel threatened by foreigners. They deepen their identification with their own "ingroups (gender, ethnic, and school affiliation)."[13]

On the other hand, persons diagnosed with a terminal illness, persons who recover after nearly dying, and the elderly (who frequently reflect on their own death) do not have such a reaction. They do not turn inward in defensiveness. On the contrary, their sustained habit of reflecting on their own death opens them to others, even to those who are different from their "in-group." They are also "less concerned with materialism, fame, and money."[14]

The practice of prayer seems to have similar effects on people. Empirically speaking, meditative prayer tends to lead to a softening of the fear of death and to greater care for others, whether or not those persons belong to the same in-group. Benedict of Nursia, who advised his monks to meditate on their deaths daily, would not be surprised. And as the author of the book of Hebrews knew, a fundamental aspect of our human predicament is that we can be slaves to "the fear of death" (Heb. 2:15). Whether one is considering the New Testament, Benedict's sixth-century monastery, or modern social psychology, a common conclusion about humanity can be drawn: our terror of death—or its softening—is a key variable underlying our action.

By what process does the fear of death underlie the actions and habits not only of individuals but of entire communities and cultures? On this question, Ernest Becker insightfully claims that "culture is in its most intimate intent a heroic denial of creatureliness."[15] This remark leads Becker to an analysis of death and coping that intersects deeply with the witness of Scripture and the church's teaching, even as it neither emerges from nor perfectly reflects those teachings.

Becker says that, as creatures who need to act in an extraordinarily complex and mystifying world, we've developed a coping skill called "partialization."[16] We shut out the mystery and ultimately the terror of being people who move from dust to dust, with some days in between. The world is too much for us. We can't take it all in. Even on our best days, we fixate on only tiny aspects of the crowded streets we walk on; people whose stories we will never know pass by us unacknowledged. Becker often calls this process a form of "fetishizing," not because there's a fundamentally sexual instinct at play but because partialization focuses obsessively on minute parts of the world. In Becker's metaphor, a person is like a lover who can't take in the wonder of his partner and thus fixates on the beloved's foot or hand or shoe. Becker claims that "the individual has to protect himself against the world, and he can do this only as any other animal would: by narrowing down the world, shutting off experience, developing an obliviousness both to the terrors of the world and to his own anxieties. Otherwise he would be crippled for action."[17] If we're to actually act in the world, we have to ignore most of it. We just can't drink in every moment. And we'd usually prefer not to, anyway. We would rather fix our eyes on a phone than take in the spectacle of faces and nonverbal cues, realizing that we're sharing the street or the subway with bipeds who puke and defecate and will be food for worms after their intricate, earthly stories end.

This notion of partialization strikes a deep chord with many who, like me, have a terminal illness. We often hear the advice to "take it one day at a time," sometimes with a verse from Psalm 90 added: "Teach us to number our days, / that we may gain a heart of wisdom" (v. 12 NIV). On the one hand, the partialization of avoiding the broader horizons of our lives and futures is wise in some ways. Taking things one day at a time can give us second thoughts about wasting time on quests for fame or indulgence in self-pity; at its best, it can be a way of releasing control and acting like the creatures we are before God.

But ironically, the advice to take things one day at a time often implies the opposite. Usually, in the cancer community "Take it one day at a time" means "Make the most of it!" and "What you do each day really makes a difference, so don't put off doing what you value until tomorrow!" This advice can actually lead cancer patients into an anxious frenzy, because what they value is related to a future that has become very uncertain. "The way forward would seem obvious, if only I knew how many months or years I had left," writes surgeon and cancer patient Paul Kalanithi. "Tell me three months, I'd spend time with my family. Tell me one year, I'd write a book. Give me ten years, I'd get back to treating diseases. The truth that you live one day at a time didn't help: What was I supposed to do with that day?"[18]

Thankfully, the context of Psalm 90's imperative to "number our days" moves in a very different direction from the oft-given advice that says, in effect, to ramp up your game in acting as a hero in your own story. It actually brings us, in prayer, to something closer to Becker's insights about partialization. In the words of the psalm:

> For a thousand years in your sight
>     are like yesterday when it is past,
>     or like a watch in the night.

> You sweep them away; they are like a dream,
>     like grass that is renewed in the morning;
> in the morning it flourishes and is renewed;
>     in the evening it fades and withers.
> ...............................................
> The days of our life are seventy years,
>     or perhaps eighty, if we are strong;
> even then their span is only toil and trouble;
>     they are soon gone, and we fly away. (vv. 4–6, 10)

The psalmist wants us to recognize something real, but something that we usually deny, even in the pious talk of the Christian community: our lives are tiny, short, a little speck. We are small. For the psalmist, this fact is magnified by contrast with the Lord: "You have been our dwelling place / in all generations" (v. 1). The eternity of God is a mystery greater than the whole of creation can comprehend.

> Before the mountains were brought forth,
>     or ever you had formed the earth and the world,
>     from everlasting to everlasting you are God. (v. 2)

We are small. We habitually "partialize," acting as if our own story is what really matters, what will really last. "Take things one day at a time." Yes, that's good advice from time to time, but the psalmist wants us to do more than that. We need to realize how little we apprehend, how little we control—how our ambitions are usually out of proportion to our tiny, creaturely lives, and how the everlasting Lord is the only one worthy of our ultimate hopes.

Perceiving and living in small ways, taking in just a tiny bit of the fathomless reality in our midst, can be a wonderful thing. When a sudden brush with death turns us inward, we tend to protect our in-group and demonize outsiders—leading us to horrific ends. But properly embracing our mortal limits can result in daily practices of wonder when we surrender to life's enormity as creatures who know we are small.

## The Beauty of Living Small

I've been learning in new ways from my son, Nathaniel, that partialization can be beautiful. When Nathaniel was six, I was at the park with him and our greyhound, who kept pointing her nose like an arrow toward one squirrel after another—even if they were already high up in the century-old oak trees. "Please come and help me," Nathaniel said, pulling the dog and me over to a clearing filled with acorns. "Help me find the acorn caps," he said, "*only* the clean caps with no dirt in them!" As I bent over and sorted through the acorns to find the clean caps, I saw how Nathaniel's intense focus opened up a world of detail that I had been missing. I was just sitting in the park, thinking about what would come next in the day. Meanwhile, he had discovered that the tiny, brown acorn tops have intricate patterns, like those found in a finely woven quilt, and that each pattern was distinct, singular. Amazingly, the acorn tops usually broke off cleanly from their nut, leaving a hollowed-out top that looked like a pointy hat. Nathaniel and I gathered some into a pile, admiring them as we collected a dozen, two dozen. "Do you think I should take this one home?" I asked, showing him a cap with particularly fine detail. "Yes, put it in your pocket!"

Earlier in the fall, Nathaniel had discovered cicada shells in this park, the outer shells of the grasshopper-like insects that provide atmospheric music in the evenings. The cicada shells looked like little bug ghosts—reflecting the body and legs of the bug with delicate intricacy. "They're beautiful!" Nathaniel would say, grabbing them from the trees where they were stuck, as if the bugs were frozen in their shells. He was so convinced of their beauty that he gathered a quantity of the shells and tried to sell them to earn money. He had limited success with that.

I had missed these treasures. I hadn't seen them; I hadn't noticed. But Nathaniel taught me how to filter out the rest of the park—with its people and dogs and grass and trees—and move beyond the urgent to-do lists in my head. Looking closely, we found the treasures of acorn caps and cicada shells. Nathaniel practiced partialization. In these moments he was not trying to take in the whole park; instead, he zeroed in on the small patterns, and in them he found beauty and joy.

As an adult, I'm aware of the dangers, the mortal decay, the seeming chaos of politics and the news, which do not appear to bother my son at his age. Can I overcome this double-mindedness, this double consciousness, of the beauty of small things as well as the fear-evoking uncertainty of adult life?

I don't think I can fully overcome it. But in prayer, and specifically in the Psalms, I see glimpses of ways to hold beauty and uncertainty together. At the end of the day, when my mind becomes cluttered with a to-do list, a worry list, and all sorts of lists that magnify the fears of my own life, I often pray this from Psalm 95:

> O come, let us sing to the LORD;
>> let us make a joyful noise to the rock of our salvation!
> Let us come into his presence with thanksgiving;
>> let us make a joyful noise to him with songs of praise!
> For the LORD is a great God,
>> and a great King above all gods.
> In his hand are the depths of the earth;
>> the heights of the mountains are his also.
> The sea is his, for he made it,
>> and the dry land, which his hands have formed.
>
> O come, let us worship and bow down,
>> let us kneel before the LORD, our Maker!
> For he is our God,
>> and we are the people of his pasture,
>> and the sheep of his hand. (vv. 1–7)

When preoccupied with my own worries, I make *my* actions the center of what's happening in the world. But they're not. The Lord is the center, the central actor in the drama of the world. I have only a small role. I'm among the creatures on the dry land that the Lord has made. I'm not a shepherd, heroically saving my flock from danger; I'm among the sheep of God's hand. What really matters is not my fear of dying, my fear of failing at my career, or my fear of failing as a father or a friend. These are small stories, and I am small. To be a creature is to partialize, to make things small. The Lord alone is the one who does not partialize, who is knowingly present to each creature, plant, animal, and star in the universe, who can be present in the details yet not be small. The God of Israel is not small. Indeed, the Lord himself is the central actor in the cosmos, the one before whom "all the earth" should, and will, "stand in awe" (Ps. 33:8). In the end, the Lord himself will judge the earth—the crazy politics, the unjust workplaces, the many other human shortcomings that seem out of my control. And the Lord will do so in faithfulness, in his steadfast love.

The depths of the earth, the heights of the mountains, seas, pastures, sheep—these are all "partialized" wonders, wonders that Nathaniel and I can both appreciate. But in Psalm 95, this way of thinking small is an entryway to thinking and living big. The best kinds of partializations are portals to life before God, not simply life preoccupied with oneself and one's own place in the universe. Destructive partialization denies our (very real) smallness, puffing us up in fear and pride rather than helping us accept our true, mortal limits. But embracing partialized wonders as a mortal before God can help us live and pray and act as creatures—decaying, dying, tiny creatures—before the magnificent and yet compassionate Lord. This Lord is the one and only Hero of the universe.

## Destructive Partialization and Hero Cultures

While partialization can be a gift reminding us that we are small, it can also be used for deleterious ends. Instead of facing our smallness as ephemeral creatures, we can seek to put a hero on a pedestal, committing ourselves to their cause as a way to taste immortality. When this happens, it results in a hero culture, or what Ernest Becker called a "hero system." Becker spent much of his life reflecting on the horrors of the twentieth century, and by the time he wrote *The Denial of Death* he believed that they typically involved a hero culture that put partialization to deadly use.

Becker specifically addressed the rise and terror-filled reigns of Adolf Hitler in Germany and Joseph Stalin in the Soviet Union. How do authoritarian leaders gain such power? Becker argued for a disquieting answer to this question: as human beings, we long for and ache for authoritarian rulers because they promise us that through the enduring power of nation, of race, of wealth, of military might, they can overcome death. The Reich or the Red Star will live on generation after generation; the world will be made new under them. We partialize this vision and block out the countless daily signs of our heroes' flaws and mortal frames. We fixate on heroes as though they are vehicles through whom we can lift ourselves beyond our mortal limits. The authoritarian leaders of the right and the left gain power because we fixate on their virtues, their causes, the promises of their respective legacies. And as we do so, we shut out and dehumanize others. The faces and voices of those opposing our "righteous cause" must be eliminated—whether poisoned in gas chambers or starved on government-owned farms—to achieve our heroic vision. Fascism and communism, the radical right and the radical left, both draw upon this shared poison of partialization. In each case, the denial of our finite creatureliness gives way to slavery—whether in the form of a dictator, a national ideology, or both. As a Jewish thinker living after the Holocaust, understanding the rise of death-denying hero cultures such as these became a lifelong quest for Becker.

Becker's theory of death-denial as culture-generating eventually led him to a more mundane (and perhaps even more disconcerting) observation: human cultures everywhere tend to become enslaved to the fear of death, weaponizing the survival mechanism of partialization to deny rather than embrace mortal limits. Becker saw the forces of partialization at work in the structures of white racism that the civil rights movement protested. White racism fixates on an imagined racial superiority embodied in white heroic ideals, pushing aside nonwhite faces and voices as obstacles to be overcome. In reference to a different realm of culture, Becker claimed that the deification of sexual love in 1960s America also emerged from death-denying aspirations, as if sexual love could take the place of God. "How can a human being be a god-like 'everything' to another?" he asked. "No human relationship can bear the burden of godhood, and the attempt has to take its toll in some way on both parties."[19] Ironically, treating one's lover like God dehumanizes both the beloved and the idolatrous lover.

These idolatries ensnare not only atheists, who explicitly deny God's existence and presence, but believers in God as well. For example, I've seen Christian brothers and sisters throw themselves behind political candidates, both Democrat and Republican, such that their candidate can do no wrong. They take joy in punishing their ideological enemies, in silencing their opponents. I've also seen white Christians like me advocate for our own in-group interests, assuming that we don't need to embrace the ethnic and cultural otherness within the body of Christ. And I saw, as a young Christian man, how many of the songs I listened to, the books I read, and the youth group meetings I participated in seemed to assume that romantic fulfillment would be the most important part of my identity. "Only the married are fulfilled and complete," they seemed to say. For the married, the message was, "If you want your marriage to last, pray and go to church." In other words: marriage first, God second. Faith was an appendage, a tool, to serve the God of a romantic and family-oriented ideal.

Not only is Christian culture *not* immune to the hero culture that elevates a nation, leader, or romance to the level of God; Christian culture often becomes the catalyst that propels these idolatries forward. Christians too often capitulate to the powers and principalities of this world that challenge the sole and final lordship of Christ.[20] At their root, hero cultures deny that God is the true Hero and Deliverer. They put on the mask of a giant to cover over our short, limited, creaturely lives. But in this attempt to transcend our mortal limits, they nevertheless fail to release us from our captivity to the fear of death.

## Steps toward Freedom

Christians desperately need to embrace the freedom that Hebrews speaks of, freedom from slavery to the fear of death. We need deliverance. We can't get ourselves out of it. On our own, we're stuck in the pit of death-terror, ignoring or attacking our neighbors as opponents, as enemies. Death is certain, but we'd rather push it away and thus let the fear move deep into our veins, living as if our heroes will never fail, as if our legacies will never end. We fail to fully embrace Jesus, the pioneer of dying and death who is also the victorious King over its final power. In the words of Hebrews, "We do see Jesus, who for a little while was made lower than the angels, now crowned with glory and honor because of the suffering of death, so that by the grace of God he might taste death for everyone" (Heb. 2:9). Death is still coming; it's still certain, and it's still bitter. But in the end, its bitterness will give way to the sweetness of resurrection, its darkness to the light of the temple.

That's cause for hope. We will continue to fear death. But death-terror need not drive us away from the love of neighbor, even when there might not be a legacy, even when such love seems to make no difference in a hurting world. Death-terror need not strain our witness to the astonishing goodness of God and his creation, even as we creatures are passing, limited, transient. As strange as it seems, when we no longer bow to the barking of death-terror's commands, we can eventually welcome, even befriend, reminders of our own death. They can be a gift. We can welcome daily death-reminders as testimonies to who we are: living and breathing and dying creatures who cannot master our future or heroically change the world or provide a lasting inheritance for our progeny. Only when we truly know that we have nowhere else to go do we fully enter into the psalmist's earnest cry:

> For God alone my soul waits in silence;
>> from him comes my salvation.
> He alone is my rock and my salvation,
>> my fortress. (Ps. 62:1–2a)

While "my days pass away like smoke," yet truly "you, O LORD, are enthroned forever; / your name endures to all generations" (Ps. 102:3, 12). We won't last all that long in this earthly life. We can either live and die in servile obedience to the terror of death, or we can live and die as servants of the King who is enthroned forever. True freedom comes in following the King.

## Discussion Questions

- According to the writer of Hebrews, Christians may fear death, but they are liberated from slavery to this fear (Heb. 2:14–15). Describe this distinction in your own words. How do you see it play out in your life? In what ways does the fear of death seek to master your life?

- We are earthly, embodied creatures living before the Almighty— and God meets us in this reality, as the Old Testament rite of circumcision and various temple regulations about the body show. Take a moment to think through a typical Sunday worship service. What moments in the service might remind us that we are embodied, mortal creatures?

- Where do you see the fear of death driving the practices of the culture that you live within? How does a culture shaped by the fear of death influence your priorities in your daily life?

- Ernest Becker says, "The individual has to protect himself against the world, . . . shutting off experience, developing an obliviousness both to the terrors of the world and to his own anxieties. Otherwise he would be crippled for action." Where do you see this instinct for self-protection in the world around you or in your own life?

- We are called to embrace the reality of our mortality in a way that honors Jesus Christ as the final Lord, rather than honoring death as our master. In your own path of discipleship, what death-defying practices can you take up (or have you already taken up) to combat this slavery to the fear of death? How does recognizing ourselves as small, finite creatures help us on this path of discipleship?

# *Four*

—— ❧ ——

# Interplanetary Exploration
## The Strange New World of Modern Medicine

"Do you feel pain all the time?"

"Yes," I said, "I feel it all the time." The question from my coworker Lisa abruptly substituted for "Good morning" on a chilly spring day in March. Then I quickly recalled the note that I had sent her the day before, excusing myself for missing a meeting due to spiking pain.

"I'm not always thinking about the pain, but it's always there." Lisa gazed at me attentively yet calmly. She had been a longtime hospice volunteer, and I knew that she had seen worse. Much worse. And thankfully, I knew Lisa wasn't trying to "fix" me; she sincerely wanted to hear my response.

"My current chemo causes muscle spasms; the intense chemo earlier in my treatment caused permanent nerve damage, which I feel in my feet. It's kind of complicated, though. I had chronic pain before the cancer, so this pain builds upon what was there before and my cocktail of meds . . ." Breathless, I stopped. *I don't want to bore her with this*, I thought—the explanations felt futile in addressing her simple question about my pain.

"Thanks for asking," I said. "Yes, I feel pain all the time." Lisa responded with a nod of recognition. Her eyes stayed focused on me, her face attentive, relaxed. Often, well-meaning friends respond to my halting explanations with eyes of pity, followed by a well-intended five-minute quest to find the golden key that will make the pain disappear. They've read an article about a new treatment, they have an uncle who tried a special cancer soup, and so on. In the end, I become the one who consoles them about my pain. I remind them that many people, young and old, live with pain deeper and sharper than mine. No easy solutions are to be found, but that's not the end of the world.

Yet Lisa calmly looked me in the eyes and then said softly, "I'll keep you in my prayers." I took a deep breath and slackened my shoulders. I didn't need to put on a poker face to hide the pain from her. Lisa had seen chronic pain before, and she was empathetic, but she wasn't scandalized by it. In contrast, when a friend responds to my ongoing pain as a terrible affront, my life feels diminished; the outrage seems to imply that this wound could never be part of "the good life."

And yet, perhaps it's exactly right to say my life is "diminished." Rather than living the life I would have chosen, I often feel like a lab rat, as I joke with friends. One medical intervention after another leads me to a place where I never planned on going.

Modern medicine, like all medicine, involves trade-offs: both potential benefits and unwanted side effects. These trade-offs are complex, both practically and morally—puzzling enough to entertain a bored college student with a semester of case studies, or to serve as fodder for a documentary on medical ethics.

In moments when I take a step back from the drama of one treatment decision after another, I realize that I've been transported to a different planet. This new place, called "modern medicine," has a distinct terrain and scent. At times, it seems safe and clean, in an air freshener, sterile hospital sort of way. But it also makes me feel trapped. It seems like the harder I try to leave, the more stuck I become. Sometimes, when I feel energized, I act as though I can treat my weakened body like a four-wheel drive and gun the gas to pull out of this place. But my stuck-ness just deepens. One treatment's solution leads to another problem requiring another treatment. There's no way out. In the midst of this, I wonder, *What is this planet of "modern medicine," really? How did I get here, and what are the alternatives? How is my very presence on this planet changing me in ways that I did not decide or desire?*

Indeed, it's a question for all of us: How should we live and die on this planet of modern medicine?

In some ways, this terrain is similar to the territory in our earlier chapters. The planet of modern medicine has numerous dark pits, deep holes of Sheol, that can leave us entrapped, on our own and far away from the light, the God of life. This planet is also a place where some hearts beat and others are still, where some muscles strengthen and others lie stiff and motionless. The prospect of illness on the planet of medicine can energize us—whether in fear of the losses that illness and aging bring, or with courage in the face of death's ever-present shadow. And yet, while this territory is familiar to us, it's also one that shapes us to hope and act in peculiar ways. In particular, the terrain of modern medicine trains us to think and feel that our final battle is not against sin and the devil but against illness and aging.

Whether conscious of it or not, all of us, whether Christian or not, are catechized in the hope that these foes and many others will be conquered by modern medicine one day. Science-fiction novels, movies, news reports of scientific breakthroughs, our consistent attempt to keep the "dying" and "healthy" separate—all of these teach us and shape us. We are taught to look forward to a coming day, not of Christ's kingdom, but of a kingdom where disease and decay are tamed so that we can live even longer, stay in the driver's seat, calculate risk, and minimize loss. We are taught to pray, "*Our* kingdom come, *our* will be done, in public health as it is in the laboratory . . ."

As one in the midst of navigating these complex medical trade-offs, I often feel lost, left in darkness. I have enough light to see where I should place my foot next. However, I'm confused and disoriented about the larger picture—about what planet I'm on, what battle I'm fighting, what all of this is for. As I've gotten to know others in the cancer community, I've come to see that I'm not alone. We're lost together. We thought modern medicine would save us from the Pit, but we've found Sheol here as well, even amid sparkling, sanitized hospital spaces. Somehow, after a lifetime on the planet of modern medicine, we are stunned when illness hits. Make no mistake: medicine is a gift. But it's only a small flashlight, when what we need is a shining sun to see what's going on, to see what it means to be a dying creature before the One whose days have no end.

## Ending Up Where We Don't Choose to Be

No one forced me to take the path of chemotherapy after I was diagnosed with cancer. I was the one who chose, who made the decision—or at least that's how it felt at the time. Sober-sounding voices and page after page of leaflets packed full of medical jargon told me the risks. Every month, I complete a questionnaire and am interviewed by a specialized pharmacist to reaffirm that I know the risks. But I feel that after taking one step, then another, then another, somehow I'm in a different country altogether. Each step of the way, the questions and answers seemed rather obvious.

*Do you want to live for only two to three years, or take the new chemo with its attendant side effects but likely live much longer?* The question was, in effect, Would you rather die before your children are out of elementary school, or be assailed by the forces of chemo?

I took a step.

*Are you and your wife willing to give up your hopes for future pregnancy?* The chemo causes severe birth defects and is also likely to make the patient infertile.

Haltingly, we took a step.

*Do you want to manage the pain that comes from your chemo, or live a life that is distracted and preoccupied because of your physical distress?*

I took another step.

*Do you want to address the anxiety and depression that results from some of your treatment, or leave it untreated?*

I took one more step.

Somehow I expected that my old (pre-diagnosis) life would continue on after these changes—just with some "quality of life" adjustments, to use the cancer center's phrase for weighing the benefits and side effects that come with medical intervention. Maybe moving from taking one ten-milligram pill a day (for chronic pain) to over a dozen pills a day would only be that: more pills. But as it happened, every new treatment brought new symptoms, which often surprised the doctors as much as they surprised me.

And the change in my daily life went much deeper than the long list of symptoms. As Duke Divinity School professor Kate Bowler noted after her cancer diagnosis, although "few people will let you admit [it] out loud . . . a tragedy is like a fault line. A life is split into a before and an after, and most of the time, the before was better."[1] At times I've resisted this sharp chasm between "before" and "after." But denying this gulf leaves me observing my life from a distance—gazing from behind glass at my former life and at the lives of others who are charging forward, continuing with energy, fortitude, and courage. Each speaking engagement called off, each friendship that's cooled, each course canceled leaves me feeling more and more alone. "You look great; you don't even look like you have cancer!" Though friends seek to comfort cancer patients with words like these, they create the illusion that we can and should compare our lives after diagnosis to our lives before it. But according to that ledger, each new day brings another unexpected loss. Maybe I miscalculated the losses in deciding to go on chemo—perhaps I should not have done it after all?

Before entering the hospital for my stem cell transplant, I was encouraged to think about what quality of life I desired in terms of bodily functions: Which functions are so important to you that you wouldn't want to be kept alive without them? Under what circumstances do you want to be resuscitated or stay on life support? Who do you designate to make medical decisions for you if you are alive but incapacitated? Those are significant discussions for all of us to have. But as a patient I've worried that there is something inherently misleading about this attempt to delineate the quality of life, as though it were something akin to the quality of coffee: Do you require Arabica? Or only dark roast? Would you drink it black if no sugar or cream were available? Or would you just opt out altogether?

Is life diminished by deteriorating quality?

If so, then admitting to Lisa that I live with pain all the time feels like a defeat. If I frame my quality of life in terms of a list of functions—of my nerves, my feet, my hands, my mental stamina, even my emotional stability—then surely I live a diminished life. Indeed, in addition to having opted for a lowered quality of life, I've also become one of those heavy users of the health insurance system in the process. My treatment is expensive; it comes with head-spinning bills that make my salary look like a middle schooler's allowance.

So why opt for this?

Unlike those rushed to the hospital because they are acutely ill or injured, patients like me *choose* to board the roller coaster of intense treatment. Or at least that's the language we're given—we "choose." We know, in theory, that the ride will twist high in the air and zoom low to the ground, that the treatment will come with both intended and unexpected consequences. If we stagger off of one ride, we can slide onto another, as long as our hearts still beat. Doctors today rarely say, "That's all we can do." There's always another ride, another treatment. We can be certain, mainly, of this: although we make individual choices along the way, we end up in a place that we did not choose to be.

## Opting Out of Modern Medicine?

Where would we be without modern medicine? In my case, I would probably be dead, one of my two children would likely have died before the age of five, and mention of the flu or measles coming to town would have shaken the neighborhood with mortal fear. For all its shortcomings, I cannot advocate for opting out of modern medicine. Over meals with my father and my brother, both physicians, I would hear about wondrous new treatments: "Patients used to die within six months, but now they can live five, maybe ten, years." I would hear about how my brother had mended torn flesh earlier in the day; a car had hit a motorcycle, and remarkably, both drivers could look forward to living decades longer, even if in an altered way because of the injuries and the trauma. Occasionally, my father and my brother would tell about patients who refused treatment, insisting that their illness was unreal or that prayer was the only proper salve. My father seemed breathless, nervous, and sometimes angry when he told those stories. He felt responsible, but he couldn't act when the patient refused medical care. Those stories never seemed to end well.

The extraordinary power of modern medicine became clear to me when I lived in a rural region of Uganda for six months in 1994. Modern medicine, which I had taken for granted in the West, was on the margins in that area. In that year, the average life expectancy of a Ugandan was lower by thirty years than the life expectancy of someone in my home country: 75.5 years in the US, 44 years in Uganda.[2] In the countryside, which had no electricity, running water, or a nearby hospital, I saw how death was woven into daily living, even as I was introduced to strangers. After an initial greeting, I would often ask, "How many children do you have?" "Seven, with four who are living," the answer would come, stated in a matter-of-fact way. Death was a part of every family and every person's life story. A brother or sister, a daughter or son—each family seemed to have loved ones who died in childhood. Extended families would faithfully attend the funerals of their kin-group members, which happened about once each month. Death was part of the rhythm of life. At the time, I wrote in my journal, "Death seems like *enya*," the staple bread-like Ugandan food that accompanied nearly every meal. Coming from the United States, where death usually presented itself through news headlines and Hollywood dramas, I wasn't accustomed to the intrusive and pervasive presence of death.

In Uganda, death announced itself through the lips of one's neighbor. Sometimes death broadcasts its coming in advance, as in the case of Ochen, a man whose wounds proclaimed his impending death. I visited Ochen while he was living several miles from my home in Uganda. The visit seared itself in my memory, and my account here draws upon notes I made shortly after my time with him.[3]

My Ugandan coworker Isaac and I walked to a compound with several grass-thatched, mud-floored huts to visit Ochen. A young woman, seated and holding her nursing child, greeted us with a nod before she rose and led us into the largest hut. Bending low to make it through the doorway, we found places to sit on the floor near a flickering flame, facing a darkened edge of the hut. "Ochen has not really eaten well for six weeks," said Isaac, pointing to him. Ochen's skin clung tightly to his bones.

Ochen, an elder in his fifties, was lying on the other side of the fire, with a massively enlarged leg resting on a stool. A second young woman moved near his leg, waving several long leaves to shoo away flies. "He accidentally cut himself with a hoe in the field. They tried to drain the pus here at home," Isaac said. "But when they cut his knee, the skin on his leg was not enough. It ripped." My eyes went to a spotted white part of his leg; I thought it was simply too large to be a wound. After a few minutes of trying to resist the almost magnetic pull on my eyes of the protruding, white wound, I asked Isaac if they could cover his leg lightly with a cloth rather than constantly waving away the flies. They did so, perhaps more for my sake than for Ochen's.

After our visit, I plied Isaac with questions as we walked away on the dirt path. Why did his family not bring him to the clinic five miles away? "They say he's unable to move and he's in constant pain. It would be very hard to do on a bicycle. And it's very difficult to find a vehicle to come here to bring him to the hospital."

I probed more. "His son is a teacher, isn't he?" "Yes," Isaac said, "he's an educated man. He should be an example to the others. He should have brought his father to the hospital right away before it got bad. But he just used traditional herbs instead."

Isaac continued, "I asked Ochen's brother if we could help Ochen in some way. He said no. He said that since Ochen's son did not take him to the hospital, Ochen will die. He's given up."

Isaac was quiet as we walked back. I felt a cool evening breeze as I looked toward the golden late-afternoon light on the savanna horizon, seeing long shadows spread behind the huts we passed.

After a few minutes, Isaac broke the silence. "I disagree with his brother. I think it's possible that Ochen could still live."

"I think so, too—if he makes it to the hospital right away." My head was spinning. "It just shocks me that something that could be so easily treated at the beginning, for just a little money, has been allowed to turn into something so big!"

"Ochen's son said it happened quickly and he was in bed soon after the wound," Isaac replied.

Later in the evening, I shared a mundane yet compelling possibility that had come to mind: although none of us had access to a vehicle, in three days I would have a supervisor visiting from the United States. He would come in a Land Rover and stay for two days. This thought energized me. Maybe the vehicle could be used to take Ochen to the hospital! Maybe I could save the life of this man!

I could hear a stirring John Williams score playing in the background of my mind as I turned the idea over and over. I could help to save Ochen!

My supervisor came a few days later. The Land Rover made it across the pothole-riddled mud roads to Ochen's house. However, instead of transporting Ochen to the hospital, the Land Rover brought us to his funeral.

## The Great Health Transition

Overall life expectancy in Western countries has doubled in the last century. Developing countries such as Uganda have seen an upswing in life expectancy as well, as various forms of modern medicine have gradually become more accessible.[4] In 2015, Uganda's average life expectancy was fifteen years longer than it was in 1994. The causes for this are numerous and include greater access to clean water, vaccines, and medical care.

In Western countries, the increasing life expectancy has been accompanied by a set of trends that place the Ugandan village I visited in the 1990s in even starker contrast to the West today. In the West, marriage and childbearing have been delayed to later and later ages; both fertility rates and family sizes have dropped dramatically; the proportion of single, never-married adults has sharply increased; and while young people used to hope to live to be sixty or sixty-five, that age range is now considered to be merely the cusp of the last third of one's life. Today in the West, expecting to live well past sixty-five is no longer an airy, unlikely hope. The proportion of Americans over sixty-five has been steadily increasing in recent decades, and was 15.7 percent of the population in 2014. That number is expected to rise to 21.7 percent by 2040.[5]

Given the choice, I would not undo the changes brought about through the complex combination of improved public health, better medical treatments, and increased economic prosperity. In key ways, these improvements are testimony to God's goodness and care, which should be received as gifts. John Calvin expressed this view of medicine as a gift of God quite forcefully back in the sixteenth century: "I can prove that medicine came from God, inasmuch as it is a knowledge of carefully using the gifts of creation, which God gives us according to the necessities to which we are subjected. . . . But I say that whoever does not take account of the means which God has ordained does not have confidence in God but is puffed up with false pride and temerity."[6]

Medicine is a gift from God, a gift of God's wondrous and good work in creation. With gratitude, we can receive and use the gift of medical care to assist in the challenges of our creaturely life "to which we are subjected." But we are not masters, and medicine is not the master.

We're dying creatures in need of the salves and comforts that medicine can help provide. Their relief is temporary, but they are nevertheless gifts on this mortal path, gifts from the One who created and sustains our bodies. Medicine, in itself, is a good gift.

However, in our rapidly changing society, in which dying has been institutionalized and the ordinary process of dying has been removed from our daily experience, medicine is often not *received* as a gift. Instead, we cling to it as a cloak to shield us from the daily reality that we are all dying. We fail to acknowledge that even the best medical treatment has no solution for the diagnosis of death. Instead of receiving medical care as a gracious gift from the Lord, we look to it as a golden calf, a self-made god that can become our tyrannical master.[7]

Effective immunizations, advanced chemotherapy, and sanitary water are all gifts in their own way, part of the great health care transition of modern times. But in the context of a highly technological society, which gives us the illusion of mastery over our fates, this great modern health transition also presents trade-offs, new deficits along with new benefits. In a very real way, the Ugandans who attended monthly funerals of relatives were consistently putting themselves in touch with the real world of mortals, the world that has confronted and corrected human hubris for centuries. When my cancer treatment immersed me in the world of the dying, where six-year-olds and eighty-six-year-olds alike are pummeled by disease, receiving treatment that at times crumbles the body as quickly as the illness itself, I felt like I had moved from one culture to another. In this new place I sensed that, truly, I live among fragile mortals.

This movement to a death-aware culture was also illuminating—for the real world is one with mortal limits, where diseases have no regard for fairness, aspirations, or race or class or wealth. In a strange way, that reality check, which penetrated daily life in Uganda, was a gift. The loss of a sense of that reality extends around the globe, as far as modern medicine does. As Ephraim Radner notes, before the great health transition, whether you were rich or poor, your life expectancy was low compared to contemporary Western standards. Indeed, "death was all around, all the time." For "mortality was fastened into your existence from your birth and through every relationship from then on and at every point in your existence."[8]

The world in which death and dying is ubiquitous *is* the real world; it is not an alien terrain. Death is inevitable and often unexpected, and its mastery is outside the scope of our medical power. For all the gains in the modern health transition, one of the losses is the widespread diffusion of an illusion: that human life can be *unfastened* from mortality at any point.

Doctors, nurses, and insurance companies are not involved in a great conspiracy to deny mortality. There is something larger that is keeping us from approaching medicine as a tool or a gift, inviting us to approach medical care as a fetish, a supreme comfort with the magical power to make the daily reminders of death go away. Very few people have made the conscious decision to suppress death. Rather, we've come to generate and inhabit a culture that prizes and rewards death-denying habits. We're faced with countless young, airbrushed bodies on our billboards and screens that make health look easy and decay seem alien. We tell our children that they can be "whatever they want to be," as if they are in control, unhindered by the embodied, mortal limits faced by earlier generations.

The death-denying stories we tell ourselves are an example of what my friend James K. A. Smith, a philosopher, calls a "cultural liturgy." Whether or not we've ever entered into a religious worship service, the "liturgies" of modern culture shape our desires, our habits, the way in which we tell our stories. Smith puts it this way: "'Liturgy,' as I'm using the word, is a shorthand term for those rituals that are loaded with an ultimate Story about who we are and what we're for."[9] For example, the consumer space of a shopping mall has a "liturgy" that shapes us as we walk through it. A mall may seem blandly secular, but its temple-like architecture invites us into a quasi-religious space, with great glass atriums and numerous banners displaying attractive models or images of the newest tech gadgets—signs and icons of "the good life." The mall's "spiritual significance (and threat) isn't found in its 'ideas' or its 'messages' but in its rituals. The mall doesn't care what you *think*, but it is very much interested in what you *love*. Victoria's secret is that she's actually after your heart."[10]

The liturgy of the mall accomplishes its purpose—creating and cultivating our desires as consumers—which is why it has been replicated around the world. But for our analogy with the liturgy of death-denial, one of Smith's points is particularly crucial: when we find our habits and desires shaped by a shopping mall, the problem is not that we've been "hoodwinked by bad ideas"; rather, it's that "we've been immersed in de-formative liturgies and not realized it." As a result, even if we have higher aspirations than to live as slaves to the gods of consumerism, we've absorbed the story of consumerism in the habits of our actions and thoughts. Without even recognizing that we're doing it, "we start to live toward a rival understanding of the good life."[11]

In a similar way, no one consciously starts their day by thinking, "I'm going to deny my mortality and suppress my bodily limits today." But the cultures that have arisen with modern medicine create death-denying "liturgies" that lead us to do just that. The geography of our daily lives and the ritual interactions we have with our phones and computers have already set the stage. The ill and the aged are not in our homes, but out of sight. Texts, tweets, and news headlines glow before us, always promising something new. Our talismans of mastery, such as the smartphone, remind us of our busy schedules. They *don't* remind us of the lonely grandfather sitting at home or the dying member of our congregation who can no longer make it to Sunday services. Our screens don't light up to remind us of our mortal limits. Instead, promises of new life—overcoming the boring, overcoming the old—greet us, hinting at new "blessings" each morning. In a thousand tiny ways, by what we've been taught to see and hear and notice and ignore, we've come to believe that death is distant, morbid, something for other people to worry about. In the words of Radner, "Death has increasingly become no longer a part of life, where once it had supplied life its background threads, running into its colors."[12]

Of course, distant echoes of death do still make their way into modern life. Those of us who have lost loved ones find ourselves expecting to see them at breakfast; or we remind ourselves to give them a routine evening call, even if cognitively we know they're gone. When death appears in our broader cultural liturgy, it's often to provide a touch of drama in order to sell a product, such as a new home-security system, or to promote a political cause, such as gun control or gun rights. In big ways and small, our desires are turned away from embracing our impotence, our limits, the smallness of our mortal lives. We have been conditioned to receive news reports of wars, drownings, and shootings as confirmation that death happens to *other* people and that we can ultimately control it—if only we buy the right products, support the right political causes, and avoid whatever may put us at risk of the kinds of senseless deaths that make the nightly news and populate our newsfeeds each day.

But where *does* this liturgy direct our attention? Does it lead us, as mortals who have very little time, to focus on how we treat our co-workers, spouses, or children? No. This liturgy fixates us on the trivial, drowning out the whispers of our fragile existence with noise. When our most consistent cultural encounters with death are attempts to sell us an idea or product, it is no surprise that we come to see death as a bluffing foe. But the truth is this: each moment, we are dying. We are parents, children, siblings, and friends who are dying—and that dying is not simply an issue of political management or marketing prowess, but a foe that we cannot overcome in this earthly life. Even with all of our ingenuity and planning and technology and wealth, in the end we are still impotent before death. And when death comes, as it always does, the liturgy of our culture encourages us to distance ourselves from it. Rather than spend time with the body of the deceased—so that the embodied reality of the death can be absorbed in our skin and our heart—we're encouraged to call the funeral home right away so that the body can be handled by professionals. The recently deceased body is treated as a contagion, a dangerous transmitter of the disease of death.[13]

How we treat the body after death is also telling. As James K. A. Smith observed at a conference on death and dying, funerals have come to mirror, in several ways, the evolution of the wedding ceremony in our consumer culture. Weddings, which were once integrated into larger congregational services focused on worship, are now often personalized events attended by friends and family. They focus on the bride and groom in a Disney-type narrative (of being "king" and "queen" for a day) rather than on consecrating to God the bodies of those gathered to worship.[14]

Christian funerals have followed a similar path. The older pattern was to bring the coffin, and thus the body of the deceased, to a congregational worship service centered on the death and resurrection of Christ. The funeral was a service for the whole congregation, important for the discipleship of both young and old. In contrast, the newer trend is to leave the body of the deceased behind, as that might dampen people's mood. The services have a positive spin, with polished videos and rousing music. While these services intend to honor the deceased, their focus on being a "celebration of life" often displaces the story of Christ's death and resurrection. Stated differently, all too often the church swaps a Christ-centered funeral liturgy for a sugarcoated "personal memorial service" to accommodate a death-denying culture.[15]

For Christians in particular, the dangers in embracing death-denying cultural liturgies like this are profound. Sidelining our mortal bodies means acting as if we are not the transient, fragile creatures that we truly are. Living into this death-denying liturgy makes us sidestep our radical need for the God of deliverance, the Lord of life who is our only hope in each new breath and our only hope in death.

## Children Learning to Be Mortal

In light of the modern cultural liturgy of death-denial, even within the church, what might be a possible counterliturgy? I face this question not only as a Christian and as a cancer patient but also as a parent. The question has a specific ring to it when I'm around my kids: Do I have the luxury of distancing my young children from the dying, or should I bring them up close? Without the liturgy of a monthly funeral, without the regular practice of sitting with the dying, we leave it to the tailored dramas of television or the highly charged outrage of the news cycle to portray the concrete process of dying. But neither medium helps my seven-year-old face the fact that his skin will one day sag, his growing body decay. Since my cancer diagnosis, I've decided that the denial of death is a luxury my family can't afford.

With this in mind, I walked with my son, Nathaniel, across the nursing home's parking lot, his hand locked tightly into mine. The sun was still bright on this warm and sticky summer afternoon. The last time we had entered this tan brick building, we'd come to visit a different friend from church. Nathaniel asked now, "Is Mr. Walker . . . dead?" He knew the answer in the abstract because we had talked about it multiple times, but we hadn't been able to arrange for him to attend the funeral, so he hadn't seen the body.

"Yes, Mr. Walker is dead," I said.

"Is Grandpa Wilbur going to die?" ("Grandpa Wilbur" was what we called the friend we were visiting today.)

"Yes, he's going to die. But let's talk to him now. He and Miss Sharon will be excited to see you!"

Walking through the outer set of doors, we felt the cool of the air conditioning, a relief from the humid heat outside. "Do you remember the combination?" I asked. Nathaniel thrust his small, stuffed, gray-and-black kitten, "Neow," toward the keypad, but Neow's memory was apparently not as good as we had hoped. After a few tries, we caught the attention of a nurse who walked over and pulled the door open for us. "C'mon in," she said. The door clicked shut behind us, locking from both inside and out. Unauthorized visitors without the combination were kept out, and unauthorized wanderers (such as dementia patients) were kept in.

A banner ahead of us down the long, carpeted hallway proclaimed, "Live this day!" in a sparkling, golden font. "Live this day, for tomorrow we die," ran through my mind as we walked. At the end of a second hallway, we found ourselves before Sharon and Wilbur's door. We knocked and peeked in.

"Come on in!" Grandpa Wilbur shouted. The couple, in their early eighties, sat in companion easy chairs in front of the TV, their usual spot. Sharon was thin; she sat up straight and looked alert. Wilbur was heavyset, with a swollen leg propped horizontally on a chair.

"Good to see you!" Wilbur shouted over the blare of the TV. "And how is Master Nathaniel?" Nathaniel cracked a smile but moved back behind the door to Wilbur's shiny blue electric wheelchair, tucked away in the room's corner.

After greeting Wilbur, I asked, "How are you, Sharon?" As usual, Sharon, who had late-stage dementia, didn't seem to recognize me. She smiled with a glance at us, then looked back toward the glow of the television.

"How have things been going, Wilbur?" I asked.

"Not too bad," he said, turning his eyes down to the floor. "Not too bad." Then, looking up into my eyes, he began his regular update: several new doctors' appointments, the doctors trying to control his pain, the seemingly vain attempts to keep fluid from swelling up his leg again—the ups and downs of life as a patient. Wilbur recited the well-rehearsed script breathlessly and seemed eager for it to end.

I pointed to a table. "Are you building a puzzle?"

"Yes," he said, "but this one kind of has me stumped right now." He relaxed in his chair, pointing to the deep greens, blues, and reds in the farm scene on the puzzle. Then his eyes rose to meet mine. "I so miss helping with the kids at church."

"Yes, we miss you too, and especially on Sunday mornings."

"I'm still going to figure out a way to make it there," Wilbur said. "This wheelchair is too big for the church bus, but I've wondered, why can't I just go outside and ride my way there?"

"On the sidewalk?" I asked.

"Why not?" he replied. "It can't be over two miles. Beverly said that she could stay with Sharon on the church bus. I could just ride along the road. It would take a while, but there's nothing to stop me." Wilbur had mentioned this idea before, and he seemed to be asking in a way that sought my approval.

As I considered what to say, Neow came out of hiding and leaped onto the sofa across from Wilbur and Sharon. "Eeeooii, eeooii," bounce, bounce. For the first time since we had arrived, Sharon focused her full attention away from the glowing screen to follow the progress of the tiny cat.

"Where is she? Where did Neow go?" Nathaniel asked, shrugging his shoulders. A smile crept onto Sharon's face as her forefinger pointed to the edge of the sofa cushion. "Meow—*there* she is!" Nathaniel shouted over the TV, as Sharon laughed gently and pointed to Neow's new location by the blue wheelchair. Nathaniel was much more successful in drawing out Sharon than I was.

Wilbur turned back to me. "Well, it's so nice to have the meals taken care of here. And they have good food," he said, savoring the words "good" and "food" as if he could taste them. "But they don't have enough hot water right now." He pointed to the shower in the small bathroom right beside the main room. "I wake up in the night with pain in this leg, and when I wake up at two or three in the morning, I'll just take a shower then. That's the only time I know that I can get warm water."

Within a few minutes, the most popular guest—Nathaniel—was hopping up and down like a manic bunny, so I suggested we grab each other's hands for our closing time. Nathaniel's small hand gripped mine tightly, and he held Sharon's hand on the other side. We closed our eyes and prayed in unison, "Our Father, who art in heaven . . ."

As Nathaniel and I pulled out of the driveway a few minutes later, he asked more questions about dying and death. Most were softball pitches that I took on one by one. A few left me halting and puzzled.

I remember thinking that these were questions, whether easy or hard, that mortals—even seven-year-old mortals—can and should ask.

My son continued asking questions about death over the following weeks. One day the tiny, spotted catfish in his aquarium at home slowed down, his deep brown spots fading to a drab yellow. He didn't bop around the rocks and the plastic castle in search of food, and his body was stiff when I poked him with a net.

Nathaniel struggled with what to do with the feelings of sadness and confusion that came with his fish's death. I wondered whether to follow one of two common parental scripts: "Your catfish had a good life" and "It's sad, but all fish have to die sometime." I had a chance to shape my son's formative liturgy. Which script was both life-affirming and mortality-accepting? While the question hung in my head, I blurted out both responses and held Nathaniel close by my side.

A few mornings later, Nathaniel popped out of bed and greeted me with an announcement: "Baby Pom Pom died last night." (The "Pom Poms" were a group of stuffed animals, tiny tan dogs.) "Baby Pom Pom forgot how to breathe, but last night Mommy Pom Pom laid an egg." So, it seemed, a life had ended and a new life had been born. "Isn't that sad news and happy news all at once?" he asked earnestly, as if he were the first person to discover this strange reality. "Yes, it is both sad news and happy news at once," I said. Nathaniel's imaginary world, where birth and death were held together in a single story, tore into the bubble of illusion frequently promoted by our death-denying culture. Who knows? Perhaps he's cultivating seeds of resistance to the larger death-denying culture that he inhabits.

## The Art of Dying as the Art of Living

My halting efforts to live—and raise my children—among the dying have a long Christian pedigree in a tradition known as the *ars moriendi*, the "art of dying." This tradition is another counterliturgy to the death-denying liturgy we encounter today, a historic path for embracing our mortality as we live and prepare to meet our Almighty Lord beyond the grave. Because of the prominence of the death-denying liturgy in our daily lives, many nonreligious persons have called for a form of *ars moriendi* as well. Consider Caitlin Doughty, a self-described millennial "none" (someone who marks "none of the above" on religious affiliation surveys). She closes her recent bestseller, *Smoke Gets in Your Eyes*, with these words: "We can wander further into the death dystopia, denying that we will die and hiding dead bodies from our sight. Making that choice means we will continue to be terrified and ignorant of death, and the huge role it plays in how we live our lives. Let us instead reclaim our mortality, writing our own Ars Moriendi for the modern world with bold, fearless strokes."[16]

In another bestseller, *Being Mortal*, Atul Gawande, a surgeon and Harvard Medical School professor, devotes a section to exploring the Christian *ars moriendi*. While not a Christian himself, he points to the "prescribed set of customs" that used to be a part of dying but have now been poignantly lost, including "reaffirming one's faith, repenting one's sins, and letting go one's worldly possessions," along with prayers for the dying and their faith community.[17] In some ways, he notes, the hospice movement attempts to revive the communal dimension of the *ars moriendi* for our age. But for Gawande, a recovery of the art of dying is absolutely vital, whether its form is historically Christian or more modern and secular: the modern "experiment" of "making mortality a medical experience is just decades old. It is young. And the evidence is that it is failing."[18]

Prayers and community, pastors and moments of reconciliation—these have receded into the background in our modern health transition. Doctors used to say, "There's nothing more we can do." These days, doctors can always do more, even if that "more" is a tortuous cycle of treatments with no hope of recovery. At the door of death, doctors have replaced pastors, and the ventilator has replaced the prayer book. And we're the poorer for it, Gawande says. As a surgeon, he has seen first-hand how the idolatry of medicine "has caused callousness, inhumanity, and extraordinary suffering."[19] Not even the best medicine can solve the problem of death, and we separate ourselves from family, faith community, and the natural process of dying when we act as if it can.

For Christians, the *ars moriendi* tradition relates not only to the end of life but also to the whole of it. Both young and old tend to live as if our lives are without end, as if our worldly accomplishments and wealth are eternal investments. In contrast, coming face-to-face with the inevitability of death, the psalmist prays,

> LORD, let me know my end,
>> and what is the measure of my days;
>> let me know how fleeting my life is.
> You have made my days a few handbreadths,
>> and my lifetime is as nothing in your sight.
> Surely everyone stands as a mere breath. (Ps. 39:4–5)

Our days are "a mere breath." Death often comes unexpectedly. In any given moment, death could be near or far—we don't know. And even for those who live seventy or eighty years, as Psalm 90 says, our days "are soon gone, and we fly away" (v. 10). Our span of life "is as nothing" before the eternal Lord. Death is the great equalizer for mortals; it comes to us whether we are ready or not, whether we feel safe and secure or in danger.

For centuries, both Catholic and Protestant pastors instructed their congregations about how to live in light of the art of dying. The pastoral advice and existential struggle of sixteenth-century reformer Martin Luther is especially instructive. According to Luther, even when our body feels vibrant, and dying seems like it belongs to a far country, we should make death a frequent acquaintance. "We should familiarize ourselves with death during our lifetime, inviting death into our presence when it is still at a distance and not on the move."[20] Why does Luther advise this? His reason, it would seem, is not a morbid proclivity but rather the same reason the psalmist refers to life as a mere breath before God: death punctures our hubris, our sense that the world is a drama in which we are the focal point. Death points to the God of life—the God who put flesh on dry bones—as our only hope, both now and in the age to come. Reminding ourselves of our mortality helps us turn to the One who is eternal, for "since everyone must depart, we must turn our eyes to God, to whom the path of death leads and directs us."[21]

Because reminders of our death can help us cling to God for life, the whole "life of the Christian," for Luther—"from baptism to the grave"—is "nothing less than the beginning of a holy death."[22] Luther's insight here is both existential and theological. As mortals, we are masters of self-deception. We deny reality—that we are creatures and that only the Almighty Lord is God. Although we were created to cling to God and his promises, sinful "man is by nature unable to want God to be God. Indeed, he himself wants to be God, and does not want God to be God."[23] Thus, a "holy death" is actually a holy way of living—a way that puts to death the old, sinful self in baptism—and a coming-to-life on a sojourn that hopes in God alone.

The possibility of a "holy death" that brings life is, for Luther, not simply an idea or an abstraction. Dying to the old self and embracing our creaturely reality are cultivated through specific practices within the context of our family and faith community. These practices, to use Smith's term, are a sort of "liturgy" that helps us embrace our mortal limits and place our deepest confidence in the eternal Lord. For example, Luther advises Christian parents to help their children prepare for death through self-denying practices such as "prayer, fasting, keeping vigils, working, worshipping, hearing God's word, and observing the Sabbath." These practices don't offer immunity from suffering, but they can certainly be part of the life-giving path of preparing for dying, learning "to disdain temporal things, endure misfortune with equanimity, face death without fear, not holding this life too dear."[24]

Yet Luther also frequently reminds his readers that these practices of self-denial and worship flow as fruit from faith—faith that is not our own work but a Spirit-given confidence in God's mercy in Christ.

Faith, experientially speaking, entails giving up our self-saving efforts as we run *to*—not *away from*—God for deliverance.[25] It is expressed in worship, fasting, and hearing God's Word—helping us to feed upon the truth that we desperately need. When we ache and hunger for God's Word, hoping in his promise, we live in faith. Indeed, Luther says that even life's trials, when approached in faith, can be "holy things" that the Lord uses to bring death and cultivate new life. "People should regard suffering and misfortune as holy things, and be glad and thank God when they strike."[26]

To my ears, Luther sounds a bit overly pious in speaking about suffering and misfortune as "holy things" when received in faith. But as his own struggles with serious illness reinforced, faith itself is not an autonomous achievement. It is an action of God, received in the community of the church. Several times, illness brought Luther near to death, and in response he was anything but stoic. Theologian Kelly Kapic describes one instance in which, "turning to everyone in the room one by one, Luther requested, 'Pray for me, please.'"[27] He cried out for prayers from the Christians around him. At times in the tumult, faith itself seemed beyond Luther's reach: "I almost lost Christ in the waves and blasts of despair and blasphemy against God, but God was moved by the prayers of saints and began to take pity on me and rescued my soul from the lowest hell."

These moments on the cliff of despair sound like a far cry from his belief that misfortunes can be "holy things." Luther doesn't claim that our calamities will make sense or be within our power to overcome; he does claim, however, that when we pray, fast, and seek the Word of God, we admit that we cannot live in faith on our own. We need the Spirit to come and enable members of the body of Christ to bear one another's burdens, binding the whole body to Christ, their head, even in the darkness. "When we feel pain, when we suffer, when we die, let us turn to this, firmly believing and certain that it is not we alone, but Christ and the church who are in pain and suffering and dying with us," Luther writes.[28]

If Christians today are to recover the *ars moriendi* tradition, we need to rediscover the value of preparing for death as a lifelong feature of discipleship. We should seek out opportunities to touch and sit with and pray with the dying. We should welcome and guide our children to come to know the dying, and we shouldn't shy away from bringing children to funerals—both for the sake of the dying and for the sake of our children and ourselves. An *ars moriendi* can also involve daily practices of remembering our mortal limits before the God who gives life—practices such as breaking bread with a friend, and expressing gratitude; attending to the ache in your feet that feels like walking on needles, and cultivating patience; tossing a squeaky toy to a neighbor's dog, and embracing the simple joys of play. These are embodied acts of mortals who owe their life and breath to the Creator. We eat, ache, and play as embodied, temporal, vanishing persons. We do so as ones who are not in charge of the universe. Recognizing our mortal limits can lighten our load and deepen our joy. We are small, and the world is not on our shoulders.

In our smallness and fragility, medicine can be an aid from the Lord of creation. However, the liturgy of modern medicine has coaxed us into seeing medicine as more than an aid. We're tempted to turn to it as a savior, a form of magic that can protect what matters most. In thousands of little ways, we come to assume that medicine gives us control over our future and perhaps even control over death.

But as my coworker Lisa knows, pain, dying, and decay are not exceptions but rules that will eventually overtake us all. My own daily pain reminds me that people in the real world have bodies that can't be "fixed." Medicine can offer a real salve in the midst of our short pilgrimage, but it is temporary; it cannot change the fact that we are fragile, dependent creatures, utterly reliant on the One who is the source of life and breath. Whether our death is perceived as timely or tragic, our warm bodies will grow cold.

For Christians, however, while death is an abrupt severing of body and soul, of individual and community, it does not have the final word.

"This world, with devils filled, . . . threaten[s] to undo us," Luther reminds us in his hymn "A Mighty Fortress Is Our God." Yet

> the Spirit and the gifts are ours through Him Who with us
> sideth;
> Let goods and kindred go, this mortal life also;
> The body they may kill: God's truth abideth still,
> His kingdom is forever.

Death may appear to win the final battle, but it does not—because God
in Christ endures, and his kingdom is forever.

As we look to God for deliverance, practices of worship—of clinging
to God's Word—have a central role. Indeed, for Luther, participation
in doxology is always the ultimate goal of the art of dying. All who
have breath are invited to join. If the breathing creatures do not sing,
then other parts of the creation will:

> The mountains and the hills before you
> shall burst into song,
> and all the trees of the field shall clap their hands. (Isa. 55:12)

One of my favorite parts of Sunday worship comes when I stand with
the congregation and sing the doxology. When young and old raise their
voices together, the song becomes more than simply about us or our
own lofty plans or even our own faith. When we sing, we sing a truth
about reality, the central truth of the cosmos—a truth that endures
whether we confess it or not, whether we are alive or not, whether any
humans join the angels in singing it or not. The doxology adores the
one Lord who endures.

> Praise God, from whom all blessings flow;
> Praise him, all creatures here below;
> Praise him above, ye heav'nly host;
> Praise Father, Son, and Holy Ghost. Amen.

## Discussion Questions

- Think about what it means to live and die on the "planet" of modern medicine. How have you seen the formative power of modern medicine affect those around you?

- Can you relate to the idea of making choices with regard to medical decisions and ending up at a destination you did not choose? What experiences do you have of this "strange new world of modern medicine"?

- Medicine is a great gift from God, but it can also become a powerful idol. In what ways do you see medicine idolized?

- The modern world can shape us with a cultural liturgy that functionally denies our mortality and our mortal limits, pulling our attention away from the dying, who are often separated into institutions. The glow of smartphones and our consumer culture lead us to think that death only happens to *other* people. In what ways do you see your own life, and the lives of those close to you, shaped by a cultural liturgy of death-denial?

- What do you think is the purpose of a funeral service? How might funerals be a way to stand against a liturgy of death-denial? Describe aspects of funerals you've attended that either cultivate death-denial or push back against it.

- How might today's church recover a corporate sense of the *ars moriendi*, the art of dying?

# Five

## The Way of Prosperity and the Christian Way

When I entered high school in 1987 in central Kansas, I thought I knew what prosperity looked like. Its color, at least, was red with black stripes.

On TV I saw the bright red lipstick on Tammy Faye Bakker's face and the black stripes of mascara running down her cheeks as she wept during a Praise the Lord (PTL) network fundraiser. She and her husband, Jim, taught the "prosperity gospel." In the words of Jim's 1980 book, which foreshadowed his television ministry, "God wants you to be happy. God wants you to be rich. God wants you to prosper, even as your soul prospers."[1]

Tammy Faye's red lipstick and black stripes were part of the drama of fundraising for the Bakkers' twenty-four-hour-a-day TV network, PTL. Later, after Jim was indicted for conspiracy and fraud, those same colors donned the covers of *Time* and *Newsweek* as "prosperity" gave way to scandal. This drama of false prosperity led my classmates and me to jeer at the Bakkers and their "prosperity gospel"—good for jokes, but not much else.

But there were other aspirations of prosperity, besides those of the

Bakkers, to mock in high school. This was also the time of the bright red Air Jordan high-tops, complete with the black Nike swoosh. Basketball star Michael Jordan, with his extraordinary leap and perfect shot, was the definition of prosperous, and my high school was filled with wannabes. Whether or not they could imitate his discipline and athleticism, they wanted to reflect the winning flare of his slam dunks by wearing red, black, and white Air Jordan high-tops.

I, on the other hand, had joined the high school debate squad. Leaving before the sun rose on Saturday mornings for debate tournaments, we could argue for or against the Reagan tax cut or the solvency of Social Security at the flip of a coin.

Among our peers, debaters were the nerds—not exactly the definition of high school success. The varsity basketball team, its games attended by hundreds of cheering locals, topped the teenage status hierarchy. But there's more than one way to succeed, we thought. "You'll be working for us someday," a fellow debater would taunt basketball players who were just out of earshot.

Eager to find our own place to belong, we launched a counterattack on the exaltation of basketball in our town. We discovered that, through a local community league, we could form our own basketball team. No tryouts were required. If we had enough people and paid the fees, we were in. We wouldn't be playing varsity, but we could still compete against classmates who were Michael Jordan wannabes.

We called ourselves Air Debate, and our jerseys fit the red-and-black style of the Air Jordan fad. Our jersey numbers shamelessly proclaimed our nerdiness. Rather than 3 or 9 or 33, the number on my back reflected the ancient theorem about right triangles: $a^2 + b^2 = c^2$.

Michael Jordan meets Pythagoras.

We had a great time playing. Yes, we lost every game, sometimes by over a hundred points. But we were the only team popular enough to have cheerleaders. We had fun. And we mocked our classmates who acted like they were Michael Jordan simply because they could beat a bunch of debate nerds on the court.

There are many ways to define success and prosperity. Jim Bakker claimed that God wanted his viewers to be rich while Bakker took their money, and he doctored the books to finance the Bakkers' lavish lifestyle. My high school jock classmates claimed to be the next heroes on the horizon, like Michael Jordan. My debate team, as well, had its own definition of prosperity. We mocked the Bakkers and our classmates, all the while trusting that our brains would one day put us in charge of the jocks at the workplace. In reality, both we and the jocks were just nervous kids in a small Kansas town, competing for status. All of these aspirations to prosperity were hollow.

And yet, when I'm honest, in my day-to-day life I feel a genuine attraction to the prosperity gospel. On days when I feel beaten down with the effects of cancer treatment, any hope leaking through the cracks is enough for me. I could despair in this darkness or respond with rage at those who are close enough to blame. But the prosperity gospel seems to point me in a more constructive direction, compared to those alternatives: reach up when hopelessness pulls you down. Think positively and go for it. I can get out of this. If I try hard or take a step of faith in the right way, I will be rewarded with the good life.

The Bakkers have faded from the headlines, and Michael Jordan no longer plays in the NBA, but the prosperity gospel has spread far and wide. While its origins are distinctly American, it shows up around the globe now. "God wants me to be happy. God wants me to prosper."

I find myself drawn to this prosperity message, even if in more modest forms. I don't want a private jet or the accomplishment and fame of a basketball star. But I would like to live long enough to see my children graduate from high school. Is that asking so much, God? Isn't that part of the prosperity that you supposedly desire? I'd like to be alive if a grandchild comes someday. Something inside me feels as though God must, or should, want these things for me as well.

However, when I hear Scripture speak about prosperity, it moves in a different direction. On the one hand, God desires *shalom*—communal peace, wholeness, and flourishing—for his creatures. Yet this flourishing differs from the kind that we pursue on our own. In the wisdom of the God of Jesus Christ, human flourishing has a cross-shaped, cruciform character.[2] Indeed, the peace of *shalom* testifies to a more fundamental reality—the rule of the crucified and risen Lord, the King of the kingdom. In the Lord's Prayer we pray for God's kingdom to come rather than for our own wishes for flourishing to be fulfilled. Indeed, we pray to die to our own wishes as we receive a reality (the coming kingdom) that we have not earned with our drive or discipline. As a cancer patient and a father of young children, I suspect God may be up to something different than providing me with middle-class American "prosperity."

## Prosperity and the Religious Turn of Terminal Cancer Patients

What does it mean to prosper? Would we know true prosperity, true flourishing, if we saw it? If your blinders of self-deception are anything like mine, exposing the notions of prosperity that really drive us can be a very complicated task. In the past six years I've become a participant-observer among terminal cancer patients. In that role, I've tried to untangle what views of human flourishing lie beneath all the chemotherapy and clinical trials and how we're encouraged to approach the future as cancer patients.

I'm reminded of a cultural anthropology class I took in college. We learned about "participant observation"—a set of methods for learning about a culture or subculture by participating in the culture while making close observations about its internal rules and codes. Shortly after the course I put this methodology into practice as a participant-observer in Uganda, working with a local community development organization for six months, as noted in my story about Ochen in chapter 4. I let myself become curious, taking notes and asking questions as I immersed myself in the culture. I was always an outsider. But to attend a wedding, for example, I needed to be part of the clan of the bride or groom, so when I introduced myself I would quip, "Ma va Nori" (I'm also [of the] Nori), which was met with whoops and laughter. The Ugandans were extraordinarily hospitable, but without a doubt I was an outsider who was learning as much as possible by acting as an insider.

Decades later, in Michigan, a formerly hidden subculture was opened to me: the cancer community. I quickly started learning its customs, norms, and values. When I wasn't manic from the steroids or listless with fatigue, I found myself curious about how to decode this new culture. Now I was an insider participant-observer, without needing a ruse to be part of the community. In the cancer clinic I met nurses and doctors who knew their patients well and seemed to have a set protocol for all the odd questions I had and the problems I was experiencing. Other patients who started off as strangers became friends as we talked about our diagnoses and our lab numbers, as we compared nerve pain and talked about our families. In countless appointments, hospital stays, and cancer support group meetings, a set of patterns became clear.

One of the striking features I noticed was that cancer patients are a religious bunch. It wasn't unusual to meet a cancer patient who was not religious *before* the diagnosis. But after? Even cynical skeptics seemed to have their hearts thawed to the point of aching in prayer, asking questions about God afresh. While most hospital-sponsored cancer groups have a thin veneer of secularism in order to be inclusive of the nonreligious, I noticed how conversations often included talk of prayer, miracles, and what God could be up to in this mess.

When I consulted the academic literature on the subject, sure enough— most cancer patients consider religion to be either "important" or "very important" in their lives. In contrast to their doctors, they considered prayer and faith to be vital in discerning a path of treatment.[3] Given the disconnect between doctors and patients on points like this, it's not surprising that these religiously animated patients find that the sterile, ostensibly secular space of the hospital leaves their lives of faith underaddressed. In one study, 72 percent of cancer patients "reported that their spiritual needs were supported minimally or not at all by the medical system." Sadly, and perhaps more surprisingly, "nearly half (47%) reported that their spiritual needs were minimally or not at all supported by a religious community."[4]

Cancer patients, as a group, are animated with religious hope—praying and believing more fervently than the population at large, and more than they themselves did before their cancer diagnosis.[5]

Interestingly, even for those who don't believe in God and whose goal is simply to be healthy and to live as long as possible, practicing religion has benefits. Empirically speaking, numerous studies from the general population indicate that high religiosity is associated with positive health outcomes, both in mental health (a greater sense of well-being, being less likely to commit suicide, etc.) and in physical health (having the self-control to avoid risky behaviors, the ability to cope with stress and loss from disease, etc.).[6] These are health benefits of the highly religious that are touted by researchers (who themselves are often *not* religious) in a wide range of cultural contexts. If religion is a tool for living longer, then cancer patients are right to turn to it.

One problem with these studies is that they define "religion" in extremely broad, formal terms, in spite of the practical reality that not all religious commitments lead practitioners to the same ends. Even among Christian patients who pray and are active in their faith, the locus of their hope can vary dramatically. As theologian George Lindbeck noted, "You can no more be religious in general than you can speak language in general."[7] Indeed, a sociologist's construct of "religion" is just that: a socially constructed category with numerous divergent (and conflicting) theological visions within it.

Stated differently, many cancer patients, especially after being diagnosed with a terminal illness, seem to recognize that we're in a pit of one sort or another. But what to do about that is far from clear. Do you pray for a cure? Do you seek the temple, the presence of the living God? Do you accept your mortality as a creature? At times I've been buoyed by hope that perhaps Christians in the cancer community can testify to the surrounding culture about the dangers of death-denial. Sometimes that happens. But as I've explored how religious fervor actually functions for many Christians with a terminal illness, I've often become more troubled than encouraged.

## Prosperity: Seeking Heroic Measures?

Patients don't choose to receive a lethal illness, but their response to a diagnosis can say a great deal about what sort of "prosperous" life they are pursuing. The new medical "liturgy" that we examined in earlier chapters includes a set of end-of-life options involving extreme or "heroic" measures. That is, terminally ill patients may be offered aggressive treatments that have little or no chance of success. Even if remission or recovery is impossible, there is always more that doctors can do. As Harvard surgeon Atul Gawande explains, "they can give toxic drugs of unknown efficacy, operate to try to remove part of the tumor, put in a feeding tube if a person can't eat; there's always something."[8] But on the whole, extreme measures do not enable the dying to live longer. Such measures are extraordinarily costly—financially, socially, and psychologically—and frequently have devastating side effects that can make communication with friends and loved ones during a patient's final days all but impossible.

Choosing extreme measures is a gamble. "We've created a multi-trillion-dollar edifice for dispensing the medical equivalent of lottery tickets," Gawande points out, "and have only the rudiments of a system to prepare patients for the near certainty that those tickets will not win."[9] A losing ticket results in increased suffering for the patient and trauma for the surviving family. A winning ticket means only a few more days or weeks of breath. Why would anyone opt for this?

Thankfully, most patients say no to this lottery ticket. But here's what, at first, left my mind spinning: the patients who are most likely to say yes to these "heroic" measures are those who are highly religious. In one major study conducted by the Dana Farber Cancer Institute in Boston, highly religious cancer patients (predominantly Christian) were more than three times as likely as other patients to opt for extreme measures.[10] This data fits with that of other studies and with my own experience as a participant-observer in the cancer community.[11]

When researchers asked patients why they chose treatments that were almost certain to fail, the patients gave very specific *theological*—rather than strictly medical—reasons. They said it was to give God a chance to perform a miracle, to give God longer to heal them. Such responses used almost exactly the same phrases I encounter so often in the cancer community, especially in the comments sections of the medical web pages of friends with terminal illnesses.

"We're praying for complete healing!"

"A miracle is around the corner!"

"Expect God's miracle."

"The resurrected Christ can answer your prayers!"

"We pray for a miracle because we believe it can happen!"

"God is an awesome and powerful healer."

In the words of one of the Dana Farber study's researchers, "It seems like those patients . . . would hold on as long as possible to give God every opportunity to grant them a miracle and save them." Yet in this sample, as in other studies of this sort, heroic measures failed to deliver on the hopes of patients. "We find that those who get more aggressive care have decrements in their quality of life," the researchers noted. Indeed, "the more aggressive care did not predict survival differences."[12]

Even apart from the decreased quality of life, extreme treatments have other very real costs. As Gawande explains, "The end comes with no chance for you to have said goodbye or 'It's O.K.' or 'I'm sorry' or 'I love you.'" There may be no opportunity for holding hands and praying the Lord's Prayer, for singing that favorite hymn. A study from the Coping with Cancer project showed that, six months after the death of a patient who utilized extreme measures, the person's caregivers "were three times as likely to suffer major depression" as caregivers of patients who did not receive those measures.[13]

What are these highly religious (mostly Christian) patients assuming about human flourishing? Shouldn't committed Christians have peace when they die? Why do they opt for this gamble rather than embracing their lives as short and using whatever strength they have to love God and neighbor? Troubling as these questions are, my participant-observation leads me to an even more troubling possibility: perhaps, for some committed Christians, it's their *faith* that pushes them to deny the reality of their mortality rather than embrace it. Perhaps that is why they are so much more likely to choose heroic measures. They assume that God works according to only one script—that of healing and reviving. Perhaps these Christians found that this script fit their path of discipleship earlier in life. But now, as they enter their final earthly chapter, the script simply doesn't fit anymore. There is no role in it for a dying disciple of Jesus.

## Maggie and Linda and the Eclipse of Resurrection Hope

As I've puzzled over these questions for several years, I've seen the drama play out through friends and acquaintances facing death. Often, after curative methods have failed and it is clear that the condition is terminal, the patient is open to the reality of dying. But accepting the reality of death is much harder for the person's spouse, children, family, and church.

In a case that is fixed vividly in my mind, the patient, Maggie, was my age. Maggie was very involved in her church, and she and her husband, like my wife and I, had two young children when she faced her cancer treatment. One treatment after another failed. Each was preceded with hope and prayers but ended with disappointment. After these multiple treatments, Maggie's body was beaten down and hollowed out.

As Maggie struggled, her mother continued to ask for prayers for a miracle. Support poured in from "prayer warriors." Putting Maggie into hospice would be a defeat, they believed. Finally, just a few days after prayers were fervently offered that Maggie would live to watch her young children grow up and become parents themselves, she went into hospice. Two days later, she died.

I can't wag my finger at Maggie's family and friends. Their loss was cataclysmic, beyond words. But again and again I have wondered: How was their Christian faith formed through their childhood, adolescence, and adulthood such that God must work according to the script of giving the young a longer life?

In the case of Linda, an older friend who was also a committed Christian, her friends responded with similar calls for prayers after doctors said her condition was dire. One day, out of curiosity, I did a word search on her medical blog site, looking through the posts and their comments. Linda's site had hundreds of references to God and prayer and healing. Not a single comment referred to resurrection hope or heaven or the life to come.

I cherish Linda's friendship, and I don't want to lose her. But she is in her mid-seventies and has repeatedly taken extreme measures to keep her heart beating, to keep her breath flowing. None of the hundreds of comments on her medical blog imply that she should be preparing to die. None of the comments imply that God might want her to prepare for death. They sing a single tune in unison: God is a healer, and true hope points toward being cured, restored to full health, because God's primary work is that of performing miracles.

Did Maggie or Linda attend a "prosperity gospel" church? Were their pastors Jim Bakker protégés who preached that God wants us to be rich? Absolutely not. Did their friends, seasoned congregation members, think that faith is a tool for acquiring money and health? Of course not.

But behind the single melody of their song lurks a question: How could God *not* desire to heal Maggie and Linda? The prayers were earnest. Often they looked something like this: "When you heal Maggie, your name, O Lord, will be famous—many shall come to know your goodness!" (How could God *not* want that?) "When you heal Linda, many will ask for the source of this miracle—and we will testify to your power alone!" (Again, would God *not* want this?)

The church families of my friends were sincere and earnest. They were not treating God like a slot machine—interested only in the "goods" they could get from God. They wanted healing because they wanted to hear Maggie and Linda sing songs of praise and deliverance. They wanted non-Christians to come to faith. They wanted wholeness for the lives and families of Maggie and Linda. And yet, in their single-minded preoccupation with physical healing, something at the center of the Christian faith had been obscured: that our hope is not for life extension, a healing that could give us five more years or even fifty more years. Our hope is for eternal life with Christ, in Christ—the joy of which we taste now and which continues in the midst of the crosses we bear, even through the indignities of death.

Healing is a good gift. We can and should long for it when struck down in pain, in illness. We rightly petition for it, just as we ask the Father for our daily bread. Yet healing, like our daily bread, is ephemeral, passing away. Whether we live only a few years or several decades, "everyone comes naked from their mother's womb, / and as everyone comes, so they depart," Ecclesiastes reminds us (5:15 NIV). When Paul mentions that he and other early Christians are "outwardly wasting away," the anchor of his hope is not deliverance from or delay in the process of decay (2 Cor. 4:16 NIV). Rather, it is our union with Christ blossoming to full flower in the coming resurrection with Christ that will inaugurate "an eternal glory that far outweighs" our troubles (v. 17).

See the body for what it is: an amazing and good gift from God, but also one that is temporal, wasting away. Take heart and put your hope in the eternal glory that is unseen now (v. 18). Moments of healing occur on our earthly journey, and God deserves the thanks, as for daily bread. But why should we fixate on the manna of daily bread when a great feast and an eternal glory is to come? Seek a greater end for our desires. In the words of the psalmist, "one thing I asked of the LORD, / that will I seek after"—to "behold the beauty of the LORD" in the temple (Ps. 27:4).

### The Prosperity Gospel: It's Not Just the Televangelists Anymore

As strange as it seems, a version of Jim Bakker's health-and-wealth gospel has become an underlying assumption for many Christians today. It comes to the surface when they face illness or tragedy. But it was present all along, animating their vision as they pursued a life of flourishing.

I recall standing in front of an audience of about forty cancer patients and swaying back and forth nervously as I thought about how
to respond to a question about my presentation on prayers of lament.
"It's hard. It's hard to keep hoping in God's promise, as you say," the
woman had said quietly, as others leaned in to hear. "But I keep hoping
in God's promise—that my oncologist is *wrong*, and that my cancer
isn't getting worse." I had been speaking about the necessity of bringing our cries to God even when things don't make sense, on the basis
of God's promise—that God is the God of life who won't abandon us,
even if things feel otherwise. Somehow my talk of "God's promise" was
interpreted by her to mean "God's promise to take away this cancer."

I paused, and the room was quiet. *This is not the moment, this is
not the moment to speak my mind*, I thought to myself. I wanted to
point out that God's promise is to be a covenant Savior and Lord. The
God of Scripture never promises to heal our every disease now. God
has not promised life extension. But the questioner had already filtered
my words through a mental screen of how she thought God acts in the
world. After some long moments of silent thought, I encouraged her to
continue bringing her concerns to God. I wasn't sure how to respond
to her hope that her oncologist was wrong.

This patient was not alone in her view of God. Indeed, in a recent
Pew Foundation study, among those in the United States who believe
in God, 56 percent think that "God will grant good health and relief
from sickness to believers who have enough faith." And this expectation
of physical prosperity often goes hand in hand with the idea that God
secures financial prosperity, with nearly half of religious Americans
(46 percent) affirming that "God will grant material prosperity to all
believers who have enough faith."[14]

These beliefs have become mainstream, spreading around the world
in a variety of Christian traditions—Pentecostal and non-Pentecostal,
Protestant, nondenominational, and Catholic alike. In fact, on these
same questions, many other countries had much higher percentages
than the United States. For example, in Kenya, 83 percent affirmed

that God will grant financial prosperity, and 90 percent that God will provide health and healing.[15] I should not have been surprised that when I speak of God's "promise" to us in the midst of serious illness, many hearers assume that God promises us health and healing—either now or after a season of petitioning and waiting.

Of course, not even the best sociological study is a transparent window into the soul. Shades of meaning differ according to the culture and the season of a person's life. Perhaps, seeing on the survey the phrase "God will grant good health and prosperity," some thought of how their own lives of addiction and deprivation had been turned around after they became Christians. Perhaps, in this process of change, they discovered the health and financial security that had seemed foreign to them before. Or perhaps some respondents' answers didn't really reflect how they would've framed the issue themselves. Theological convictions are often more nuanced than a sociological survey can fully assess.

And yet the Pew Foundation study identifies something central that lines up with the studies of highly religious cancer patients I referenced earlier: What do many patients think God is interested in? Apparently, health, healing, miracles, and life extension. These answers top the list, while other responses are crowded out. In cancer communities I repeatedly encounter the earnest conviction that God wants us to prosper according to *our* definitions of "prosperity," definitions that don't include stumbling or weakness.

Although common today, these assumptions about a prosperous life are quite bizarre for Christians, of all people, to hold. On the one hand, it is true that our bodies are created good—worthy of honor—and that our bodies are "intricately woven" by the Lord himself (Ps. 139:15). But if God's *primary* concern were to prosper our health and finances, one would have expected the Messiah to come in earthly glory. The contrast with *Jesus* as the Messiah is startling. Jesus, the son of a carpenter, was mocked, beaten, and crucified in disgrace, never reaching the "golden years" of old age. It is strange, then, that the followers of this crucified Lord should expect worldly comfort and ease.

## A Different Prosperity? The Apostle Paul's Gospel

In their favor, prosperity Christians can make a logical case for their theology. One pastor, Joseph Prince, sets out the case with particular clarity. Prince is senior pastor of New Creation Church in Singapore, with over thirty thousand people at its weekly services and a wide global broadcast audience. Prince writes,

> My Bible tells me clearly that God is a God of love and that He is a good God. . . .
>
> This means that if you are sick, God's heart is and will always be to heal and restore health and life to you. He so desires for you to walk in health and life that He gave you His beloved Son, Jesus, so that you might have life and have it more abundantly (John 10:10). [God's will] is for you to walk in abundant health and life. He does not want your body and life sapped, incapacitated or debilitated by pain, sickness and disease, and He will never withhold healing from you.[16]

Prince's reasoning flows from one thought to another without the discomfort of paradox: God loves you. Because he loves you, God doesn't ever want you to be sick. He wants abundant life for you—and, of course, abundant life is incompatible with sickness. Since pain, sickness, and disease sap our life and energy, God "will never withhold healing from you."

What does this mean for readers who are plagued by chronic pain and ongoing illness? One possibility is clearly ruled out: that God could ever desire this for you. God desires flourishing, and flourishing requires health.

Why are the ill afflicted with sickness, then? The response is a familiar one in prosperity gospel circles: it's the fault of the sick. No other response is possible when the idea that God would permit you to be ill has been ruled out. Sickness is a sign of a lack of faith, so we need to reach out and claim God's promises by faith. As one friend told me after my cancer diagnosis, trying to smile as he looked me in the eyes,

"Cancer is just a spiritual condition. It's already been healed through the cross of Christ, since 'by his wounds we are healed'" (Isa. 53:5). In other words, if my kids lose their dad while they're still in elementary school, I am the one to blame, not God.

Such reasoning has a directness that can be attractive to patients and caretakers looking for certainty. When the psalmist faces sickness, he laments, "O LORD, heal me, for my bones are shaking with terror. / My soul also is struck with terror, / while you, O LORD—how long?" (Ps. 6:2–3). The prosperity Christian can bypass such laments. If you are sick, don't lament to the Almighty, "How long?" The Almighty has already done what he can; through Jesus, according to Joseph Prince, "your healing has already been paid for at the cross."[17]

This way of thinking is directly counter, however, to the teaching of the apostle Paul—and the teaching of Jesus, as we will see below. Paul's proclamation of "Christ crucified" did not lead him to reflect on the visible, bodily benefits of Christ's cross—quite the contrary, in fact. "For Jews demand signs and Greeks desire wisdom, but we proclaim Christ crucified, a stumbling block to Jews and foolishness to Gentiles" (1 Cor. 1:22–23). In the cross we see that "God's foolishness is wiser than human wisdom, and God's weakness is stronger than human strength" (v. 25).

This was Paul's message, which takes on a stingingly personal character when he speaks of his "thorn in the flesh" in 2 Corinthians. Paul prayed in faith to be delivered from an affliction, but his petition was not granted. And Paul confesses that the power of the crucified and risen Lord is displayed in the midst of "weaknesses, insults, hardships, persecutions, and calamities for the sake of Christ; for whenever I am weak, then I am strong" (2 Cor. 12:10). Far from seeing prosperity as a transparent sign of God's blessing, Paul boasts of his "weaknesses, so that the power of Christ may dwell in me" (v. 9).

How do prosperity preachers like Joseph Prince respond to Paul's teaching about his thorn in the flesh? Prince argues that it refers to Paul's enemies, those persecuting him for the sake of the gospel. Interestingly,

Prince claims that Christians should expect to suffer *persecution* for the gospel. But, he says, neither Paul in the New Testament nor Christians today suffer because of *sickness*, since illness has been defeated by the cross.

The stakes are high for Prince and other prosperity preachers in denying that Paul's thorn in the flesh was an illness. Most scholars, examining Paul's language in its ancient context, speculate that the thorn in the flesh was indeed an illness—probably a chronic illness. But since illness, for prosperity preachers, has already been overcome by the cross, this interpretation is deeply threatening. So they promote a heroic view of the Christian life—the healthy Christian boldly preaching the gospel, opposed by the enemies of the gospel. According to the prosperity gospel, Paul and true Christians experience very little ambiguity; their experience is not at all like that of the psalmist, who cries out for healing but continues to be afflicted with illness.

Historically speaking, we cannot be sure *what* Paul was referring to as the "thorn in the flesh." We do know that three times Paul "appealed to the Lord about this, that it would leave me" (2 Cor. 12:8). It did not. Instead, the risen Lord says to him, "My grace is sufficient for you, for power is made perfect in weakness" (v. 9). Moreover, as troubling as this may seem, Paul's Greek grammar is quite clear on one point: although there is nothing good about the thorn in the flesh in and of itself, and although it comes as "a messenger of Satan to torment me" (v. 7), it's the Lord himself who allows this thorn to afflict Paul. The line "a thorn was *given* [to] me in the flesh" is a "divine passive," indicating that "God is the unseen agent behind the bitter experience."[18] Thus, both the revelatory words about God's power made perfect in weakness and the thorn in the flesh are ultimately given by God.[19]

This means that we can't be content with the logic of Joseph Prince and others, even though it seems so utterly straightforward and clear: God is a God of love, so "God's heart is and will always be to heal and restore health and life to you."[20] Apparently this was not the case for the apostle Paul, nor was it the gospel he proclaimed. Paul did not proclaim a gospel that promised to heal all diseases, but one in which the followers of Christ sometimes receive afflictions for reasons we can't understand. In the words of one commentator, "The Lord neither effects nor promises removal of Paul's thorn in the flesh. In this respect, the apostle's prayers go unanswered. Rather—and this is what Paul himself now wants to impress on his readers (see vv. 9b–10)—the apostle is directed to understand his affliction as part of that weakness in and through which God's powerful grace is operative."[21]

Paul, like Job, was right to be confused and even in anguish about why he received this affliction. He was not given a reason—for example, that the thorn was a sign of his faithfulness (i.e., because of persecution). He's simply told by the resurrected Christ that "my grace is sufficient" and that the people of the crucified Lord display his power in a peculiar way: "in weakness." In Paul's words from another part of his letter, we are "always carrying in the body the death of Jesus, so that the life of Jesus may also be made visible in our bodies" (2 Cor. 4:10).

Far from granting "prosperity" through status or health, the power of the gospel is shown in the cross, in suffering that doesn't seem to make sense. In the words of Martin Luther, a great rediscoverer of Paul's theology of the cross, "The holy Gospel is a powerful Word. Therefore it cannot do its work without trials, and only he who tastes it is aware that it has such power. Where suffering and the cross are found, there the Gospel can show and exercise its power." Does that mean that the gospel leads us to pursue suffering as an end in itself or to turn from the light toward the darkness of Sheol? Absolutely not. We turn to the temple when we're in the Pit, to the Lord of light in our darkness. But we shouldn't be surprised that, in this turn, the God who displays his love to the world in Christ does not free us from suffering and trials. He loves us and displays his power through us in our weakness, in our creaturely, mortal dependence upon him. The gospel "is a Word of life," Luther declares. "Therefore it must exercise all its power in death."[22]

## Prosperity and Lifelong Discipleship

Whether we are young or old, Paul's theology of the cross is not an easy word for us to hear. Recently a friend shared an example of this. She was working as a counselor with middle school youth at a Christian summer camp. On a designated day, the whole camp participated in an activity designed to help the campers understand how they might approach the world if they lost the use of part of their body. Some were blindfolded, others had their ears covered, and others sat in a wheelchair for the day's activities. The goal was to develop empathy, though, of course, the exercise could not fully capture the daily experience of someone living with a physical disability.

Partway through the day, a girl named Hailey ripped off her blindfold and refused to put it back on. She had a theological rationale: "If I became blind, God would heal me." Hailey had faith in Jesus. She knew that she could count on God to give her a prosperous life because of her faith. If she became blind, God would fix that. And, we could ask, why not? Doesn't God desire good health for her? Doesn't God desire that she prosper?

Hailey's view of "prosperity" is that, if she lives the Christian life and has faith in God, he will respond by giving health and healing to her. What makes Hailey's approach contrary to Paul's gospel of the cross—and dangerous for her ongoing life of discipleship—is not that she believes God can perform miracles. Jesus performed miracles, including the healing of people who were blind. And he did so freely. Sometimes those seeking healing displayed faith, but often they had no apparent faith, as biblical scholar David Crump has pointed out.[23] The issue is not *whether* God can heal or perform miracles or *whether* God loves us. The issue is that the God of Scripture never promises the type of prosperity that Hailey expects. We can and should pray for our daily needs. But there is no mechanism to make God give us the type of prosperity we desire, and the words of Jesus himself about prosperity and "blessedness" sound much closer to Paul's theology of the cross than to Hailey's hopes for a life insulated from senseless suffering.

Blessed are the poor in spirit, for theirs is the kingdom of heaven.
Blessed are those who mourn, for they will be comforted.
Blessed are the meek, for they will inherit the earth. (Matt. 5:3–5)

In the Sermon on the Mount, it is good to be blessed. But this "blessed" is a far cry from the "#blessed" that adorns so many photos of status and physical prospering on social media. Being blessed, in Jesus's sermon, doesn't mean flourishing with health or material prosperity; it also doesn't mean masochistically seeking to suffer. Rather, it involves an ache, a lament, a looking forward to a coming order in which the kingdom of God turns our notions of status and prosperity upside down. Blessed are the poor in spirit, those who mourn, the meek—not those who think they've already achieved victory. Blessed are those who seek the temple from the Pit, who "hunger and thirst for righteousness," who are "pure in heart," for they will be prosperous— but not in our usual way of conceiving of prosperity. The pure in heart are blessed, Jesus says, "for they will see God" (Matt. 5:8).

Indeed, if we look to the New Testament Gospels for what it means to be blessed, it's quite clear that life in Christ's kingdom is not primarily about personal victory, about bodily or financial flourishing. We should expect, instead, the blessing of aching and longing for the kingdom to come, of knowing that our blessedness does not depend on our pocketbook or our physical prosperity (see Matt. 19:16–30; 25:1–13; Luke 6:46–49). As other parts of the New Testament repeatedly emphasize, Christians should *expect* a life with unexplained suffering. Because we have an extraordinary gift—Christ dwelling in us now by the Spirit—we are "heirs of God and joint heirs with Christ," which means that right now "we suffer with [Christ] so that we may also be glorified with him" (Rom. 8:17).

In the words of 1 Peter, in this present time Christians should expect to "suffer various trials" (1:6). In contrast to the way in which Christians with serious illnesses are often told to "expect God's miracle now," 1 Peter points to the flowering and culmination of our present union with Christ in the resurrection, an eternal inheritance that does not deliver us now from terrible diseases or economic woes. Instead, we look to "a living hope through the resurrection of Jesus Christ from the dead, . . . an inheritance that is imperishable, undefiled, and unfading, kept in heaven for you, who are being protected by the power of God through faith for a salvation ready to be revealed in the last time" (1 Pet. 1:3–5). The God of Jesus Christ promises something much better than a prosperity defined by financial and physical blessing: God promises us an inheritance as children of God through the resurrection of Christ that is "imperishable, undefiled, and unfading"—kept safe by God in heaven and revealed in its fullness only on the last day.

## Against Future Hope: The Law of Faith and Heaven Now

When read in isolation from the rest of the biblical canon, certain Old Testament passages can sound a bit like modern-day prosperity preachers. For example, in Proverbs 10 we read,

> Lazy hands make for poverty,
>    but diligent hands bring wealth.
>
> He who gathers crops in summer is a prudent son,
>    but he who sleeps during harvest is a disgraceful son.
>
> Blessings crown the head of the righteous,
>    but violence overwhelms the mouth of the wicked. (vv. 4–6
>    NIV)

In the Bible's Wisdom literature, creation is good, and humans are created to act as active stewards of the earth. As Proverbs frequently notes, wise actions can bear good fruit, and wicked actions can lead to terrible consequences. The Lord blesses the righteous, sometimes with long life, as with Abraham, who "breathed his last and died in a good old age" (Gen. 25:8). Within the Old Testament, however, these themes of prosperity are set in the context of God's gracious initiative. For example, God's blessing of Abraham is grounded in his covenant promise; it is not a reward for righteous conduct. Moreover, the Old Testament Wisdom literature is filled with examples that undermine any attempt to see a mechanistic link between obedience and prosperity. These include the narrative of the righteous Job, who loses his wealth and health, and scores of psalms of lament that reflect experiences of illness, loss, and tribulation not tied to anyone's actions or disobedience.

Interestingly, prosperity preachers today generally assume that we've reached a higher stage in salvation history, one in which the Old Testament's Wisdom literature—which claims that tragedy and illness strike both the righteous and the unrighteous—no longer applies. They encourage us to claim through faith the fullness of new covenant promises that surpass the old. Christians today should command healing and prosperity, claiming their new authority in Christ.

One prosperity preacher of the late nineteenth and early twentieth centuries, E. W. Kenyon, gave a particularly influential theological account of how this could be the case. For Kenyon, Christ's death not only breaks the power of sin; it also delivers believers from the power of a material world that has been under Satan's rule for all too long. Kenyon drew inspiration from the nineteenth-century faith-healing movement, which rebuked those who prayed for healing only "if it is God's will."[24] Instead of asking for healing only if it is God's will, the ill should act as if the healing has already happened, even if this means ignoring ongoing signs of pain or symptoms of sickness. Just act in faith. Broadening this principle more generally, Kenyon claimed that we need to ignore the "sense knowledge" that seems to contradict our faith and live into the life that we have legally inherited in Christ.[25] There is no reason for God's children to endure sickness or poverty. When we pray in the name of Jesus, we have the legal right to command the blessings of health and finances, and the Holy Spirit will assist in the execution of this authority. Indeed, far from giving credence to the sense observations about our limited, dying, mortal bodies, Kenyon claims that Holy

Spirit–filled believers are "supermen": "The World has not known that there is a superman in their midst today."[26]

While I disagree with Kenyon's theology, he is right on one crucial point: according to the New Testament, believers have been united to Christ not only in his death but also in his resurrection. In fact, in two places the apostle Paul suggests that we have a foretaste of being raised with Christ in the present life. Yet, once again, sharing in Christ's resurrection now is not framed in terms of *worldly* triumph and victory. In Ephesians 2:6–22, Paul speaks of union with Christ in his resurrection to encourage Christians to take costly steps to overcome the enmity between Jews and Gentiles and live into the "new humanity" of Christ (v. 15). This foretaste of the resurrection, while still looking forward to the coming age for its completion, indicates that we need to enter into the costly work of reconciliation and communion with one another right now.

Paul's other reference to sharing Christ's resurrection now is even more telling in indicating what it means for a Christian to "prosper" in this present age: "So if you have been raised with Christ, seek the things that are above, where Christ is, seated at the right hand of God. Set your minds on things that are above, not on things that are on earth, for you have died, and your life is hidden with Christ in God. When Christ who is your life is revealed, then you also will be revealed with him in glory" (Col. 3:1–4).

Union with Christ reveals our true identity: creatures who "have been raised with Christ" and are "seated at the right hand of God." But rather than suggesting that this means ignoring the aches and decay of our mortal bodies, Paul goes in the opposite direction. "Set your minds on things that are above," he says, because "your life is *hidden* with Christ in God." Our current lives *do not* reflect the resurrection blessing that we will experience in the age to come. Indeed, as one commentator notes, "Paul's own apostolic ministry, marked as it is with suffering and affliction, provides a graphic instance of a life 'hidden with Christ in God.'"[27] Don't ignore your bodily aches and pains, but remind yourself that your true life *has not yet been revealed*. Do you experience daily pain? Have the healing waters passed you by? Does financial security seem out of reach? Paul's response is clear: remember you are *hidden*. Signs of health and wealth do *not* testify to who you really are. Who you really are—one who has died and risen with Christ—will only be disclosed on a coming day: "When Christ who is your life is revealed, then you also will be revealed with him in glory." Don't ignore your body, with its needs and pains; but seek the kingdom.

As Jesus proclaimed, "Do not worry about your life, what you will eat or what you will drink, or about your body, what you will wear. Is not life more than food, and the body more than clothing? Look at the birds of the air; they neither sow nor reap nor gather into barns, and yet your heavenly Father feeds them. Are you not of more value than they? And can any of you by worrying add a single hour to your span of life?" (Matt. 6:25–28). Food and clothing are necessary, and "your heavenly Father knows that you need all these things" (v. 32). But to seek these temporal goods first—above all—is a foolish act. It's pursuing prosperity on our own terms. Instead, seek the temple, the kingdom, the God who alone has life in himself. "Strive first for the kingdom of God and his righteousness," Jesus says, "and all these things will be given to you as well. So do not worry about tomorrow, for tomorrow will bring worries of its own. Today's trouble is enough for today" (vv. 33–34).

Jesus repeatedly reminds us of our mortal frailty: we need food, we need clothing. He doesn't deny the dangers we face, given our frailties. Nevertheless, his imperative—"Do not be anxious"—is nearly the opposite of our fight-or-flight tendency in facing threats. Don't *deny* your weakness or the frailty of your mortal state, acting as if you could command the material world to bend to your will. Instead, delight in what is beautiful, be grateful for each day, and expect trouble ("Today's trouble is enough for today"). Take joy in the daily gifts of the Creator. But remember that you won't make it out of this journey alive. Use each day's strength to seek the temple, the kingdom, and the King.

## Kingdom Prosperity at Death

What does it look like to seek the kingdom form of prosperity as we face
our own mortal ends? Although the issues of this chapter apply to the
entire life of discipleship, I will close with two examples that illustrate
how Christians can bear witness to Christ's kingdom as they face their
own deaths. In each case the dying person navigated the cultural liturgy
of modern medicine, attempting to seek the kingdom. They show us
what it may look like to turn away from the glow of "prosperity" that
energized the Bakkers and the status-hungry Air Jordan imitators. Both
examples reflect a tiny morsel of kingdom prosperity, which Scripture
indicates involves fellowship with others that simultaneously kneels to
the risen King who will return again.

"I've given up fighting," Jack said to me from his wheelchair. Perhaps
I looked surprised or shocked. He had been fighting for his life the last
few years, in and out of the hospital with his degenerative illness. After
several moments, while breathing through his oxygen-tube nosepiece, he
added, "But I haven't given up hope." Jack smiled, as if to reassure me.

Jack's body was battered by the extensive testing and the treatments
for his illness. He had a lightness about him as he explained what a
relief it was to him and his wife to enter hospice care, giving up on
"curative" treatments. He had always wanted to read more of the Old
Testament; now he was doing that, and he had questions. What did
I think about Micah? Jack had been writing to former students and
longtime friends, expressing gratitude and also curiosity about life and
faith. He welcomed children, showing my daughter his classic train set
with enthusiasm when she joined me in his apartment. He marveled at
the glories of nature and would spend hours birding through his apartment window. Several times he sent me bird photos he had snapped
with his camera. On my birthday I received an email with a photo
of a cedar waxwing outside the window—with its soft, golden belly,
rust-colored head, and brown, sharp-cornered wings. Jack no longer
worried about his next medical decision or about how his wife would

cope with another ER visit. He was able to read the Bible, converse, pray with friends, and delight in the gifts of glory outside his window. Jack was a gift to me while he was in hospice; he had an eye for beauty, while I just wanted to empty my inbox.

Ironically, after Jack gave up fighting his illness through the more extreme treatments, his health stabilized. He lived in hospice longer than doctors expected. He chose this path not in order to live longer but to use his last days of breath in fellowship with God, with others, with nature. He was flourishing. But he flourished by giving up fighting and by hoping in the Resurrected One. "For since we believe that Jesus died and rose again, even so, through Jesus, God will bring with him those who have died" (1 Thess. 4:14).

A second example. As Claude's pastor (a friend of mine) entered the hospital room, the bed was circled not with doctors and nurses but with family and close friends. Only a ventilator was keeping Claude alive now, given the advanced stage of his degenerative illness. Even with the ventilator, each breath took work. Medically speaking, recovery was not possible.

And so his loved ones gathered and formed a circle, and one by one they told Claude how much they loved him. There were smiles and laughter as well as tears at this goodbye. After others had spoken, the room was quiet for a moment, shifting the attention to the pastor. Just as my friend was beginning to speak about the bold Christian trust that we belong to God, ready to commend Claude to the Lord in prayer, Claude reached up and pulled the ventilator off his face. The circle of people gasped, as did Claude, who would not be able to breathe more than a few minutes without the ventilator. But with the ventilator off and his mouth free to speak through labored breaths, his lips delivered words he had learned as a child:

> What is your only comfort in life and in death?
> That I am not my own, but belong—body and soul, in life and in death—
> to my faithful Savior Jesus Christ.[28]

The words of the first question and answer of the Heidelberg Catechism trailed off as Claude's final breaths quietly punctuated his last earthly moments. My pastor-friend was in tears when he told the story, as was I by the time he finished.

Many Christians today try to combine the prosperity of status and health with the gospel of Jesus Christ. More than a few cannot imagine a terrible sickness followed by death to be anything other than a defeat. But Claude, in this final scene of his earthly life, gave his family a taste of a different kind of prosperity. He witnessed to the prosperity that cannot be measured by status, a bank statement, or even a life span. In an ordinary hospital room, with no video cameras or journalists, he embraced his weakness. He pulled off the mask—and those gathered both gasped for breath and yet breathed in the scent of *shalom*, wholeness, the peace of someone who belongs to Jesus Christ. In the boldness of his weakness, he commended his own body and soul to the King of the kingdom, the priest of the temple, the crucified and risen Savior, the One who embodies true flourishing in his very person.

### *Discussion Questions*

- This chapter reframes our understanding of prosperity. As you look at your life, what has been your own definition of prosperity?
- A recent study found that highly religious (predominantly Christian) cancer patients are more than three times as likely to opt for extreme treatment measures. What might this say about common Christian understandings of God's plans?
- Online comments in response to health updates often refer to God as the "Great Healer," which seems to assume that God's primary work is to perform miracles. What do you think of

this? What implications might Paul's theology of the cross have for this approach?

- Matthew 5:1–12 and 6:19–34 present a vision of kingdom-shaped prosperity for mortals. Read those passages. What implications do they have for the kind of prosperity that we should expect here and now?

- This chapter closes with the story of Claude, whose final words were from the Heidelberg Catechism, Question and Answer 1: "What is your only comfort in life and in death? That I am not my own but belong—body and soul, in life and in death—to my faithful Savior Jesus Christ." How are these words a comfort? How do these words contrast with widespread Christian understandings of a "prosperous" life today?

# Six

## The Fracturing of Our Stories, and Life after Death

My college's winter break had just finished, but winter had not. I squinted at the red taillights ahead, but it was hard to see beyond the blanket of soft, wet snow covering my windshield. Warm, dry air surged out of my heater. Squeaky wipers swung back and forth. Then a truck barreled past on my left. I pushed down the gas slightly. I didn't want to get run over because of my slow speed.

But then I was moving too quickly toward the red lights of vehicles in front of me. My foot pushed the brake pedal hard, and I could feel my front-wheel-drive Honda Civic twist and then spin in a circle as my locked wheels skated across the road. No traction on this snow and ice.

My entire life didn't flash in front of my eyes, but a single thought gripped my tightened body: *It should not end this way!* A few hours earlier, I had been talking to friends about my plans for the future, how that related to what I was studying in college, and when I would see my family next. But as I spun across the road, those stories were threatened. The logic of the quick "not end this way!" seemed to be: "My stories don't fit this ending. The stories of my education and friendships and family would become nonsense if I died this way."

In our day-to-day lives as students, as daughters and sons, as workers, as friends, we assume that our story's end will somehow make sense, that it will not be incoherent, like shards of broken glass scattered randomly across the terrain of our life. *It should not end this way.* To muster the courage to live, and love, and learn each day, we need more than senseless stories.

We want more than a broken ending. Imagine attending a baseball game at Dodger Stadium and hearing "The Star-Spangled Banner" sung by a soloist who stops with the words "o'er the land of the—." The song moves from what musicologists call the "home key" to heightened levels of tension and variation. But then, intuitively, the song returns to the home key. If this return were lacking, the fans would probably sing the resolution ("free and the home of the brave") themselves. Or else they would feel the irresolution so sharply that it would create painful tension in their bodies. We are deeply wired to desire an ending with resolution.[1]

Sometimes, though, the music stops before reaching home. When Harvard professor James Kugel was diagnosed with an aggressive form of cancer, he had the sense that "the background music had suddenly stopped." This background music, he says, was "the music of daily life that's constantly going, the music of infinite time and possibilities. Now suddenly it was gone, replaced by *nothing*, just silence."[2] This silence reminds us that we are small and dispensable. But silence, in the midst of a melody that promises to finish in harmony, is deeply dissonant. Not only does it change the song's ending; it affects the integrity of the song as a whole. To replace a musical resolution with silence threatens to make the whole song seem farcical, as if the hope and promise expressed in earlier parts of the song were a cruel trick.

For Christians, the unsettling reality of broken endings does not simply go away because of Christ's victory. We may hear the apostle Paul's words touted at Grandma's funeral: "Death *has been* swallowed up in victory." Amen. This is a central Christian confession. But this cosmic turnaround has not yet happened—not even for Grandma, who has already died and is with the Lord. Paul's verb tense in the preceding sentence is key: "*When* this perishable body puts on imperishability, and this mortal body puts on immortality, *then* the saying that is written *will be* fulfilled: 'Death has been swallowed up in victory'" (1 Cor. 15:54).[3] We have a steady promise from God that this will take place, but it hasn't happened yet. In the words of Saint Augustine, since "death is dead" in Christ, we can rejoice that "death will die in us also." But when will this happen? "At the end of the world, at the resurrection of the dead."[4] Death will not be dead in us until that final day, the day toward which both the dead and the living look: the day of resurrection, when Christ returns to "judge the living and the dead"[5] and bring about the consummation of his kingdom. Death will not be dead until the glory of the Lord in the temple is spread across the whole of creation. And that hasn't happened yet, not even for Grandma.

Thus, whether the funeral we're attending is for an elderly grandparent whose time of dying was expected, or for a young person for whom the music stopped in a moment of irresolution, Christian hope does not enable us to bypass the unsettling questions presented to us by our broken endings. The moments of each day are meaningful to us because they are connected by a story. But since death is not yet dead, this tapestry of meaning can be torn when death cuts into our story. Dying, as a final earthly chapter, is something that happens *to us*; it's not a chapter we write ourselves. And the loved ones left behind are often left with open questions and raw wounds—challenged to make sense of their ongoing life in new ways.

The purpose of this chapter is to explore how we make sense of our life stories as dying creatures and how this relates to our longing for connection with God and others. Our life stories have been ruptured by death, and we want to do something about it.[6] The challenge we face is to discern true Christian hope amid the myriad stories we tell ourselves about death and about life beyond the grave.

## Fumbling to Mend Ruptured Narratives

As humans, whether we speak English or Mandarin, Arabic or sign language, we are constantly narrating our lives to one another and to ourselves. But what happens when death comes as a rupture to those stories? In my case, what would've happened if my Honda Civic had crashed, ending my mortal life? Or what will happen if my next doctor's appointment shows that my cancer has come back with full force, and I'm struck down within a matter of months?

At that point, I would cease to be the narrator of my life and history. And my family and friends would be driven to ask the questions exposed by my narrative rupture. Whether expressed or not, a number of questions are present in grief. How do we go forward without this friend? How do I make sense of life without my dad? Where was God the King in Mom's car crash? Why couldn't my sister be granted one more remission?

When a young child dies, the parents may never make narrative sense of the child's abrupt end. And yet, for the living, the storytelling always continues. It's true for those who are religious and for those who are not: we narrate our hopes about a day to come in the afterlife. Indeed, about a third of those who do *not* believe in God still believe in life after death.[7] Such belief in the afterlife appears to be on the rise. A University of Chicago study indicates that, while belief in God and affiliation with a particular religion have been in decline in the United States in recent decades, a growing number believe in "life after death"—80 percent in 2016. "It was interesting that fewer people participated in religion or prayed but more believed in an afterlife," a researcher at San Diego State University noted. Why would more believe in an afterlife? Researchers can only speculate, but one suggested that "it might be part of a growing entitlement mentality—thinking you can get something for nothing."[8] Whatever the reasons for this growing belief, stories about the afterlife continue to have a prominent place in Western culture, even in contexts where religious hopes are proscribed from polite conversations.

I observed an example of this, on a broad cultural level, when George H. W. Bush died in the course of my writing this chapter. The former president held numerous high posts of office and certainly had wide spheres of global influence during his career. But many news articles at the time of his death focused on a tender wound that he and his wife, Barbara, felt: the loss of their daughter, Robin, more than half a century earlier. Robin appeared to be a healthy younger sister to her older brother, George W., for her first three years. While she would "fight and play" like other children, her father noticed "a certain softness" and peacefulness about her personality.[9]

In her third year, Robin became lethargic and sluggish. A blood test showed that she had leukemia. Despite aggressive medical treatment, Robin died six months after her diagnosis, before reaching her fourth birthday.

Decades later, George H. W. Bush, then vice president, visited a children's hospital. A small boy who had leukemia came forward to greet him, and Bush began to cry. Later that day, Bush detailed the account in his diary. "My eyes flooded with tears. And behind me was a bank of television cameras. And I thought, 'I can't turn around. I can't dissolve because of personal tragedy in the face of the nurses who give of themselves every day.' So I stood there looking at this little guy, tears running down my cheek, hoping he wouldn't see. But if he did, hoping he'd feel that I loved him."[10]

After decades in the world spotlight, Barbara and George H. W. Bush circled back to this ruptured narrative in their final years. Nothing had mended the wound of losing Robin. Nothing could make sense of the loss, it seemed, except for hope in an additional chapter of the story—one after death. Barbara Bush once said that, upon George H. W.'s death, Robin "is who he'll see first." "In our grief," George W. Bush said in his father's eulogy, "let us smile knowing that Dad is hugging Robin and holding mom's hand again."[11]

In a rare bipartisan moment, many who were sharply critical of Bush's career paused before the story of Robin, giving it a place of honor. A widely circulated political cartoon showed the elderly Barbara Bush holding the hand of a young girl with blond curls, bouncing on a cloud in the sky. "We waited for you," Barbara says as the elderly George H. W. takes the girl's other hand.

## Family Reunions after Death: More Than Wishful Thinking?

What are we to make of this family reunion story, which played such a prominent role in how the Bush family understood their own living and dying? George H. W. and Barbara Bush felt an acute sense of loss for their daughter. And after the sudden loss of Barbara's mother three years earlier, losing a young child made death's sting all the sharper. So a skeptic might say that the Bush family engaged in "wishful thinking": an imagined family reunion after death.

Is the Bushes' hope in an afterlife simply wishful thinking? Is the prominence of such belief today—even with religious adherence in decline—the product of a culture that assumes God *owes* us an afterlife to patch up our broken stories?

The attempt to mend our stories with the idea of a family reunion after death has been a prominent part of many Christian funerals I have attended. Family members speak of their assurance that the departed is now reunited with other family members who have died, participating in the activities they once enjoyed—playing baseball, hunting deer, eating ice cream. A song I heard at one funeral calls this a "hello after goodbye," where there will be "a blessed reunion, promised in time." The song confidently proclaims that more time will be spent with loved ones after death than before: "We will be with them far longer than we were without." A friend of mine in his eighties was grieving his wife, and he spoke again and again about how this song was "just right." His wife had gradually slipped away because of dementia, and now she was gone. Hunching forward in his wheelchair after her funeral, his hands grasping mine tightly, he spoke of a time when, in the words of the song, they would "laugh and talk like before."

Are such hopes simply a reflection of wishful thinking or of an entitlement mentality? Some observers who are skeptical of the supernatural will quickly say so. Ironically, many Christian theologians share similar skepticism about such hopes. They do not deny the supernatural, but they do question the grounds for such common hopes and speculations.

I think these theological concerns are legitimate, because the "family reunion" narrative sharply contrasts with biblical hope for life after death. Scripture speaks about the age to come as a *theophany*, a coming and appearance of God, and the primary context is corporate and cosmic. Biblical hope centers on the presence and dwelling of God in a renewed creation. As we will explore in some detail in the next chapter, this coming of God in a temple to dwell with creation culminates in none other than Jesus Christ in the New Testament. In the cosmic theophany on the final day, Christ will return bodily to dwell with, rule, and be worshiped by people from all tribes and nations. In an astonishing fulfillment of God's purpose in creation and the Lord's promise to Israel through Moses that "I will take you as my people, and I will be your God" (Exod. 6:7), God's people will sing in harmony to the Lamb of God, Jesus. In the words of Revelation,

> See, the home of God is among mortals.
> He will dwell with them;
> they will be his peoples,
> and God himself will be with them. (21:3)

The climax of God's covenant promise is a great, cosmic encounter with the Lord himself, and a reconciled communion with others flowing from that. The center of Paul's hope is the cosmic "coming of the Lord" to his creation on the final "day of the Lord" (1 Thess. 4:15; 5:2).[12] Likewise, in Revelation, when the Lord comes to dwell among his people in the new Jerusalem, "mourning and crying and pain will be no more"

(Rev. 21:4). But this is not in order to fulfill our fondest human wishes; rather, it's because the living God has come to make his "home" among "mortals," fully dwelling with the creation as in a temple (Rev. 21:3).

While individuals and family members are not at the center of this great drama, they are implicated nevertheless. As Paul hopes for the coming of the Lord, he also assures the Thessalonians that they need not be overwhelmed with grief as those who have no hope, because their brothers and sisters in Christ who have died will rise again on the final day (1 Thess. 4:13–16). This is an important word of encouragement. Yet it hinges on the larger, cosmic hope in Christ's return on "the day of the Lord" (5:2).

Ultimately, it is significant that the Bible contains poetry and song praising Jesus Christ, the covenant Lord, who will come dwell with his spouse, his people. But it contains no songs climaxing in the reunion of separated family members or friends. Such reunions are not at the *center* of Christian hope.

Thus, this coming of God in Christ to renew the creation is the breathtaking Grand Canyon of Christian hope—so wide and deep and expansive that we are left in wonder. It's hard to take it in. And our life stories, which can seem so big when we're driving on a winter road or when a loved one dies, are tiny, minuscule, like specks of dust in the midst of staggeringly deep valleys, high cliffs, and wide-open spaces. As we face our own deaths, and those of loved ones, we are right to ask with the psalmist, "What are human beings that you are mindful of them, / mortals that you care for them?" (Ps. 8:4).

And yet, while as a Christian I seek to keep my eyes on the center—the renewal of the cosmos at Christ's return—perhaps I can trust that the great symphony of redemption includes some small riffs on the grand themes for specks of dust like me, like the Bush family, and like my friend who lost his wife. Indeed, while the New Testament doesn't speak of family reunions, it does include deeply personal language about how those who die in Christ are consciously present with him, even before the grand movement of the bodily resurrection of the dead at the culmination of the kingdom.

While the apostle Paul writes about the world-shaking day of Christ's return and the resurrection, he also writes from prison to the Christians in Philippi that "living is Christ and dying is gain." How could this be? Because his union with Christ defines his present living so deeply, he is confident that this union will continue—and even deepen—immediately after death, before the final resurrection. Indeed, "to depart and be with Christ" would be a transition to a "far better" state; yet to be alive in the body is to be preferred for now because he can offer "fruitful labor" to Christ's church (Phil. 1:21–23). Elsewhere, in 2 Corinthians 5, Paul says that the grand, symphonic movement of the resurrection is our central hope, and yet life immediately after death—what theologians call the intermediate state (before the resurrection)—will still be one in fellowship with Christ. For even while we are "away from the body" after we die and before we are resurrected, we will be "at home with the Lord" (2 Cor. 5:8).[13]

The New Testament provides very few details about this intermediate state, except that it is in union with Christ. It does not provide a theory for exactly how it occurs after death, or even a precise anthropology of how body relates to soul. The final consummation following the return of Christ is depicted with image after image: a wedding banquet, a heavenly city come to earth, the temple, and many more. But in comparison, the New Testament passages about the intermediate state seem to give a mysteriously two-dimensional, black-and-white vision rather than the full-color, three-dimensional vision of the final consummation.

Ultimately, the hope for life immediately after death is an appendage to the heart of cosmic hope rooted in Christ's renewal of creation. Still, while usually in the peripheral vision in the New Testament, this hope is nevertheless present and proclaimed. The Gospels, the book of Revelation, the book of Hebrews, and the letters of Peter join Paul in both implying and teaching that personal identity will continue on through Christ, while the body decays. And all of this happens before the next great act of God's drama—the resurrection. The intermediate state is not the central movement. But when Jesus says to the thief on the cross that he will be present "this day" in paradise, when the souls of the martyrs in Revelation await the coming judgment, and when Paul proclaims that neither life nor death will separate us from the love of God in Christ, we have grounds for such hope (Luke 23:43; Rev. 6:9–11; Rom. 8:38–39).

And yet, in many Christian funerals and in the popular Western imagination at large, this secondary hope is frequently emptied of its central focus on union with Christ and awaiting cosmic restoration. In most funerals that speak of heaven, it's implied that the dead ascend to heaven, and that's the end of the story. The conflict is resolved, and the dead continue on in more or less the same way that they had lived on earth, only without pain, as they await the coming of their relatives. Functionally, this is a one-stage eschatology: a child like Robin dies and is whisked away to heaven—end of story.

The historic Christian tradition, in contrast, has a two-stage hope about the end. In this version of the story, Robin is dead and in fellowship with Christ; she awaits the great drama to come—the day in which the dead will rise in new bodies, when Christ will "come again to judge the living and the dead" (Apostles' Creed), when every knee in heaven and on earth will bow to Jesus Christ. This drama culminates in the renewal of all creation, when heaven and earth are reunited and the Lord dwells with his creatures as in a temple.

But then, what are we to make of our tender hopes to be reunited with loved ones after death? To fully explore this question requires probing the nature of death itself—a reality for mortals that underlies our aching desire for mended stories and reunited fellowship after death.

## Approaching the Earthly End: Knowledge and Helplessness

Flowing water, with its bubbling sound and fresh scent, can calm my nerves. When I sit by a forest stream, I am refreshed and at peace. But when I heard the splash of water in my office a few months ago, it was different. Contrary to habit, I had forgotten to put the lid on my water bottle. When I clumsily hit the bottle with my forearm, water splashed right onto my laptop keyboard. At first I froze, still caught in the thought I had been typing on my computer. Then I charged into action, grabbing a paper towel and frantically rubbing the keyboard, trying to soak up the moisture. Unfortunately, as my IT colleague let me know after attempting to dry out the computer over the next several days, my efforts to contain the spill had been to no avail.

The image of water spilling and escaping our grasp is used in the Bible to portray death itself. In the course of a larger speech, a "wise woman" from a village near Bethlehem confronts King David with these words: "We must all die; we are like water spilled on the ground, which cannot be gathered up" (2 Sam. 14:14). We, like water, are spilled onto dry ground—or laptop keyboards. Helpless to stop the process, we slip through the cracks and soak into the ground. Attempts to deliver ourselves (or others) from this end are in vain.

Of course, many of my fellow Christians would be quick to say that biblical images like these do not give Scripture's final word about death. I agree. But we misunderstand victory in Christ when we downplay the sense in which death is a precipice, a cliff with a steep drop-off to a destination we cannot see.

We can try to analyze death scientifically, in a way that may appear to vanquish the mystery. Rather than a precipice, maybe death is just the next step in a biological process that can be fully understood. The heart stops beating. Air is no longer inhaled. Brain activity ceases. In some sense, the transition from a living body to a corpse can appear to be a transparent process. Occasionally there are ambiguities, such as in near-death experiences (discussed below). But in most cases, can't science explain this mystery of moving from life into death?

Scientists can give certain explanations about the process, but the experience of approaching death as a mortal creature can never be fully explained by scientific analysis. It's like someone describing the various chemical properties of honey, including its sugars, its viscosity, and so forth, thinking they understand honey; but if they haven't tasted the sweetness and stickiness of honey for themselves, their knowledge of honey will fall haltingly short.

As creatures who have not yet tasted death, our attempts to speak about moving beyond this precipice are always partial. In the words of Sigmund Freud, "We cannot, indeed, imagine our own death; whenever we try to do so we find that we survive ourselves as spectators."[14] We have not tasted the honey—or bitter herbs—with our own tongues.

As a result, death always eludes our full knowledge as living mortals. We cannot master it or control it. There may be life after biological death. I not only wish for that; I believe and hope that will be the case. And yet we cannot put such hopes to the test in the laboratory. As Paul says, "For now we see in a mirror, dimly, but then we will see face to face" (1 Cor. 13:12). As mortals awaiting redemption, we see now by faith in Christ, by the Spirit—sight that points beyond itself, looking forward. But we see with the help of a mirror—our sight is indirect, accommodated to our weakness, partial. The Greek term translated "dimly" in Paul's statement shares a root with the English word "enigma." We are left with a puzzle, a kind of riddle. We see neither God nor our future in a "face to face" fashion.

Along with adherents of many other religions, Christians believe that biological death will not be the final chapter of our stories. And yet, for Christians at least, this belief takes the form of hope in God's promise, not journalistic knowledge about the future. We trust God's promise, even when the spilling of life into the ground seems to contradict it, because "faith is the assurance of things hoped for, the conviction of things not seen" (Heb. 11:1). These "things not seen" are events that have not yet happened, as theologian Anthony Thiselton points out.[15] Writing after nearly dying himself, Thiselton notes that "when facing imminent death, we may seem to reach the edge of an unknown world, and, in understandable panic, may even contemplate an unwelcome encounter with an unknown God." Yet through hope in God's promise, which we have heard and experienced through Word and sacrament, we can dare to hope for what we have not seen.[16] Facing death, none of us can see or verify that biological death is *not* our final chapter; but, like the children of Israel in the desert, longing for the land of milk and honey, we are called to trust in the Lord and his promise.

While Christians rightly look to the New Testament witness to Christ's decisive victory over death, sometimes we skip over the Old Testament witness about death. Most Old Testament books do not present a clear expectation of life after death, though there are strong hints and intimations. Frequently, the psalmists lament the way in which dying is an entry into a silenced, cut-off state: "The dead do not praise the LORD, / nor do any that go down into silence" (Ps. 115:17). The Preacher in Ecclesiastes explains that "in the realm of the dead, where you are going, there is neither working nor planning nor knowledge nor wisdom" (9:10 NIV). As theologian Karl Barth starkly noted while reflecting on these Old Testament passages, "The dead exist in a state of utter weakness and helplessness." For the living, a dead person "exists only as one who has been."[17]

When Old Testament writers do express hope for life beyond biological death, it's not because our human stories are so grand that they must find a proper ending. Rather, the hope is centered in God instead of humans. Old Testament writers approach life after death, as Carol Zaleski has argued, "never daring to assert that the human being possesses it by rights, and yet daring to hope that God would bestow a share in eternal life upon those who belong to him."[18] The dead are silenced and cut off, utterly helpless; even so, there remains hope for the Old Testament authors that God, the only source of life, will grant the dead some of his life.

The enigma of death has always evoked wonder. Archeologists have found evidence that humans have memorialized their dead for thousands of years in varied yet carefully wrought burial rituals. While visiting the Cairo Museum in Egypt, I found myself drawn to the mummy of the great pharaoh Ramesses II. After a brief viewing, I sensed I should leave the room to see other treasures in the museum. But I kept coming back to the mummy. Here was the mighty pharaoh who in popular legend was the king who kept the Israelites in captivity, confronted the prophet Moses, and endured the ten plagues. As king, he did not live as most mortals: he had more than two hundred wives and concubines; he was a war hero and the commander of thousands of soldiers, masons, and other workers. Yet as we can tell from his body, he also had "dental problems, severe arthritis, and hardening of the arteries."[19] I could still recognize his facial features: his skin was preserved, covering his nose and ears; his eyes were closed; and long, golden, stringy hair covered the back side of his scalp.

Why did wealthy and powerful Egyptians such as Ramesses draw upon the most sophisticated science of the time to try to *control* what would happen after their death? Certainly, part of the reason relates to beliefs about the afterlife. But I wonder whether the energy expended to preserve the king was so great, in part, because of the nature of death itself: it's an abrupt end; a corpse is so helpless; death seems so final; it seems so out of our control. Whether for ancient Egyptian pharaohs or for today's transhumanists, like Aubrey de Grey, who seek to "solve" the problem of aging, the finality and mystery of death taunt us so deeply that they can actually energize our efforts to bring it under human mastery.

Still, memorializing and burying the body does not, in most times and places, involve placing a mummy into a gold-plated Egyptian coffin. Memorializing itself reflects the deep human instinct to set the dead into a larger myth or story. After a zebra fish from my son's aquarium died, Nathaniel cried out in grief but then led me to the backyard. I dug a small hole in the dirt with a stick in one hand, as I held a fishnet containing the tiny corpse in the other. "He will lie in the ground for two days," Nathaniel said solemnly. "But then he will go to Nathaniel-world!" "Nathaniel-world" is an imaginary place where Nathaniel's favorite things always seem bigger and better than in the "real" world. Nathaniel cupped his hand to receive the tiny body, placed it in the hole, and then spontaneously improvised words to a song in memory of his fish. The song sounded a bit sad at first, but the tempo picked up as he went along. Then Nathaniel asked me to pray to commit the fish to God. As we walked back in the house after the prayer, he exclaimed, "We will see him again in Nathaniel-world!"

The zebra fish did something that Nathaniel himself has never done: it died. Not only did Nathaniel honor the little creature's body and memorialize its life, but he also told a story with a particular shape: one of *passage*. In the passage story, the dead "pass away," as through a tunnel, into a realm that we mortals have not yet experienced. Through stories of passage, Nathaniel, the ancient Egyptians, and scores of other cultures tell us something profound about death itself: it's a moving over from one side to another, and as such, it's something we don't understand until we've tasted it. Scripture indicates something similar when it speaks of the dead "going down" to Sheol (Job 21:13).

As noted in chapter 1, at times it is the living who cry out from Sheol in the Old Testament, from a place of alienation from God's presence. As Jonah cries from the fish,

> I called to the Lord out of my distress,
>     and he answered me;
> out of the belly of Sheol I cried,
>     and you heard my voice. (Jon. 2:2)

But in other instances in the Old Testament, such as in Job, Sheol is the place where the living go *after* they have died. In this image, the dying travel to where none of us have gone. Indeed, apart from the Old Testament, and even if there were no afterlife, the passage story would still reflect this truth: only living creatures who then *die* truly know what death is; only they have tasted death.

All of this may sound like a twofold counsel of despair: the dead, Old Testament writers testify, are utterly helpless; and in the passage story, the face-to-face knowledge of what death truly is comes too late—after one passes from this earthly life.

But this knowledge about the reality of death—that it's a passage into helplessness—is actually a word of mercy for mortals like us. Helplessness seems frightening when we imagine ourselves alone in the universe. We could feel like chips of wood taken where we don't want to go by a whitewater stream. But what if the stream, the moving force, is the love and grace of God? Then the very fact of our helplessness, as those who are carried by the flowing stream, can be a comfort. The helpless dead don't have to earn love. The helpless dead don't make a wrong turn of the steering wheel on a snowy evening, devastating their lives and those of others. The helpless dead rest, as we customarily wish, "in peace." Such a thought is reassuring when this rest is in the gracious hands of the Almighty.

Although the Old and the New Testaments frequently use the metaphor of sleep when speaking of death, in light of the event of Christ's death and resurrection, this "sleep" is not unconsciousness. Rather, it is rest in the conscious presence of the Lord, a taste of Christ's temple presence that will come to fullness in the great cosmic event of judgment and resurrection, when all of creation will be God's temple, his place of dwelling.[20] But it is rest all the same. As the Spirit indicates to John in Revelation, because of Christ, "blessed are the dead who from now on die in the Lord," for "they will rest from their labors" (Rev. 14:13).

In addition, the underlying assumption of passage stories—that only those who have died *truly understand* what death is—has special significance for the living who look to Christ in life and death. None of us have tasted the sweetness or bitterness of death. Yet that's precisely what Christ, the priest of the temple who willingly offered himself as a sacrifice, did for the sake of the world. In the words of Hebrews, Christ shared in our flesh and blood, tasting death himself "so that by the grace of God he might taste death for everyone" (Heb. 2:9). We have not tasted death. But we serve the crucified and risen Lord, who met John at Patmos with these astonishing words: "I was dead, and see, I am alive forever and ever; and I have the keys of Death and of Hades" (Rev. 1:18). He tasted death. He was dead—and thus, as the Living One, when he holds the keys of Death and Hades (the translation of "Sheol" in Greek), it makes a difference for mortals like us. As a sojourner, he has passed away, passed through death.

Thus, in union with Christ, we encounter what we don't know in a face-to-face way. Indeed, baptism itself involves a foretaste of death through union with the One who died and rose again. As Paul says in Romans 6, "All of us who have been baptized into Christ Jesus were baptized into his death" and thus can trust that we will "be united with him in a resurrection like his" (6:3, 5). The baptized cannot claim to have tasted death, but they do belong to the One who has tasted death. Through God's promise made visible to us in the splashing of the water on the body, we're united to the One who pioneered a passage through it. In baptism, recognition of our helplessness can be part of the gift of impotently floating on the roaring river of God's potent grace. In the restful abandonment of the words of the African American spiritual "Give Me Jesus,"

> Oh when I come to die
> Oh when I come to die
> Oh when I come to die
> Give me Jesus
> Give me Jesus
> You may have the world
> Give me Jesus.[21]

## Near-Death Experiences and the Stories That Fascinate Us

Of course, it's possible that death isn't that mysterious after all. In our day, the testimony of personal experience bears heavy weight. More than a few have claimed to see their own incapacitated body, to have experienced a movement toward a great light and then an encounter with Jesus or other religious figures. I recall chatting with my friend Deanna in a food court at the San Antonio airport. Deanna, like me, is a late-stage cancer patient and a theologian. Over our drinks and sandwiches, we were talking about death. A middle-aged man sitting a couple of tables away from us looked up and came over after a few minutes. "You are talking about death, right? I've done that before," he offered in a matter-of-fact way. "When *I* died," he began, and my mind just started to spin as he described his separation from his body, going toward a light, and coming back after about fifteen minutes. His comment ushered in a moment of silence while Deanna and I tried to figure out what to say.

Millions of people have given similar testimonies. In the modern context, these kinds of experiences were popularized by Raymond Moody, who coined the term "near-death experiences" (NDE) in his 1975 book *Life after Life*. Moody identified a common set of patterns that his patients described in their NDE stories. After hearing doctors or spectators pronounce them to be dead, these people are flooded with "feelings of peace and quiet."[22] Often they begin to hear beautiful music and then perceive a tunnel or a funnel that pulls them from the darkness through space, out of the body, toward a great light.[23] There they often meet others, becoming "aware of the presence of other spiritual beings in their vicinity."[24] Frequently, a "being of light" with "unearthly brilliance" communicates with them.[25] At this point in the encounter, "it is often obvious that the being can see the individual's whole life displayed" as people undergo a "rapid" and "vivid" review of their own life experiences.[26] Then, though often people would rather stay in the presence of this being of light, they come back, experiencing a "return to physical life."[27]

Moody's book became a blockbuster, selling over thirteen million copies. Yet it was relatively modest in intent. Moody tells the story of how he encountered a few people who had had vivid experiences during short periods of time when they were clinically dead.[28] Later, as a philosophy professor, he engaged students in discussions of the immortality of the soul and began to ask them about NDEs. "To my amazement, I found that in almost every class of thirty or so students, at least one student would come to me afterwards and relate a personal near-death experience."[29] A polymath, Moody went back to school and received a medical degree. He recalls nervously speaking to a medical society in Georgia about NDEs. "As I spoke, I began to notice something I would never have expected. One by one, jolts of recognition appeared in the eyes of the doctors."[30] They too had patients who had described such vivid near-death experiences to them.

So Moody wrote his book to "draw attention to a phenomenon which is at once very widespread and very well-hidden," as numerous people who had these experiences were embarrassed to share them with others. "I am not trying to prove that there is life after death. Nor do I think that a 'proof' of this is presently possible."[31] But he wanted to expose these NDE stories to a wide audience so that they could be openly discussed and explored. Moody was clearly successful; his work helped to generate widespread interest in near-death experiences among adherents of many religions and of no religion at all.

In the opening decades of the twenty-first century, NDE accounts have become the focus of scores of books, documentaries, and other forms of media. Particularly striking is the overwhelming interest in testimonies that not only fit the basic pattern Moody gives but also entail an encounter with Jesus. In a series of colloquies I facilitated with pastors from 2016 to 2018, we found that these stories—distributed through bestselling books, radio programs, and movies—have shaped their congregations' imaginations about life after death deeply, quite possibly more than any other source. Within the first five years of its publication in 2010, the book *Heaven Is for Real* sold over twelve million copies and became a motion picture that brought in over $100 million.[32] Don Piper's *90 Minutes in Heaven* has sold over four million copies, and Dr. Mary Neal's *To Heaven and Back* also topped the *New York Times* bestseller list.

In many Christian congregations, NDE stories come not only from famous books and movies but also from the ground up, from within the congregation itself. One pastor shared with me how an elder at his church experienced an NDE and quietly came to him, unsure what to make of it.

These experiences are powerful and vivid, and empirical studies indicate that the NDE itself becomes formative for the person who has undergone it. In addition, in the popular imagination these stories counter a cold materialism in parts of the culture that consider science to be the final authority in all matters. For many both within the church and outside of it, these stories point to a softening of the so-called war between science and religion, with an empirical, experiential entryway to the transcendent.[33]

Do such stories, with their vivid accounts of passage, really tell us what it is like to taste death, thereby removing the mystery of what will come after death? And do they tell us anything about the afterlife? Many people approach these questions assuming all-or-nothing answers. Either NDEs are complete fantasy, or they are direct, eyewitness accounts of what all of us will experience after death. In the all-or-nothing paradigm, skeptics often charge that the content of a religious person's NDE reflects his or her own upbringing rather than a coherent vision of the afterlife that would apply to everyone. As Maud Newton wrote in the *New York Times* about the *Heaven Is for Real* publishing phenomenon,

> The visions children have in near-death situations often have a great deal to do with what they already believe. Culture to culture, these experiences involve bright light, celestial figures and a sense of watching your own body from above and sometimes all three. According to Kevin Nelson, a neuroscientist and the author of "The Spiritual Doorway in the Brain," adults often have a sense of looking back over a life; young children, lacking that perspective, tend to report "castles and rainbows, often populated with pets, wizards, guardian angels, and like adults, they see relatives and religious figures, too."[34]

The story of the young boy Colton Burpo in *Heaven Is for Real* fits this pattern. The son of a pastor in a small Nebraska town, he speaks about meeting Jesus, who had a "rainbow horse." "I got to pet him," Colton said. "There's lots of colors."[35] This is consistent with Newton's account in that Colton's experience reflects his religious background and childhood imagination. It's not surprising, then, when Muslims report meeting a mufti (an expert in Islamic law), while Hindus report encounters with various Hindu gods.[36] The bestselling author Eben Alexander claims that his NDE confirms the doctrine of reincarnation.[37] If we look to NDEs as sources for divine revelation or religious knowledge, we are faced with claims as different as those of the beliefs of the patients themselves. To combine them into a synthetic portrait of the afterlife would leave us drowning in incoherence.

Carol Zaleski, professor of world religions at Smith College, has written two insightful books that have helped to shape my reflection on NDEs.[38] She shows that NDEs are far from new phenomena; they flourished in various forms in earlier eras. In particular, medieval Christians frequently reported visionary experiences connected to death that have much in common with contemporary NDEs. In that context, however, stories of visions were accompanied by imperatives not to accept the visions in a "literal" fashion.[39] In the words of Pope Gregory I in the sixth century, these visions often contain "illusion" and can sometimes "arise from a full stomach or from an empty one."[40] Positively, they could be gifts for personal edification, but they must be received as symbolic encounters. The content of the vision is accommodated to the receiver; it is not a direct encounter with heavenly realities. The visions are not a source of Christian doctrine.[41] These vivid visions, we might say, are still seeing "in a mirror, dimly," in Paul's words, rather than a "face to face" encounter with the resurrected Lord (1 Cor. 13:12).

For some of my readers, even this medieval appropriation of visionary encounters may be too sanguine. And I think their strong caution is warranted. New Testament scholar Scot McKnight, author of *The Heaven Promise*, sums up his response to near-death experiences in a 2016 interview:

I confess I'm skeptical about a lot of things people say about heaven [based on NDEs]. I'm skeptical because near-death experiences are (1) a common human experience that (2) have been occurring since the beginning of recorded civilization and (3) those experiences, while there are some common themes, are shaped deeply and sometimes entirely by that person's religion, culture, philosophy or religion embedded in the "experiencer's" brain, and (4) the near-death experience stories vary wildly from one generation and culture to another.

Near-death experiences are unreliable guides to what life is like beyond the grave. This is not least because they are "pre" or "near" death experiences not "post" death experiences.[42]

I share McKnight's sense that NDEs give us knowledge of the ones experiencing them more than they give us direct knowledge of life beyond the grave. Christians in particular should pause before allowing these stories to shape their views of the life to come. Christians hope for the great coming together of heaven and earth, the cosmic temple fellowship, as all knees bow to the Lamb of God. Still, it doesn't follow that we should simply dismiss NDEs as no more than self-serving illusions, as we will explore below.

## Myths and the Question of Truth

The question is ultimately inescapable: Are the narratives we tell ourselves in light of the ruptures of death true or false? Are they wishful thinking and illusion, or do they point to reality? We know that the ruptures in our lives cannot be fully mended. But in the face of fractured stories, we have a deep inclination to mend them through narratives of life after death. These narratives are what I will call "myths"—not in the sense of a childish fable or something untrue, but in the sense of stories that orient our living each day.

The hopes embedded in these myths may show themselves to be real or illusory, but such myths function as life stories either way. Was there a week that went by that George H. W. or Barbara Bush did not think of Robin and long for reunion? I doubt it. Most parents who have lost a young child live each day with the presence of that absence, and many long for reunion, even postmortem reunion. Whether religious or not, we are relational creatures, and family connections mark our identity in deep ways. It should not surprise us that one of the most common themes that hospital chaplains hear from the dying is a longing to meet with departed loved ones. This same longing becomes the "myth" that the living lean into as they cope with the death of the departed, at the funeral service and beyond.

But what will really happen? Which myths that we live by in relation to death disclose reality as opposed to illusion? And how can we really know the difference?

On the one hand, I don't think that we can "know" in the sense of having proof. We cannot perform controlled experiments to discover whether there is life after the grave or which stories about life after the grave are true. Yet every day, each of us properly believes all sorts of things about the world that cannot be "proved" empirically. As philosopher Alvin Plantinga has shown, the vast majority of our beliefs cannot be proved, yet they are proper and warranted for us to hold. Even true beliefs involve a certain amount of guessing, one might say. I could be in a dream at this very moment rather than typing on my computer. But because my body seems to be functioning properly, and I haven't been sleepwalking recently, I have a pretty good guess that I'm here at the computer. I could be wrong. But as a living creature, I make such (warranted) judgments without proof all the time.[43]

Given that we cannot prove a particular view of the afterlife, how are we to sort through the different sources that claim to give us knowledge about it?

As a Christian, I believe that, rather than stories about family reunions or NDEs, the most reliable source for hope in an afterlife is found in the Old and New Testaments. This claim is not arbitrary. It's rooted in a particular historical event: two thousand years ago, the God of Israel became incarnate in the person of Jesus Christ. Christ received the Old Testament as God's Word, and the apostolic testimony of the New Testament testifies to one who lived, tasted death, rose again, and still lives as the exalted Lord. In Revelation, Christ proclaims, "I am the Alpha and the Omega, the first and the last, the beginning and the end" (22:13). If this testimony is true, then Christ himself, who speaks through Scripture, cannot be overruled by later claims of testimony to life after death. Instead, again and again in Scripture, we are given a story, a myth, that does not focus on family reunions but rather looks to the day of the Lord, when God will appear in the return of Jesus Christ. The dead will rise bodily; the world will be shaken, judged, and remade; and God's reign will be present in its fullness. This is the great and cosmic story—the story at the center of Christian hope, repeated weekly by Christians around the world in the Apostles' Creed—that the dead will be resurrected, the risen Christ "will come again to judge the living and the dead," and those resurrected in Christ will enjoy "life everlasting."

In light of the biblical witness, then, should other stories—of family reunions, or the vivid encounters of NDEs—be dismissed as complete illusions or, even worse, as idolatrous falsehood? Here I think we should tread cautiously. On the one hand, Scripture indicates that humans are subject to illusion and idolatry in many forms. Yet, on the other hand, humans are created in the image of the living God, designed for a relationship with God. The apostle Paul goes so far as to say that "ever since the creation of the world [God's] eternal power and divine nature, invisible though they are, have been understood and seen through the things he has made" (Rom. 1:20). Some theologians speak of this as a "seed of religion" that is universally planted by God in the human heart. Indeed, the creation itself is a theater of God's grand glory.[44] It may be that humans reflect this glory, however imperfectly, even when they don't intend to. Perhaps the family reunion and NDE stories that we tell in the face of death imperfectly testify to our place as creatures made for communion with one another and with the transcendent God.

An illuminating perspective on what these stories say about us comes from the terror management theory (TMT) school of social psychology, discussed in chapter 3. Recent TMT studies indicate that the stories we tell ourselves as humans presuppose that our lives partake in a larger mythic purpose. We are wired, whether through processes of natural selection, through God's design, or both, to tell stories about ourselves that require the transcendent. In fact, even the vast majority of atheists are, in practice, unable to do otherwise. The details of these recent studies are synthesized by Clay Routledge in his 2018 book, *Supernatural: Death, Meaning, and the Power of the Invisible World.*

In numerous studies on how people make sense of their lives in light of their mortality, Routledge found that the vast majority of subjects spoke in terms that require a "teleological meaning." "Teleological thinking is when people perceive phenomena in terms of purpose."[45] At the larger level of their self-understanding, this becomes "supernatural" thinking, because it violates a strictly scientific approach to the universe, in which neither God, nor nature, nor the world has a will or design that is at work in our lives. "Even in the absence of religious faith or belief in a deity, people are attracted to teleological meaning. They treat the universe as if it has intentions or a plan. They treat nature as if it has a will or desires."[46]

Indeed, even atheists with PhDs in the hard sciences had a difficult time avoiding teleological ways of thinking. In one study, more than three-quarters of atheists gave teleological explanations about their lives, even as they struggled not to speak that way. For example, one "made it clear that he does not believe in fate, but at the same time when he lost his job he couldn't help but have the feeling that it was meant to be."[47] Moreover, those who disavowed God's existence seemed to have an ache for transcendent thinking that they would satisfy in other ways. For example, "atheists are more likely than theists" to believe that "intelligent alien life is monitoring and influencing human behavior."[48]

In sum, the vast majority of humans, including atheists, narrate their lives in ways that assume a transcendent design or Designer. Even after decades of acculturation into naturalistic ways, what atheists "preach" (that there is no God or transcendent design) rarely fits with what they practice. In the words of Routledge, "perhaps there are those with the preparation and discipline to live a life nearly free of supernatural inclinations, but I doubt there are many. And, based on the research, many of the people who think that supernatural ideas and beliefs do not affect their attitudes and behaviors are simply wrong."[49]

Does this data prove the validity of belief in God and the narratives that many religious people tell about the afterlife? Absolutely not. In fact, some would interpret the evidence as pointing in the opposite direction. The scholarly literature shows that "supernatural thinking" and participation in religious communities help people make meaning in their lives when faced with a crisis or the death of a loved one. Numerous studies show that this participation has positive outcomes for both mental and physical health. "Regardless of age, adults who don't have a sense of meaning in life are at greater risk of death than those who perceive their lives as full of meaning."[50] As humans, we are deeply wired to live by myths that connect our lives with meaning, wired to believe that our lives belong to a transcendent purpose. It takes an extraordinary amount of effort over decades to convince anyone to coherently narrate their lives otherwise, and few are able to do so. Yet, skeptics say, this may be why humans have evolved to be religious. Rather than these myths reflecting any genuine reality about the world, perhaps religion itself—and stories of the afterlife with it—has evolved as a "narrative-rupture corrective," as a human adaptation to the vulnerabilities of creaturely life. Rather than reflecting the glory of the Creator or any other transcendent reality and purpose, perhaps these myths are helpful illusions for us to live by.

There is no definitive way to respond to this skeptical concern. The skeptics may be right about God, the universe, and the afterlife. Perhaps personal identity is annihilated at death. Perhaps we deceive ourselves when we assume that our lives belong to a larger narrative fabric—so we grieve when that fabric is torn by death. Yet this would simply be to tell another story: atheists have not tasted death, and so they can tell the story of death as annihilation. It cannot be verified or disproved.

Perhaps the (empirical) fact that humans are wired for "supernatural" thinking, for telling the stories of our lives with purpose, and for believing in afterlives that include connection with others and with God testifies to an element of truth. Perhaps rather than supernatural thinking being a kind of disease of human consciousness, it is a God-given seed of something true.

In fact, it seems much more likely that if there *is* a transcendent truth, there will be scores of myths that approximate it. Here, C. S. Lewis is helpful. In *God in the Dock*, he responds to a scholar of comparative religion who documented the areas of commonality between different religious visions and stories around the globe. Lewis, a former religious skeptic himself, grants that Christianity is a myth—a story that provides meaning in life and in dying. Yet "the heart of Christianity is a myth which is also a fact."[51] The stories and hopes and legends of peoples from around the world about a Creator God who comes close to us, even to taste death, and then brings new life become concrete historical fact in the person of Jesus Christ, born of the virgin Mary, crucified under Pontius Pilate, and raised bodily on the third day. But "by becoming fact it does not cease to be myth: that is the miracle."[52] For as myth, it is a grand story that nourishes and cultivates the lives of peoples and cultures, "claiming not only our love and our obedience" as truth "but also our wonder and delight" as a beautiful drama in which we find ourselves.[53]

Thus, if Christianity is the true myth, such that human creatures reflect the image of God with a "seed of religion" implanted within them, a third way opens up for the stories of the Bushes' postmortem reunion with Robin, the widespread stories of encounters with the transcendent in the light of love and peace in NDEs, and other stories we tell ourselves in the face of the ruptured narratives that characterize our lives. Perhaps they are neither purely illusory nor reliable anticipations of the life to come. Perhaps they reflect who we are as humans—soaked in the grandeur of God's glory, testifying to our transcendent purpose of knowing and glorifying God, even in the face of death. They are imperfect myths, stories that we tell ourselves because we are so deeply designed by God for connection with God and one another.

When a pastor hears a church elder talking about having an NDE or about longing for the hug of a departed spouse, the pastor should not respond as if the person is expressing only a self-deceiving illusion. Rather, these people—squeezed and broken—are telling stories that point beyond themselves. They pray prayers that ache for more than merely seeing their losses as random events in a world of chance. They may not be giving us any direct "information" about the life to come, from a Christian standpoint, but they are expressing their God-given longing for the temple, the loving presence and reign of God.

The songs of our lives can bring unexpected joy and moments of delight as dissonant chords melt into an unexpected harmony. At other times, orchestral movements that stir our deep anticipation are cut off, ruptured, like my spinning Civic on a winter road. When life's music suddenly stops, what are we left with? We are left alone in silence, as small creatures in a vast universe. We can't see what will come next.

But we can trust a promise that comes from the Triune God rather than ourselves. We can trust that rupture and tears will not have the final word. To those who are tiny and small and helpless, the risen Christ reaches out his right hand, as he did to John of Patmos, and says, "Do not be afraid; I am the first and the last, and the living one. I was dead, and see, I am alive forever and ever; and I have the keys of Death and of Hades" (Rev. 1:17–18). Death is a mystery to us. Yet the Living One has passed away, passed through death, holding its keys. We can grieve when our loved ones die, but in the words of the apostle Paul, we need not "grieve as others do who have no hope. For since we believe that Jesus died and rose again, even so, through Jesus, God will bring with him those who have died" (1 Thess. 4:13–14). Through God's promise in Christ, we can glimpse enough to hope for an ending that is neither annihilation nor a permanent family vacation. We're free to hope that the Lord of the universe will give mortals like us life through Christ and come to dwell in fullness among his people. We're free to hope that even the dissonant breach of death in our earthly song can eventually lead back into a stanza of joyous praise.

## Discussion Questions

• In what ways do you tend to think about your life in terms of a story? Who are the central characters, and what are some major plot points? How would different possible endings impact the story itself?

• We long for resolution in our stories of death and life after death. One way we do this is by speaking of heavenly "family reunions." How have you heard this narrative expressed? How is Christian hope for life after death similar to or different from the family reunion story?

• Another way we narrate death is by describing it as a passage or journey. How does this narrative help us as we face the unknown of death? What does it mean to belong to Christ as the one who has journeyed through death to new life?

• Scripture, rather than cultural understandings or stories of near-death experiences, should serve as the final authority on what we believe about life after death. While the chapter engages a range of passages in the Old and the New Testaments, some key parts of the biblical witness on this point are 1 Corinthians 15:42–58, 2 Corinthians 4:16–5:10, and Philippians 1:20–26. Read these passages. What do you notice about how they speak about life after death?

• One way to speak about the frameworks we use to narrate our life stories is to use the language of "myth." Describe your own guiding myths. In your own words, what is the "true myth" for our ultimate end?

## Seven

# Hoping for the End as Mortals

My favorite hymn since childhood bears imagery intoxicated with the coming age. I still remember looking up at my father with a bit of embarrassment as he held the hymnbook and belted out the refrain more loudly than anyone standing near us in the congregation, his voice cracking. My daughter rolls her eyes as I do the same now, boldly singing,

> Crown him with many crowns,
> the Lamb upon his throne.
> Hark! how the heavenly anthem drowns
> all music but its own.
> Awake, my soul, and sing
> of him who died for thee,
> and hail him as thy matchless king
> through all eternity.
>
> Crown him the Lord of life,
> who triumphed o'er the grave,
> and rose victorious in the strife
> for those he came to save;
> his glories now we sing
> who died and rose on high,

who died eternal life to bring,
and lives that death may die.[1]

I've joined in the "heavenly anthem" to "the Lamb upon his throne" with many congregations on Sunday mornings, as I did in the sanctuary of the Baptist church of my youth. I've hailed "the Lord of life, who triumphed o'er the grave" at funerals, with a chorus sung before we took our loved one's body to the grave. I've sung this refrain accompanied by the birds of the Great Plains on an early morning on a Kansas farm. I sing and confess and pray the hope of this song. With the last verse, I believe "thy praise shall never, never fail throughout eternity."

And yet, as I live each day, caught up in the pressures and tasks of the moment, what difference does this belief about the culmination of history in Christ make? This is my hope, I sing. But in my mortal life, do I hope for the coming age in a *mortal* way? That is, is it just tucked away as information in the back of my head, along with the names and dates of American presidents and famous peace treaties that I learned about in history class? Or is this hope truly present with me each day, animating my aches and delights as I get up each morning and enter into the day?

The truth is, when the choruses of the Easter hymns die down, I'm afraid I often turn my Christian hope into an abstraction for another day, information I can put on the shelf. In those moments, I don't *disbelieve* in Christian hope, but it is crowded out. In the words of David Foster Wallace's memorable commencement address at Kenyon College,

Everything in my own immediate experience supports my deep belief that I am the absolute center of the universe, the realest, most vivid and important person in existence. . . . It is our default-setting, hard-wired into our [circuit] boards at birth. Think about it: There is no experience you've had that you were not at the absolute center of. The world as you experience it is right there in front of you, or behind you, to the left or right of you, on your TV, or your monitor, or whatever. Other people's thoughts and feelings have to be communicated to you somehow, but your own are so immediate, urgent, real.[2]

Wallace calls this out as an "example of the total wrongness of something I tend to be automatically sure of." When it comes to mortality and hope for the life to come, there is a corollary: we tend to assume that "I am the absolute center of the universe"; thus I can live forever, without creaturely limits. We don't consciously think this, but it's how we tend to live.

Recently I was on my hands and knees on the living room floor, doing my best to persuade Gabby, our rescue greyhound, that getting her nails clipped was not the worst thing that could happen to her. Gabby was not convinced. At one point, I moved my head down toward the rear of her resting body to pursue a back paw. Without warning, Gabby abruptly sat up. Somehow her long limbs acrobatically maneuvered so that her front paw scraped against my left ear. I noticed this in passing but didn't think much of it as I focused on getting the rest of her nails trimmed.

Later that evening, as I glanced in the mirror before bed, the face reflected back at me looked familiar, but . . . my ear—my left earlobe, to be precise—what was that red goo covering it? Suddenly it had my attention. *My ear*, I thought. *What an odd little appendage—two of them, in fact, and one is covered with red goo right now. Am I bleeding?* I grabbed a washcloth, ran some water over it, and started to gently wipe the wound. My mind continued to buzz: *Ears . . . Yes, I do have ears. How does an earlobe actually work? What does it do? Could a cut like this affect my hearing? Since I'm prone to infections because of my cancer treatment, should I call my doctor?* All I could think about was ears.

Like most mortals, I tend to think about my body mainly when something goes wrong—when my ear is bleeding, when my body aches with pain. Perhaps Wallace's observations guide us toward even subtler questions: In day-to-day life, how am I aware of the world? What do I assume? Do I live and act with awareness of all the ways in which my body is a gift, the ways in which its many specialized parts enable me to experience the world—as when my ear, for example, allows me to receive and process sound waves? Most of the time, no. More often than not, I live as one who is unaware.

When it comes to the final things of Christian hope, my mortality forces me into a place of modesty. Do I know that I am mortal? Yes. Do I live like I am mortal? Not much of the time. But on my cancer path, strangely enough, the tingling and sharp pain in my feet, the ache in my back and my neck, and the heavy cloud of fatigue can actually be strange daily gifts. They are frequent bodily reminders to me: "You are dust, / and to dust you shall return" (Gen. 3:19). The pain reminds me in the morning, in the afternoon, and in the evening that my life is like a passing breath; I am a small yet beloved creature belonging to the Creator. I cannot save the world. I cannot do all I have ever imagined or desired to do. Like the hundreds of generations of mortals who have come before me, my body aches, I am small, and I am dying.

My mortality does something else for me, too: it evokes wonder. I haven't seen the age to come. I don't have "speculative" knowledge in the most literal sense of the word—I cannot directly *see*. "For now," the apostle Paul says, "we see in a mirror, dimly, but then we will see face to face" (1 Cor. 13:12). The direct objects of Christian hope—the return of Christ, the new creation—are not before my mortal eyes to be fully comprehended, mastered, and manipulated.

In addition to the limits of our knowledge, it is difficult for us to embrace the limitations of our power. Whether or not you or I approve of it, God will determine his own action in the age to come. Will God come in judgment? Will there be a hell? It's tempting to talk of the life to come as if we're major stakeholders in a company or members of an electoral college. We think that if we hold out on our vote, it could change the outcome. But precisely in this we deny the earthy, embodied fact that we are creatures and not God. Death and what follows will come, and there are no voting booths in the entryways to cemeteries.

Rather than assuming that God needs our approval in choosing among various possibilities for the life to come, we would do better to return to our skin and practice surrender. Whenever we fall asleep, we practice a little death, a surrender of sorts. Our attention to racing thoughts, throbbing aches, and desires for new experiences must slip away. We are overtaken by sleep. Here, within our creaturely rhythm, is a regular reminder of mortality, one that points to the reality that we are not ruler and judge of the universe. In the words of the famous eighteenth-century prayer for bedtime,

> Now I lay me down to sleep,
> I pray the Lord my soul to keep;
> If I should die before I wake,
> I pray the Lord my soul to take.

We don't *think* ourselves to sleep. We surrender our bodies to being overtaken, just as we surrender our bodies to God in death. The Jewish morning prayer Modeh Ani reflects this view of sleep as a mini-death as it thanks God for returning "my breath of life" to me in the morning.[3]

Just as we relinquish our control in entering into sleep, so the dying relinquish their agendas in entering into the life to come. It is not a policy proposal that we get to debate and vote on; it is reality—the reality of what will be when we are overtaken, when breath is taken from us.

For Christians in particular, this surrender to death is utterly fitting. The center of Christian hope is that God has tabernacled among us in the garden of Eden, in Israel, and most fully in Christ—and these mighty actions of God have implications for the future in ways we have not yet seen. Our entry into this God-shaped future is inevitable. We're living as creatures with a terminal condition, and we won't make it out alive.

Our hope, then, rests not in a speculative vision of the future but in God and his promise. Lacking a journalistic account of the future leaves us with many unanswered questions: What will we "do" in heaven? What exactly will it feel like and look like? My most basic answer to questions like these is "I don't know." As a theologian I love to discuss such questions, just as I enjoy discussing recent policy proposals in health care or foreign affairs. And those kinds of discussions have value. But they often lead us to assume that we have a face-to-face knowledge of what is to come. Martin Luther stated it starkly: "As little as children know in their mother's womb about their birth, so little do we know about life everlasting."[4]

It would be a mistake to use Luther's statement to justify complete agnosticism about the life to come. But his analogy is insightful with regard to the character of our knowledge. We are held in communion with Christ, we know Christ in part, and we know that Christ, who is our life, will be the center of the life to come. But the *information* we have about life everlasting is tiny, minuscule. Just as we surrender ourselves to the little death of sleep, we can do little more than anticipate something that will happen *to us*, not by our own power or imaginings, but rather by the mighty act of God the King. Christ is risen. And yet in the body he is absent from us. We cannot calculate in human terms exactly what it will be like when Christ comes again.

Nevertheless, we are not left without hope, direction, or comfort. Scripture gives us concrete handholds onto God's promise, which extends into the future. God's own rhetoric, through strange and wonderful scriptural testimonies, can enliven our imaginations. This chapter does not seek to answer our central speculative questions. Instead it immerses us in some episodes of God's speech to mortals, God's manna for us, as we hunger for the promised land. For as Isaiah the prophet proclaimed, "The grass withers, the flower fades, / but the word of our God will stand forever" (Isa. 40:8).

## Barren Wombs and Hope: God's Promise in the Face of Death

Resurrection hope, enabled by the great appearance and return of the living Lord, is magnificent and cosmic in scope. Handel's "Hallelujah" chorus, especially when sung by a large choir, reminds me of how magnificent Christ's return will be.

> Hallelujah!
> Hallelujah!
> Hallelujah, Hallelujah, Hal-le-lujah!

Hardly able to keep my mouth shut, I listen as the chorus exults in the coming triumph of the reign of Christ.

> And he shall reign forever
> And ever and ever
> King of kings
> Forever and ever
> and Lord of Lords
> Hallelujah, hallelujah!

Each time I hear this glorious chorus, I am captivated. We can and should savor the declaration that Christ the risen Lord is victorious and coming again to reign as the King of all of our present kings and lords.

But strangely enough, as I return to Scripture to hear once again its testimony to this great day of redemption, I'm surprised to find that, rather than in a deafening chorus, the pathway to resurrection hope occurs in silence—or, perhaps, as we will explore in the next few pages, in the soft tones of a solitary woman weeping, praying in desperation for her womb to be gifted with a child. This is a peculiar backdrop for the great cosmic renewal of resurrection and new creation! But perhaps I shouldn't be surprised. After all, the King of kings I'm waiting for is the Lamb who was crucified. This is the Lord who declared to Paul that his "power is made perfect in weakness" (2 Cor. 12:9).

At key points in God's covenantal history with his people, God's surprising victory over death occurs in stories of infertility that take unexpected turns, resulting in fruitfulness, new life given by God's power. For many of us today, infertility is a highly personal struggle, a source of grief and shame. It was similar in ancient Israel. Then as now, many couples who prayed for children, who were faithful to each other for decades, who grew old together and died, did so without ever receiving a child. For many couples, this is a desolate path. But in ancient Israel, infertility often involved an additional layer as well: infertility threatened the very promise of the Lord to his people.

The paradigmatic example of how infertility threatens God's covenantal promise is the story of Abraham and Sarah. The Lord calls Abram, at age seventy-five, to leave his homeland on the basis of God's covenant promise: "I will make of you a great nation, and I will bless you, and make your name great, so that you will be a blessing" (Gen. 12:2). Years come and go, with no signs of this "great nation." When the Lord comes to Abram in a dream, Abram cries out, "O Lord GOD, what will you give me, for I continue childless?" The Lord does not spurn Abram's question but raises the numerical stakes for this divine promise even further: "Look toward heaven and count the stars, if you are able to count them. . . . So shall your descendants be" (Gen. 15:5). In spite of the unlikelihood of this promise coming to pass, at this point Abram "believed the LORD; and the LORD reckoned it to him as righteousness" (Gen. 15:6).

Yet as the years go by, infertility seems to block the Lord's promise. God's promise is breathtaking and glorious, but in order for it to take root an impossibility must be overcome: a completely infertile couple must become fruitful. When the Lord promises specifically that Sarah will give birth to a son, Abraham bitterly laughs. When Sarah later hears of the promise that she will become pregnant, she laughs as well. It's impossible. But, responding to her laughter, the Lord declares he can overcome this impossibility: "Is anything too wonderful for the LORD?" (Gen. 18:14). Sarah becomes pregnant and gives birth to the promised son.

In this foundational biblical narrative, as in stories such as those of Rebekah, Hannah, and Elizabeth, a womb that seems completely barren is impossibly filled by the Lord. For Abraham and Sarah, infertility threatens *the very existence* of the people of God. Thus, God's filling of the womb is, in the words of Kevin Madigan and Jon Levenson, a "restorative action of God" that actually "opposes the natural course of things." The Lord miraculously reactivates the "powers within nature—principally the power to procreate—that had shriveled and virtually disappeared before God's new intervention."[5] In this, God fulfills his promise of an everlasting covenant with Abraham and Sarah, even though they still die.

God's promise in Genesis is not that Abraham and Sarah will pass through death into an individual afterlife. That is not how God counters death in this foundational narrative. Rather, the Lord turns the tables on death by upending the infertility that threatens his covenant promise. Abraham and Sarah die, but God's promise for life does not die—the promise and the people of the promised covenant live on. Permanent infertility for Abraham and Sarah would have resulted in the obliteration of God's promise to their descendants; the miraculous gift of children reverses that death.[6]

It might be tempting for some to claim that such stories of infertility being overcome by fertility are the norm for God's people. With the prosperity gospel, we might be tempted to think that we have victory now over all sickness and ill health. Perhaps all couples who are faithful to God should be able to overcome infertility. But the true point of these biblical stories could hardly be further from this conclusion. Neither Abraham's covenant nor the new covenant in Christ promises that infertility will always give way to fertility for those with faith. In fact, the extreme rarity of a barren womb being filled with a child points to its source in the power of God. Jon Levenson says it this way: "Death is universal in the Hebrew Bible and seldom reversed, but God promises, offers, and prefers life and saves his chosen people from annihilation."[7] The Israelites did not expect God to overcome infertility in the vast majority of circumstances. Rather, in the cases in which God reverses death by providing children to the infertile, God offers testimony to his unique power to reverse death in fidelity to his covenantal promise. These miracles are rare, and that is essential to their power: to the infertile, the dying, those unable to save themselves, such miracles testify to the divine promise, which is immutable and reliable.

In this, these miracles point beyond themselves. After Hannah, who was taunted for her infertility, is gifted with a child by the Lord, she sings a song of praise to God. In her exultation we hear praise of the Lord's power—a hint that death itself might not be the final word for God's people: "The LORD kills and brings to life; / he brings down to Sheol and raises up" (1 Sam. 2:6). The Lord is King over both life and death, and even Sheol, the place of the dead, does not escape his reign. The closed womb of Hannah is opened, and Samuel, whom Hannah dedicates to the Lord as a priest and prophet, is born.

Thus, it's not surprising that in other Old Testament narratives, stories of overcoming infertility are connected with stories of raising the dead back to life. In 2 Kings 4, a barren woman known simply as "the Shunammite woman" is promised a child by Elisha. Years after his birth, the child becomes ill and dies. The Shunammite woman calls for Elisha, who comes and prays that the Lord would bring life back to this promised son. Then Elisha "got up on the bed and lay upon the child, putting his mouth upon his mouth, his eyes upon his eyes, and his hands upon his hands; and while he lay bent over him, the flesh of the child became warm" (2 Kings 4:34). Like Lazarus in the New Testament, the boy was revived. But also like Lazarus, his new life was temporary. He continued aging and eventually died. Nevertheless, his story points to the Lord's power and preference for life for his covenant people.

All of this may sound fanciful to us. What is the point of miracle stories if we are not promised that *our own* infertility will be overcome or that *our own* children who die will come back to life? As strange as it may seem, the fact that it is not about us is part of the point of these stories. C. S. Lewis states it this way in his book *Miracles*: "If [these miracles] have occurred," Lewis writes, "they have occurred because they are the very thing this universal story is about. They are not exceptions (however rarely they occur), not irrelevancies. They are precisely those chapters in this great story on which the plot turns. Death and Resurrection are what the story is about."[8] Put differently, stories of miraculous births and the dead coming back to life are, by definition, rare. But rather than being exceptions to a rule, these miracles are signposts of the truth of God's promise that death is not the final word.

Indeed, generations after Sarah, Hannah, and the Shunammite woman, an angel appears to a virgin named Mary and explains that an impossible birth will give her the promised son of the covenant. The Lord's great promise to Abraham—to bless all the nations through his offspring—finds covenantal fulfillment through an unlikely means, all the way from Sarah to Mary: wombs are impossibly opened to life. Death is reversed. And when Mary's promised Son meets an unjust death, the Father raises him up, just as Elisha did for the Shunammite woman's promised son. The culmination of the covenant is Jesus the Messiah, raised to a life so permeated with God's power and glory that death cannot touch it again. Through it all, the intimate, messy, and painful process of bearing a child is a central sign of God's faithfulness to his promise, a vehicle for God's blessing of the nations and the whole of creation.

In our daily lives, I wonder, does this interplay of infertility and new life really matter for authentic Christian hope? Can't we just skip to the rejoicing part, to humming along with the tune of "For unto Us a Child Is Born" and readying our legs to stand for the "Hallelujah" chorus?

And we do rejoice—we should rejoice—for Christ has been born of a virgin, and Christ has been raised from the dead! But as we saw in our chapter on the gospel of prosperity, miraculous truths can be distorted when separated from the gospel of the cross and God's power made perfect through weakness. Unless we frankly recognize that Christ's birth and resurrection come forth from places of hopelessness and helplessness, we've not understood their meaning. Until we embrace the fact that God's promise of life comes to us in the midst of the tears of barrenness, as we are completely unable to generate new life ourselves, our rejoicing in Christ's birth and resurrection will be an abstraction.

I still remember the evening years ago when my wife, Rachel, and I had dinner with another young couple our age. At one point it became so quiet that all we could hear was the clinking of our forks on the salad bowls, as if the forks themselves had become the most outspoken conversation partners. Our friends had opened up to us in a vulnerable way about how much they longed and ached to have children. After hearing and processing this, it was time for Rachel and me to share. This led to some long moments of awkward silence.

"I'm not in a hurry to collect my own children," Rachel said. "I've spent enough of my life taking care of other people's kids." The oldest sister in a large family, Rachel had frequently been in charge of her younger siblings. She was tired.

"But what about when we get old?" I asked. "Think about yourself at seventy or seventy-five. How would you look back on your life? Would you want to have children you could go and visit? And possibly grandchildren?"

"Well, maybe so, as long as we realize that when we visit our children, we might be visiting them in federal prison." All of us looked up at Rachel. "On the street where I grew up, there was a very nice older lady, and her son was in federal prison. That's where she visited him."

Speaking about children growing up to go to federal prison is not normal fare for middle-class conversations, but I was struck and refreshed by Rachel's lack of sentimentality. Sure, babies are cute, they have big eyes and funny hair, and they can take away your breath with a smile. But having children is an encounter with death as well. Bearing and raising a child keeps time for the parents—reminds them of the arc of their aging as the child grows, and ultimately of their deaths as the child goes their own way.

Many conversations between Rachel and me followed that dinner. An intractable dynamic in them was awareness of our own mortal limits. We knew we couldn't control our own futures, let alone the futures of our children. We also knew that, as aging and dying persons, we couldn't mull over this decision indefinitely. I thought of various scenarios for our future that would not involve children; but somehow these scenarios seemed disconnected from our bodies, our marriage, our calling to be salt and light in the world.

The decision to have children, we came to see, was not ultimately within our control. There were things that we could do. We had learned about natural family planning and the times when pregnancy would become possible. But one pregnancy test after another came back negative—no positive line on the test indicating pregnancy. We started on some modest fertility treatments, and those did not produce the desired results either.

Along the way, we entered into the multiyear process of adoption, not only as a way to grow our family but also in hopes that we could bless a child and another family. Ironically, after we adopted our daughter, Neti, and stopped fertility treatments, Rachel finally got a positive result on her pregnancy test. She gave birth to our son, Nathaniel. (Perhaps, though, in light of the Old Testament stories of the Lord filling the womb, this is not ironic at all.) But in both the adoption and Rachel's pregnancy, admitting our mortal limits meant opening our hearts with joy and brokenness, making a commitment and covenant, for we would always be the father and the mother of these particular children.

The point here is not to say that Rachel and I, in facing our mortality, wanted to live on through our progeny. Rather, we were forced—or invited—to surrender to the illusion of living on and to offer up our mortal bodies to God. We handed over our children to the minister's hands in baptism, a sign of God's covenant promise; we handed our children over to the promise of death and of new life in Christ alone. In giving our children in baptism, we recognized that they belong first and foremost to the Lord of Abraham and Sarah, who is the promised Son Jesus Christ—the living God who alone can give and sustain life—not to us. Rachel and I do desire for our children to follow in the way of Christ and live as witnesses to God's kingdom. But that would be the fruit of the Spirit's work, part of the baptismal drama of dying and rising with Christ. To desire to live on through a kind of "immortality" would be as absurd as Abraham and Sarah, or the virgin Mary, thinking they could generate life in a barren or virgin womb. God's promise for new life is alone worthy of trust for mortals. God's promise alone is worthy of our hope.

Likewise, whether or not one becomes a parent, we are completely helpless—utterly unable—to bring about God's new, life-giving creation on our own. We are utterly impotent, powerless to bring about that end. We can trust, we can hope—we can look for passing glimpses of the new life here and now. But in ourselves, in our own power, in the natural course of things, we are completely barren. We can pray and cry out, "Come, Lord Jesus!" But we cannot force him to come in fullness. We trust in the miracle of the incarnation, cross, and resurrection of Christ, and we look to his royal consummation. But neither our faith nor our faithfulness will make the kingdom come.

## Heavenly Hope and the End of the Christian Life

Earlier in this book, we saw how those who *know* they are in Sheol connect with a key facet of reality: they cannot find life in themselves; they cannot bring deliverance. From the desperate place of Sheol, we can choose to look to idols for deliverance, perhaps by putting medical science on the throne as the Deliverer or by granting kingship to a political hero or cause. As we seek to overcome the dusty taste of death in our mouths, we can even exalt our own act of faith to a royal place—as if God *owes* us deliverance when we pray in a certain way, according to a certain formula.

Instead of these idols, which tend to reflect back to us our own desires and wishes, I've sought to point our gaze toward the dwelling place of God, to heaven. Or have I? Repeatedly, I've suggested that we need to join the psalmist, who "longs" and "faints" for the temple. In the temple, rather than Sheol, is life and breath, for "a day in your courts is better /

than a thousand elsewhere" (Ps. 84:2, 10). Have I been elliptically refer-ring to heaven all along?

It depends on what one means by "heaven." Biblically speaking, what is heaven? It is where the Lord of the universe dwells in fullness. As heaven relates to us as creatures, it's a dwelling place with a center. For Israel in the Old Testament, because of God's promise, Jerusalem is the center of the earth, the temple is the center of Jerusalem, and the holy of holies is the center of the temple. In the holy of holies, heaven and earth come together.

As we will explore further below, the New Testament draws upon that context to claim that *Jesus himself* is the holy of holies, the temple, and Jerusalem. Jesus embodies all that they represent. He is the promised land in his very person. For this reason, the eschaton, the "final things" of Christian faith, is not primarily a set of journalistic predictions about the fate of the world and humanity. Rather, it is hope for the appear-ance and return of a *person*: Jesus Christ. Jesus Christ *is* the eschaton. He embodies the Christian hope that is to come.[9] This is the end and ultimate hope of the Christian life: that the crucified and risen Jesus Christ, to whom we are united now by the Holy Spirit, has ascended to his throne; and that when he returns to us bodily, and the bodies of the dead are raised to meet him in judgment and glory, heaven and earth will join back together in harmony, as God has intended all along.

And yet all of this can sound wispy and ethereal. That's one of the reasons I've used a common biblical term for God's dwelling place—the temple—rather than speaking of "heaven." The temple is concrete; in its various forms it occupies a particular place at particular times, with a particular structure and form. It gives our reflections a starting point other than the question "What will heaven be like?" I have to admit, though, I do enjoy asking children that question.

"In heaven, you will be able to eat ice cream," a child said to me after finding out that I cannot digest dairy products. "You'll be able to eat as much ice cream as you want."

"In heaven, there will be no homework! No chores!"

"In heaven, people won't die anymore, like the girl who died at my school."

Children make their views of heaven concrete, often reflecting the assumptions of the adults in their midst who would not put the matter so directly.

In Scripture the dwelling place of God is also concrete—material, not ethereal, filled with symbols and smells and spaces for particular purposes. Yet the earthly temple is not the same as the "heaven" that is to come. It is an accommodation to our weakness, not the dwelling place of the Lord in its fullness. The Lord gave Moses instructions to build the tabernacle on the basis of a divinely given pattern (Exod. 26:30)— what the book of Hebrews later describes as "a sketch and shadow of the heavenly" tabernacle (Heb. 8:5). Yet if we want to know, as bodily creatures, what it means to long for the dwelling place of God and why it matters that Jesus is the embodiment of the temple, then it is worth revisiting the character and structure of the Old Testament temple itself.

## The Story of the Tabernacle and the Temple

The psalmists point out that other nations have gods that appear beautiful, made with "silver and gold." These gods are "idols" that "have mouths, but they do not speak; / they have eyes, but they do not see; / they have ears, but they do not hear, / and there is no breath in their mouths" (Ps. 135:15–17).

We might expect the true Lord, in contrast, to eschew all silver and gold. For the God of Israel, the psalmist declares, "is in the heavens; / he does whatever he pleases." In comparison, in other nations "their idols are silver and gold, / the work of human hands" (Ps. 115:3–4). Nevertheless, the Lord actually instructs Israel, through Moses at Sinai, to use gold, silver, and precious stones in his sanctuary. This is the concrete form the Lord commands, so that through human hands Israel should "make me a sanctuary, so that I may dwell among them" (Exod. 25:8). Indeed, in Exodus, the Lord describes in great detail the different spaces of the tabernacle, as a movable "dwelling place," that were later adapted to the stationary temple in Jerusalem.

The tabernacle's outer court was open to the sky and contained a laver with water for ceremonial washing and an altar for burnt offerings. The inner court was a covered tent with two parts, both of which could be approached only by priests. First was the holy place, with an altar of incense, a table of showbread, and a golden candlestick; the second inner court was the heart of the tabernacle, behind a great curtain: the holy of holies with the ark of the covenant.[10] Only the high priest could enter the holy of holies, and only once a year, on the Day of Atonement. The high priest would spend multiple days in cleansing rituals before his entrance into the Lord's presence, and he would enter wearing bells. If the ringing of the bells stopped, the Israelites could assume that the high priest had died in the presence of the Lord.[11] As biblical scholar Sandra Richter states, the tabernacle structure and rituals connected with the holy of holies communicate that "God lives here. And anyone who draws near must either be holy . . . or dead."[12]

This description of God's dwelling place may strike us as strange. Didn't the psalmist declare his desire to go to God's dwelling place? But if the dwelling place of God requires that we be either holy or dead, this seems much more fit as a *house for God* than a house for creatures like us. Indeed, the imagery within the holy of holies, the center of the tabernacle, may reinforce our sense of unease. Embroidered on the curtains of the holy of holies were cherubim, who also adorned the ark of the covenant within. Far from being chubby angels, cherubim are, according to the Lord's instruction to Israel, fearful creatures who would have been recognized as "guardians of sacred space" among Israel's neighbors in the ancient Near East.[13] Cherubim combined human and animal features as creatures who point to the Lord's glorious kingship. They also stood watch over the garden of Eden (Gen. 3:24)—the garden-temple, the sanctuary where the Lord dwelt with his creation. Now the cherubim guarded the sanctuary of the tabernacle. On the ark, they were carved as heralds of Yahweh's throne. This indicated that the tabernacle was a kind of paradise—not first and foremost for human dwelling, but the dwelling of a holy and glorious God. As inhospitable as it may seem, the tabernacle offered a taste of Eden, a taste of "heaven," we might say. Precisely because it was the dwelling place of the Lord (rather than a place of wish fulfillment for humans), it also offered the Lord's people a taste of the *true life, which is the life of God.*

The concrete realities of the divinely ordained temple may make us uncomfortable on several levels. Why don't the temple and the heart of it, the holy of holies, welcome whoever wants to enter? Wouldn't the psalmist long for a dwelling place in which anyone is welcome? Here the Old Testament makes a connection we often do not: the heart of the temple contains the ark as the Lord's throne *and* the covenant law given to Moses on Mount Sinai. In the words of Jon Levenson, since the temple is a form of paradise, one cannot drag the "filth" of disobedience into the physical temple "and expect to benefit from paradisiacal existence."[14] Mount Sinai and Mount Zion are joined at the hip.

We may also worry that the Lord's choice to dwell in the temple means he is *limited* to that particular location. Yet the Old Testament frequently counters such a misconception. For example, in Isaiah's vision of the temple, he hears the seraphim proclaim, "Holy, holy, holy is the LORD of hosts." But what is their next line? "The whole earth is full of his glory" (Isa. 6:3). The Lord's presence in the temple does not dilute his presence elsewhere. The Lord created the world such that heaven and earth would dwell together. The temple is a portal for this communion, a glimpse of the Lord's abiding presence, a taste of the Lord's ongoing communion with the cosmos.

At the heart of Jesus's criticism of the temple practices of his day was the way in which the glorious promise of God's dwelling place at the temple could be resisted by human disobedience. The physical tabernacle and temple were divinely ordained—God's gift of loving fellowship to his covenant people. Yet even the physical temple could be used for ends foreign to its God-given purpose as the portal between heaven and earth, as Matthew's Gospel so vividly portrays. "Then Jesus entered the temple and drove out all who were selling and buying in the temple, and he overturned the tables of the money changers and the seats of those who sold doves. He said to them, 'It is written, "My house shall be called a house of prayer"; / but you are making it a den of robbers'" (Matt. 21:12–13).

In the Gospel of John, after Jesus overturns the tables, he boldly proclaims that he himself is the temple in his death and resurrection. "Destroy this temple, and in three days I will raise it up" (John 2:19). In the incarnation and the cross, the alienation of sin and the contamination of death are exhausted. Human sin—with its alienation and rebellion—kept all but the high priest excluded from the holy of holies. But in Christ the priest and the new temple, this exclusion was overcome. When Jesus breathed his last, "the curtain of the temple was torn in two, from top to bottom" (Matt. 27:51). All at once, the divine intention for the physical temple was honored, and yet the physical temple was also judged—as Christ's body, rather than the physical temple, becomes the true site for the union of heaven and earth.[15] Christ's crucified and risen body, then, makes "available to all people a new, bold, unrestricted access into God's very presence" in the holy of holies.[16]

And so it is, in Paul's words, that in Christ "all the fullness of God was pleased to dwell," as in the temple, "and through him God was pleased to reconcile to himself all things, whether on earth or in heaven, by making peace through the blood of his cross" (Col. 1:19–20). Precisely because he is the temple, hope in Jesus Christ is cosmic. Precisely because he is the holy of holies, his atoning sacrifice offers mediation. And precisely because the crucified and risen Jesus has ascended to heaven, we have some clue about what heaven is. Heaven is where God dwells in fullness. Heaven is where Jesus is, as the one who *is* the holy of holies in his person. Indeed, when we petition in the Lord's Prayer, "Your kingdom come. / Your will be done, / on earth as it is in heaven"

(Matt. 6:10), we pray and ache toward that final day—when the ascended Lord who unites heaven and earth in his flesh comes again to culminate his kingship on earth. Certainly, his kingdom has already started to come, and Jesus is present now through Word and Spirit. But this petition in the Lord's Prayer longs for its ultimate fulfillment, not unlike the Christian cry of lament and hope, "Come, Lord Jesus!" (Rev. 22:20; see 1 Cor. 16:22).[17]

## Embodied Hope for Heaven

But what about heaven after death? Christian hope for life after death builds upon the temple promises given to Moses and to David and the visions of Isaiah, Ezekiel, and other prophets who looked forward to a renewed temple in the future. That temple will bring together heaven and earth, the holy God with wayward but forgiven people, such that the original purpose of creation can be fulfilled—indeed, even exalted higher in glory. Thus, John of Patmos uses temple imagery as he speaks of the glorious return of Christ: "God's dwelling place [literally, "tabernacle"] is now among the people, and he will dwell [literally, "tabernacle"] with them. They will be his people, and God himself will be with them and be their God. 'He will wipe every tear from their eyes. There will be no more death' or mourning or crying or pain, for the old order of things has passed away" (Rev. 21:3–4 NIV).

The final Christian hope, the end of the Christian life, is not life extension or self-fulfillment. It is for God to "tabernacle" among his people—as in the garden, as in the people of Israel—as those united to Christ by the Spirit in the church, culminating in fullness in the age to come. In ourselves, we have no right or entitlement to enter into the life to come. We do not "deserve" an afterlife. All of this is gift.

And yet a gift can be abstract. That's why I love the concreteness of the way the covenant promise comes to us when Scripture speaks of the temple. Sociologists have summarized the beliefs of many Americans about the age to come with the proposition that "good people go to heaven when they die."[18] That seems logical, to us at least. But the assumption that good people go to heaven when they die seems more like a math equation than a tabernacle leading the people of Israel with flaming fire by night and cloud by day. Couldn't a computer perform the calculations to determine which "good people" get to "go to heaven when they die"? Indeed, the popular television series *The Good Place* playfully built on exactly these sorts of assumptions: each individual earns points in their earthly life that give them either eternal reward ("the Good Place") or punishment ("the Bad Place").[19] In such a scenario, we are not in the pit of Sheol, in need of rescue. We're on a path that we make ourselves. As long as we don't bother others and are basically good, we'll be rewarded with what we deserve: heaven.

In contrast to these abstractions, the temple promises of the Old and the New Testaments engage our imaginations, awaken our desires, and quicken our senses. Christian hope is a gift grounded in the promise of God alone. Yet it's not an abstract promise but one that comes to us with texture and concreteness: the river of life flowing from the temple (Ezek. 47:1–12) and the splashing water of baptism; the call to love the Lord and the neighbor that Moses receives on Mount Sinai and the stunning command of Jesus on a mountain in Galilee to "love your enemies and pray for those who persecute you" (Matt. 5:44); the bitter herbs of Passover on the tongue and the burning sweetness of wine at the Lord's table; the communal procession to the temple with dancing and singing (Ps. 149:3) and the joy of "passing the peace" to young and old in the church as the people of God's dwelling. In all these tangible and concrete ways, we taste and are shaped by our hope for the age to come—in joyful worship, anticipating face-to-face communion with the Triune God.

## The Temple and the Body: You Are Not Your Own

Recently, I met another cancer patient for coffee. As a brother in Christ, he had often sought to comfort me in the past. Then he was diagnosed and thrust into treatment. He seemed out of breath after walking just ten feet from the barista's counter to the table. His hand shook as he grasped his cup of coffee. But then I saw the smile of the man I had known in years past. A hollowed-out body could not shut out the splendor. No less than the body of an Olympic athlete forty years his junior, the dying, thinning body of my friend was a temple, a place of divine dwelling.

This is truly a miracle. In the New Testament, Christ is the temple; yet those who belong to Christ—body and soul—are temples as well. The believer's own flesh and blood becomes a dwelling place of God. "Your body is a temple," Paul tells the Corinthians (1 Cor. 6:19). And the church—the imperfect people hoping in God's promise to Abraham, to Moses, and to David—is the temple as well. Using the plural "you," Paul asks the Corinthian church, "Do you not know that you are God's temple and that God's Spirit dwells in you?" (1 Cor. 3:16).

That the human body, and the gathering of bodies in fellowship, could be the dwelling place for the Almighty makes my head spin. The Lord gave Moses intricate instructions for the sculpting of beautiful and fearful cherubim to adorn the ark as the dwelling place of God. In Christ, instead of moldings of shining gold, the frame and shape of the human body serves as a dwelling place for the Lord. In Solomon's temple there were "bronze stands [that] were decorated with carved cherubim, lions, palm trees, and wreaths."[20] Instead of these decorations, the individual and gathered bodies of believers are carved by the Lord as a dwelling place that we regard alternately with pleasure, awkwardness, and shame in daily life. The sublime human form has fascinated sculptors and painters for centuries with its subtle and sharp turns; our broad foreheads and our protruding noses; even our rectum and our anus, through which we excrete waste. Our bodies—whether battered from war or energized for sport, whether lively or exhausted—can be the temple of the Lord.

In my own congregation, it is not uncommon for an elderly member to die and be commended to the Lord on Saturday and then, on

Sunday, for a child to be welcomed into the church through baptism. It's astonishing: the King of the universe chooses to dwell in the bodies of both young and old. Indeed, as Paul says, "we have this treasure in clay jars, so that it may be made clear that this extraordinary power belongs to God and does not come from us" (2 Cor. 4:7). It is possible for a physical temple to stand for centuries. Our bodies, in comparison, are fragile "clay jars." But decaying temples (such as human bodies) may be more appropriate than great buildings in serving as throne rooms for the King who was crucified. "While we live," Paul says, "we are always being given up to death for Jesus' sake, so that the life of Jesus may be made visible in our mortal flesh" (2 Cor. 4:11). Being "given up" or "delivered up to death" involves enduring persecution, for Paul; but it also points back to the character of these brittle clay jars, the mortal character of our lives. In the words of John Calvin, the aches and pains of our mortal flesh can stir us "to meditate on the termination of the present life" and "to have death constantly before our eyes." In a breathtaking way, precisely because "Christ's *death* is the gate of life," as mortal temples encountering death we are appropriate vessels for Christ's presence. For "if in this world we submit to die with him," then "we shall be partakers of his life" in "the blessed resurrection."[21] Christ the King uses crumbling, mortal temples as the place where the treasure of his presence dwells.

## The Cosmic Shaking

Our bodies are temples, and the church is a temple—and indeed, the King of the universe made the whole of creation to be a sanctuary, a temple, as the picture of the garden in Genesis 1 communicates. But in another sense, all of these are *not yet* fully indwelt temples. Like the tabernacle in the wilderness and the temple in Jerusalem, these temples are not our own possession, and they do not guarantee divine presence. In exhorting believers to flee immorality and sin, Paul writes, "Do you not know that your body is a temple of the Holy Spirit within you, which you have from God, and that you are not your own? For you were bought with a price; therefore glorify God in your body" (1 Cor. 6:19–20). Your body belongs to God. Therefore give your body as a thank offering back to God, as the dwelling place of God. For you are not your own but belong to Christ. Just as "two shall become one flesh," so believers have been united to Jesus Christ and have become "one spirit with him" (1 Cor. 6:17). Being a "temple" does not make God our own possession; on the contrary, it reminds us that we do not belong to ourselves.

Of course, this is a problem.

To enter the heart of the temple, the dwelling place of God, one must be either holy or dead. I'm not either one. The church, as the people of God, is not either one. The cosmos, the good yet corrupted creation, is not either one. Speaking of the temple on Mount Zion, the psalmist asks,

> Who shall ascend the hill of the LORD?
>   And who shall stand in his holy place?
> Those who have clean hands and pure hearts. (Ps. 24:3–4)

We can no more enter the holy of holies on our own than we can give an infertile couple, at age ninety, a healthy baby in the womb. We can no more enter into the temple in its fullness than a virgin can bring a son into the world.

The cosmos, the people of God, a person—all of these, divinely intended as temples, need to be shaken.

Although surveys of religious belief in America indicate that a high percentage of people believe in an afterlife, the numbers dip when questions shift toward divine judgment. While it's still the case that a solid majority of American Christians affirm the truth of divine judgment, in keeping with the teachings of both the Apostles' Creed and the New Testament about Christ's coming to "judge the living and the dead" (2 Tim. 4:1), we also tend to focus on this judgment in individual terms, as evidenced by our ways of talking about the afterlife and what it means for Grandma, for our neighbor, and for others we know who have died. Certainly it's true that when the Bible speaks of judgment, the individual is included. But this is not the main story. At the most basic level, divine judgment is cosmic in its scope.

Handel's *Messiah* gets this right. In a joyful melody familiar to many of us, the choir sings of the coming theophany prophesied by Isaiah: "And the glory of the Lord shall be revealed, and all flesh shall see it together: for the mouth of the Lord hath spoken it" (Isa. 40:5 KJV). Less familiar to the ears of most is the Bass Recitative from Haggai that immediately follows.

> Thus saith the Lord of Hosts; Yet once, it is a little while, and I will shake the heavens, and the earth, and the sea, and the dry land; And I will shake all nations, and the desire of all nations shall come. (Hag. 2:6–7 KJV)

The bass singer returns to the word "shake" repeatedly. He slides his pitch from one note to another, "shaking" his voice as he sings of the Lord's shaking. Haggai the prophet looks forward to the coming appearance of the Lord, which brings an earthquake, a shaking of heaven and earth, a shaking of all nations, in order for the Lord to return to his holy temple (Hag. 2:6–9). The coming of the Lord and the judgment of the Lord—the shaking away of all that is unfit for the presence of the holy God—is one and the same event. God the King shakes heaven and earth, reclaiming them as his own possession in order to dwell with the temple-creation that belongs to him.

This section in Haggai, along with dozens of other references in the Old Testament both to theophanies (divine appearances) and to the coming day of the Lord, points toward a time of cosmic cleansing— ultimately, temple cleansing. In the New Testament, the common phrases "the day of the Lord" and "the final day" similarly refer to the day of the Lord's appearance and judgment—though in the New Testament, this is clearly connected to a resurrection on the final day, which is rarely mentioned in the Old Testament.[22] Nevertheless, the pattern is clear enough: on the final day, the Lord God will return to shake and judge the earth in order to cleanse it. Then heaven and earth can again kiss and come together in fellowship, and the Lord will dwell with his people.

As the visionary, apocalyptic language of Revelation portrays this judgment, "Babylon" will be thrown down, defeated by the Lord. For Babylon "has become a dwelling place of demons" and "the kings of the earth have committed fornication with her, / and the merchants of the earth have grown rich from the power of her luxury" (Rev. 18:2–3). Human rebellion—in the collective, downward-spiraling forces of greed and iniquity—together with the powers and principalities of this world will be overcome, so that an angel calls out, "Fallen, fallen is Babylon the great!" (Rev. 18:2). The temple was a mini-paradise, a microcosm of the cosmos, and required purification for those who entered it. Now, in a lavishly expanded new temple, John tells us that in the new heaven and earth "nothing unclean will enter it, nor anyone who practices abomination or falsehood, but only those who are written in the Lamb's book of life" (Rev. 21:27). Creation itself will be cleansed so that the Lord can dwell in it once again in fullness.

Like many, I have unanswered questions about Christ's return and final judgment. Perhaps this is to be expected. Human systems of justice are a response to human enmity and sin, but even in the best of circumstances the results are partial, incomplete, and often unsatisfying in comparison with the fullness of life for which we were created. And human tribunals, as was the case at the trial of Jesus, sometimes deliver verdicts that make a mockery of the term "justice" itself.

Perhaps one solution is to hope for an afterlife *without* any sort of judgment. If everyone went to some kind of "heaven," wouldn't that be an afterlife without judgment? Consider a hypothetical scenario for a "heaven" like this, with Herod and the infant boys he murdered perhaps sitting side by side on a beach, enjoying the sun and sipping cold drinks. Is this life after death without judgment? No. The very fact that life is continuing on in the afterlife is a kind of judgment—in this case, it could be one that implies of Herod's horrific actions, "This is the way things are supposed to be." Alternatively, this "heaven" could be one in which Herod himself is so drastically *altered* after death that some kind of postmortem reconciliation can take place without this heaven being a reward for his treachery. That scenario would require a "shaking" and judgment as well. Any view that connects life after death with our earthly stories makes claims on what is true and beautiful and false and terrible right now. An afterlife *without* any sort of judgment is simply not a possibility.

In the biblical vision, on the last day God the King brings judgment against sin and the powers of evil that corrupt and distort his good creation. The temple of creation must be cleansed if it is to be the dwelling place of God and his people. Yet talk of sin, the powers of evil, and judgment goes against the sentiments of Western culture, especially middle-class culture, in which regular violence can seem more like a distant spectacle than a genuine reality. In a novel by P. D. James, a detective shares a common modern sentiment, saying, "I don't go for all this emphasis on sin, suffering and judgment. If I had a God I'd like Him to be intelligent, cheerful and amusing." In response, her Jewish colleague says, "I doubt whether you'd find him much of a comfort when they herded you into the gas chambers. You might prefer a God of vengeance."[23]

A God without wrath is a God who whitewashes evil and is deaf to the cries of the powerless. A student of mine who grew up in a gang culture and had many whom he loved taken from him by violence told me with profound honesty that "if God will not avenge, I am tempted to avenge." Precisely because God is a God of love, he is also a God of holy wrath. Indeed, God's judgment is an *expression* of his love, making the way for covenantal communion with his creation. To use an environmental analogy from Fleming Rutledge, "If poisonous contamination has been released into the air and water, it must be permanently eliminated in order for God's new creatures to breathe and have eternal life."[24]

Nevertheless, many of my questions are left unanswered. I see through a glass darkly. But one aspect of biblical hope is very clear: the final, divine judgment is simply not in our hands. I am not the one who is able (or qualified) to judge. The Lord does not even ask for my approval before the shaking begins. Unlike politicians, the Lord is not pivoting his plans on the basis of poll numbers.

In my case, the more I've reflected on my creaturely limits and mortal end, the more at ease I've become with my unanswered questions about the final judgment. The wounds of the world are deep and complex and seemingly intractable. It's a relief to realize that I'm free to be a creature rather than the judge who decides what in this beautiful and terrible world will be shaken. I've been able to join the psalmist in looking forward to that day of cosmic shaking—for the judge will be not a tyrant but God the King who comes in his loving-kindness.

> Say among the nations, "The LORD is king!
>    The world is firmly established; it shall never be moved.
>    He will judge the peoples with equity."
> Let the heavens be glad, and let the earth rejoice;
>    let the sea roar, and all that fills it;
>    let the field exult, and everything in it.
> Then shall all the trees of the forest sing for joy
>    before the LORD; for he is coming,
>    for he is coming to judge the earth.
> He will judge the world with righteousness,
>    and the peoples with his truth. (Ps. 96:10–13)

Creation itself will rejoice and praise the King for his coming, for his shaking, for his cleansing.

Who is this King who will come again to cleanse and rule the cosmos? Jesus Christ, the crucified and risen Lord. He is both the Lord and our brother in the flesh. He is the one in whom we find our life and our future. "Who is to condemn?" Paul asks. "It is Christ Jesus, who died, yes, who was raised, who is at the right hand of God, who indeed intercedes for us" (Rom. 8:34). This same Christ was the one through whom "God was pleased to reconcile to himself all things, whether on earth or in heaven, by making peace through the blood of his cross" (Col. 1:20). On the final day, the heavens will rejoice, the earth will be glad, and the trees of the forest will sing with joy.

## The Shaking and Being Clothed in Christ

Within the context of this great cosmic shaking, of what significance is the life and death of a single person? In approaching the life to come, we can easily fall into the illusion that David Foster Wallace critiques: "I am the absolute center of the universe, the realest, most vivid and important person in existence." But the great cosmic vision of the day of the Lord, the day of God's judgment, restoration, and consummation, displaces such a self-centered vision. Indeed, what am I but dust, returning to dust? Thousands of people around the world die each day. What could be more predictable for a human—of any culture, creed, or age—than death? In the vast expanse of the cosmos, my death will be like a drop of rain on the ocean—minuscule, utterly expected, and laughably far from earth-altering.

And yet, while the great expanse of God's covenant promises is for the whole of creation, Christian hope meets us in our personal stories of dying as well. As I stood by the bed of one friend facing death, he agonized about angry words that he had spewed at his father shortly before his father's death. That had been decades ago. But repeatedly my friend worried about whether he could be forgiven. "I can't make it right!" he cried to me. His dad was gone. He couldn't reconcile with him. He couldn't receive a word of forgiveness from his dad. He worried that he was not ready to "meet his Maker."

In one of his most personal letters, the apostle Paul wrote from prison to the Christians in Philippi. Perhaps, like others who wrote from prison—such as Martin Luther King Jr. or Desmond Tutu—his mind was stripped of pretension, sharpened to what should be directly spoken. In his opening, Paul prays for his readers that "in the day of Christ," the coming day of the Lord when Christ returns, "you may be pure and blameless" (Phil. 1:10). Yet Paul knows that he himself is not a "pure and blameless" temple of the Lord, able to face judgment on his own. He regards his efforts to be righteous on his own terms as "rubbish"—quite literally, "garbage" or even "excrement, manure" (Phil. 3:8).[25] Instead, as he finds his identity in Christ, his hope is to "gain Christ and be found in him, not having a righteousness of my own that comes from the law, but one that comes through faith in Christ, the righteousness from God based on faith" (Phil. 3:8–9).

My dying friend longed for forgiveness and new life. He longed, ultimately, for something that mortals cannot attain on our own. For Paul, precisely because his confidence was in Christ as the holy temple, the sacrificial priest, and the true king, his own personal death became an opportunity for testimony to Christ's kingship. "Christ will be exalted now as always in my body, whether by life or by death. For to me, living is Christ and dying is gain" (Phil. 1:20–21). Christ, the dwelling place of God, so deeply *owns* Paul that both living and dying will be life with God, life with Christ. Indeed, on the final day, when Christ returns, he "will transform the body of our humiliation that it may be conformed to the body of his glory" (Phil. 3:21). Then our bodies will be soaked in the temple presence, enlivened by the Spirit, through and through.

Throughout his letters, Paul declares that the righteousness and new life for which he hoped are completely outside of his own capacity to produce: his hope is in Christ, the perfect sanctuary and sacrifice, to whom he is united in baptism, in faith, and in the practice of the Lord's Supper.[26] Paul teaches that believers are justified—declared righteous—through faith: "In Christ Jesus you are all children of God through faith. As many of you as were baptized into Christ have clothed yourselves with Christ" (Gal. 3:26–27). Clothed with Christ and declared righteous in God's household, I have a hope that extends to the very end, to the seat of judgment. This gift that will come in fullness in the future, I receive now in part in the preached and sacramental Word received in fellowship—which points beyond itself to a future in which those who have suffered with Christ also participate in his glory. As the risen Christ says in Revelation, at the judgment "I will confess your name before my Father and before his angels"—that is, he will confess the names of those clothed in the robes of righteousness, whose names are in the book of life (Rev. 3:5). My own voice is weak, and the thundering, re-sounding harmony of the heavenly chorus would be just fine without it. "Crown him with many crowns, the Lamb upon his throne." But I'm given hope that even my small voice can join in the praise, because the Christian life is defined by my belonging to Christ and to the future that I enter into through him alone.

## Expecting Oblivion or Expecting God

In our day-to-day lives, do we expect that God himself will be the center of our life's drama, in the end? Do we live in an awareness that this end is, in a real way, already upon us? In a sense, we are all like Job. We are being stripped of our relationships, our possessions, our loves—whether little by little as we age, or in one big loss, as with Job. We have much to lose when illness, accident, and catastrophe hit. The loss of our health, our relationships, our wealth—all of that will eventually come, whether by death or before death. As Jonathan Edwards noted in a sermon on Job, "worldly good things are very uncertain, and oftentimes come to an end before death."[27]

"And what if a man doth live to grow old and none of those acci-dents happen?" Edwards asks. The experiences of Job still ring true. Indeed, "there is but a little part of this life that man is capable of tasting worldly pleasures." Aging itself will break down the body and take away many of our delights. The aging experience mirrors Job's "crash," but it occurs more gradually, over a longer period of time. We are afflicted by illness. Our balance is off; our foot doesn't work; we give up running, driving, or walking. We are no longer able to talk. To eat. Little by little, the indignities of dying take over.[28]

In his novel *Everyman*, Pulitzer Prize–winning author Philip Roth narrates this process in tender detail. The unnamed protagonist, "everyman," lives his life in a way that banks on the present moment, pursuing the liaisons and interests that strike his fancy. At thirty-four, he thinks to himself, "Worry about oblivion . . . when you're seventy-five! The remote future will be time enough to anguish over the ultimate catastrophe!"[29] He takes prides in his stark rejection of religion and the way his unbelief is unsentimental about death. "No hocus-pocus about death and God or obsolete fantasies of heaven for him. There was only our bodies, born to live and die on terms decided by the bodies that had lived and died before us."[30]

And yet, as "everyman" ages, he finds his family unraveling into alienation and his accomplishments dimming. To his surprise, he finds himself in a Job-like story of devastation. He had taken pride in the prowess and powers of his body. But as he loses those capacities, he reflects that "should he ever write an autobiography, he'd call it *The Life and Death of a Male Body*."[31] Indeed, although he thought he had been honest with himself about death—that he was just a dying body, that thoughts of "oblivion" could wait until he was seventy-five—he realizes that he had been assuming another story. "Once one has tasted life, death does not even seem natural. I had thought—*secretly I was certain*—that life goes on and on."[32] Yet here he is, finally facing death as one of the aged, "in the process of becoming less and less and [seeing] his aimless days through to the end as no more than what he was—the aimless days and the uncertain nights and the impotently putting up with the physical deterioration and the terminal sadness and the waiting and waiting for nothing. This is how it works out, he thought, this is what you could not know."[33]

Unlike Job, Philip Roth's "everyman" does not plead with God to show his face or expect an appearance by God. Indeed, the contrast between a Christian approach to dying and a secular one that continually defers reflection on death to another day is not between a story of plenitude (the Christian) and one of loss (the functional agnostic). Both approaches involve bodily and worldly loss. The difference is between expecting oblivion and expecting God. Christian hope expects God to be the unrivaled King in the end, so that sin, the devil, and even death will be destroyed. As the apostle Paul says in his great chapter on the resurrection, the resurrected Christ, as the firstfruits of those resurrected at his second coming, "must reign until he has put all his enemies under his feet. The last enemy to be destroyed is death." And then all will be subjected to the Triune God's rule, "so that God may be all in all" (1 Cor. 15:25–28). The Lord will appear in Christ and deliver a final defeat of the powers of evil. God's royal rule will finally be uncontested, and templelike fellowship will penetrate each body, each worshiping mouth, each molecule of the city of God. "I saw no temple in the city," John of Patmos says, "for its temple is the Lord God the Almighty and the Lamb" (Rev. 21:22). No temple building will be necessary because the whole cosmos will be the temple of the Lord.

## Waiting in Hopeful Praise

On that day there will be no temple. But in the meantime we need our temples—the crumbling temples of our bodies and the imperfect temple of the church—seeking each day anew to offer them as dwelling places to the Lord, Christ Jesus, to whom we belong. In our daily lives we're much like Zechariah. Grateful for the Lord's gifts, he offered himself in worship to the Lord at the temple, even as he and his wife grieved that they "had no children, because Elizabeth was barren, and both were getting on in years" (Luke 1:7). Energized by hope yet still wounded with sorrow, Zechariah nevertheless sought the Lord's presence and entered into the Lord's presence in the holy place. There the Lord appeared through an angel, telling him that he and Elizabeth would receive a taste of new life—a son—but even more importantly, that his son would prepare the way for a much greater theophany, the Savior.

Zechariah didn't believe this word of the Lord at first, and his mouth was silenced. But after Elizabeth's womb received new life and the promised son was born, Zechariah's lips opened to sing a song of praise that was also a prophecy, as it hinged on the coming culmination of God's promise.

> Blessed be the Lord God of Israel,
>> for he has looked favorably on his people and redeemed
>>> them.
> He has raised up a mighty savior for us
>> in the house of his servant David. (Luke 1:68–69)

Zechariah's song culminates in the hope of the Savior who is the King, the son of David. This song points beyond the physical temple's lovely but temporal form to a divine visitation that is yet to come.

> By the tender mercy of our God,
>> the dawn from on high will break upon us,
> to give light to those who sit in darkness and in the shadow of
>> death,
>> to guide our feet into the way of peace. (Luke 1:78–79)

God has tabernacled among us in Christ. But, with Zechariah, we still wait in hopeful praise for the coming "dawn from on high" that "will break upon us." For we are people who know the pit of Sheol. In the words of the psalmist, which Zechariah reflects, we have "sat in darkness and in gloom, / prisoners in misery and in irons" (Ps. 107:10). We are not yet in the promised land, and we pray for full deliverance and freedom to worship the Lord unhindered by our own alienation and rebellion. As we do so, we cry out, "Come, Lord Jesus!"

## Closing Prayer

*Lord, come visit us again, bringing with you the age to come that only you can bring. As ones washed and fed in fellowship with you,*

*O Christ, fill our collapsing bodies and our flawed congregations with your Spirit to give us new life. May the Spirit's work give the world glimpses of your kingship, your sacrificial love, your holy joy and blessedness. As your creatures, we give thanks for the wonders of creation, for each breath, for each taste of communion and fellowship. Until the final day, when dawn breaks upon us from on high and your will is done on earth as it is in heaven, "May our Lord Jesus Christ himself and God our Father, who loved us and through grace gave us eternal comfort and good hope, comfort [our] hearts and strengthen [us] in every good work and word" (2 Thess. 2:16–17). We pray all of this through Jesus Christ. Amen.*

## Discussion Questions

- Sometimes our hope for the age to come is buoyant, as in my own experience of singing songs like "Crown Him with Many Crowns." But sometimes, in the course of daily living, that hope can be crowded out. As you think about your daily experiences, how do you find your Christian hope crowded out? What sorts of things tend to lead to the crowding out of hope in your life?

- Think of a time when your body did not function as you had expected it would. How do experiences like these help us live like we are mortal? Why does that matter as we consider our ultimate hope?

- How do Old Testament stories of barren wombs being filled give us a picture of resurrection hope? Similarly, what characteristics of the temple give us a way to speak about heaven as the dwelling place of God?

- If you can, find a recording of Handel's *Messiah*, specifically the section from Haggai, "Thus Saith the Lord." As you listen,

212 The End of the Christian Life

notice: What does this stir in you as you reflect on the cosmic scope of God's judgment and shaking of the cosmos?

- Many people are comfortable with belief in an afterlife but not with belief in the final judgment. On the other hand, some who have experienced great hardship and oppression feel that hope in a final judgment may be the only way they can overcome the desire for vengeance in the present life. What do you think about a final judgment? If you are uncomfortable with it, how would you articulate that discomfort? How might a final *cosmic* judgment inspire lives of mission and witness in the world?

- As you come to the close of this book—acknowledging your creatureliness and mortality before the everlasting Lord—what is your hope for the life to come?

# Conclusion

You are mortal. You are not indispensable to the world. Your life will come to an end. And yet, in light of genuine Christian hope, a daily embrace of these realities can refresh our parched souls, freeing us to generously love rather than cling to methods of self-preservation. Rather than being a pathway to morbid despair, embracing the daily reminders of our mortal limits can free us to experience sorrow and joy as earthly pilgrims—"strangers and foreigners"—looking forward to a homeland that will be the very home of God (Heb. 11:13).

Although under the shadow of alienation and sin, this world is beautiful and good—"charged with the grandeur of God," in the words of poet Gerard Manley Hopkins. As we look upon lofty trees and hear the calls of birds in the woods, as we encounter a stranger who becomes a friend, and as we participate in corporate songs of praise to the Lamb of God, we glimpse a goodness and love that we could not have generated ourselves. In the sorrows and joys we experience while walking this pilgrim path, we can open our hands to serve and receive. Life is sheer gift.

Even so, our lives are also ephemeral and vanishing. Until heaven and earth come together through the One who comes to make all things new, we still join the psalmist in praying,

> LORD, let me know my end,
>> and what is the measure of my days;
>> let me know how fleeting my life is.
> You have made my days a few handbreadths,
>> and my lifetime is as nothing in your sight. (Ps. 39:4–5)

What is the measure of your days? How do you live each day with the realization that life is fleeting, a few mere breaths before an ever-lasting Lord?

One way is to learn how to live small. During my time in the hospital for cancer treatment, I recall thinking, "Wow—I'm small and expendable to the universe, yet I've still been given breath. What grace is this!" That thought and the accompanying feeling of gratitude sometimes return to me as I experience my body's daily aches and pains. I don't like it when I feel the sharp nerve pain in my feet, like I'm standing on glass; it makes me want to push back and fight it away, or hide, or fume with anger. But gradually I've come to approach this pain with a strange form of gratitude, a recognition that it is not simply an obstacle, a barrier to accomplishing my goals, which can seem all-important in the moment. The pain slows me down, and it can even give me a merciful reminder that I am small, that each and every breath is a gift. Whatever life I've been given, no matter how it compares with the chronological time span of other human beings around me—it is undeserved, radiant light from above that comes down into my pit of Sheol.

At points in this book I've explored the value and joy of living small in this sense. When you are in darkness, in the pit of Sheol, you need not act like a deliverer. You can't make your way out. Open your eyes. Admit it: you have no superpowers. Look toward the light, toward the temple. You are small; you need deliverance. And you are not alone, even in Sheol, for the One who is the light has pioneered the way even into your place of darkness. He's been there already. You're still in the Pit, but you are not alone, and you can look to the day when even this pit will become covered with the radiant light of temple fellowship.

At other times we may not feel stuck in the Pit. Life is busy, full of motion. The music of your own life seems to drown out other sounds. On those days, turn off your phone, stop moving your feet, and look down. Notice the acorns—the beauty of their rough, ridged caps. Pick one up and feel the smooth seed. Sense the wonder of its potential to sprout into a giant oak. These are not realities you can master, and they are not listening to your own song. They are listening to another song—a song of thanks to the Creator.

As you feel the acorn in your fingers, remember those who have died. Many among the dead also admired the acorn. At times those mortals acted as though they were big, invincible; some put their trust in heroes who became tyrants; perhaps they trusted medicine as if it could defeat death, or trusted their own faith in God to bring one life extension after another. They are dead now. That's OK. The world still goes on. We grow old, but the everlasting Lord who upholds the universe does not.

In certain moments, these mortals felt the acorn in their hands, and they were moved to awe. In those moments they remembered that they were small. They took joy in the wonder of the garden in our midst. And some of them looked forward to the garden-temple in the age to come, one with "the river of the water of life, bright as crystal, flowing from the throne of God and of the Lamb." Beside this river is "the tree of life," and "the leaves of the tree are for the healing of the nations" (Rev. 22:1–2). Enjoy, give thanks, and wonder.

Live small when the news headlines make you feel powerless. You cannot fix the great catastrophes of our day. You are impotent, in that sense. But as one who lives small, you can extend hospitality to and make friends with someone the culture says should be your enemy. You can visit an elderly member of your church whose family and friends have died. You can pray a psalm of lament with a family reeling from an unexpected death. You can offer the peace of Christ to a neighbor grieving the burden of guilt or the affliction of violence. You are small, so do small things. Bring a loaf of bread or scones. Bring yourself. Bring a hope in Christ that is durable enough to lament and ache and rejoice and laugh. You can meet others in Sheol, and you can reflect the light of the Deliverer. But you cannot empty out the Pit. You are not the ruler of the universe. Feel the freedom of that as you act in the world.

Small gifts, given and received in gratitude, can open up a wide-angle lens to help us see the fuller picture, to measure our days, as Psalm 39 suggests. The psalmist sees the short breaths of our fleeting life in relation to the broad, expansive horizon of God's eternity; and our lives appear to be nothing in comparison. While this expansive vision may sound life-denying, it's actually life-giving. It can open up our tightened fists and release the flow of love for God and neighbor.

Our culture gives us a liturgy that shapes our loves in a hundred ways each day, teaching us to exalt our own lives and to act as if we belong completely to ourselves. Whether through the algorithms guiding social media or through the profound but often unacknowledged privilege of indoor plumbing and automobiles, the message that is conveyed is clear: we are what matters most. Our to-do lists, the glowing pixels of our cell phones, our aspirations to receive the recognition we're told we deserve—all of these prove we are special. Mortal limits, we assume, shouldn't apply to us.

But the psalmist expresses good news—namely, that orienting our deepest energies toward temporal things is not the true end of the creaturely life. While our goals and strivings and plans may be good and worthy endeavors, investing our deepest loves in them will not lead to true flourishing. Peter Craigie, a particularly insightful Psalms commentator, notes how, for the wide-angle lens of the psalmist, life's value must be understood in light of its finitude. "Life is extremely short," Craigie writes, and "if its meaning is to be found, it must be found in the purpose of God, the giver of all life." Indeed, recognizing the "transitory nature" of our lives is "a starting point in achieving the sanity of a pilgrim in an otherwise mad world."[1] Craigie wrote these words in 1983, in the first of three planned volumes on the Psalms in a prestigious scholarly commentary series. Two years later he died in a car accident, leaving his commentary incomplete. He was forty-seven.

Craigie's life was taken before he and his loved ones expected, before he could accomplish his good and worthy goals. Yet in his transient life he bore witness to the breathtaking horizon of eternity. He bore witness to how embracing our mortal limits goes hand in hand with offering our mortal bodies to the Lord of life. We're not heroes of the world, and we can't do much. But we can love generously, and we can bear witness to the One who is the origin and end of life itself—the everlasting Lord, the Alpha and the Omega, the crucified and risen Savior who has accomplished and will bring about what we could never bring about ourselves.

To what and to whom do we give ourselves in this short life? In our day, unprecedented innovations in technology can give us a sense of mastery over our world. As we've explored in this book, the dying are often put out of sight, into institutions. Visionary prophets of medicine and the grind of endless medical options can give us the impression that the realities of unsolvable pain and mortality apply to other people, not to ourselves. An ever-increasing number of Christians, it seems, assume that God promises health and financial prosperity if the right formula is used in prayer. We can be masters.

Alongside this sense of mastery and invulnerability, however, is another trend of more people reporting deep loneliness, of feeling alienated and exhausted. In the words of one commentator, our culture, which tends to put the individual at the center and our mortal limits on the sideline, has become "a conspiracy against joy."[2] Joy is not found in living as if we are immortal—or in a universe that always conforms to our wishes. Joy is found in giving ourselves away, in all of our temporal and crumbling weakness. Joy, for the Christian, is delight in the gift of the Spirit's presence as we are "given up to death for Jesus' sake, so that the life of Jesus may be made visible in our mortal flesh" (2 Cor. 4:11). We experience joy when we turn *toward* the wounds of our mortal limits, leaping into the arms of the living Lord, offering our bodies back to God as temples, hoping for the return of Christ, who is our life. He will appear on the final day and make things right.

In our anxious age, in which shots of adrenaline and distracting tweets seem to provide the winning combination in the race for status, we have good news that can slow our speeding heartbeats and calm our shaking hands. There is a promised land, and we can feel its cleansing in the waters of baptism; we can savor its taste in the bread and the wine of the Lord's Supper; we can hear its echo in the Word proclaimed to us in worship. There is a land of milk and honey, and we can long for it.

Indeed, the promised land, the temple of Zion, has come to us. The Lord's holy and merciful presence has dwelt in our midst. Heaven and earth have come together in Jesus Christ, who embodies the holy of holies in his person; he offers himself as a sacrifice and makes a way for our flesh to enter into the very life of God through Christ.

Yes, taste the sweetness of fellowship with Christ with the brothers and sisters in your adopted family, the church; delight in the garden of creation in our midst.

But also remember that we haven't yet reached the promised land, and our feet won't make it there by our own persistent efforts. You can breathe a sigh of relief as your great utopian plans are allowed to crumble. The kingdom has not come in its fullness, and we cannot bring it in. You are liberated to delight in the acorn, to love the neighbors forgotten in the shadows. Together we're freed to lift our frail voices to join a multitude of others in resounding praise, trusting that even when our voices cease, the song will continue.

A few times a year, with the gracious permission of my wife and kids, I go away to a monastery in the woods for several days. I leave my phone in the car—the place is too remote for cell phone coverage anyway. Walking in the forest, I hear the sounds of frogs and crickets and occasionally what I suspect is a snake sliding through the grass. I join the monks in praying the Psalms at various times during the day in the chapel—a dark space with long shadows, illuminated mainly by tiny lamps to show us the pages of our Psalters. But on days when the sun hangs bright in a cloudless sky, natural light breaks into the chapel through high windows, cutting through the dark shadows in laser-like beams.

In the chapel, we join our voices to pray the words of the Psalms in unison—words of anger and joy, gratitude and vengeance, thanksgiving and frustration. After each psalm, whether a searing lament or a soaring psalm of praise, we stand, bow slightly forward, and pray these words of doxology: "Glory be to the Father, and to the Son, and to the Holy Spirit. As it was in the beginning, is now, and ever shall be, world without end."

Outside the chapel, a cemetery lies in an area cleared of trees. The cemetery has several dozen simple graves. Each has a white cross engraved with the name of a monk, along with the years of his birth and death. As I stand by a cross that marks one of the more recent graves, I consider how that monk had prayed the Psalms, giving glory to the Trinity, not long ago, just a few hundred yards away. When he prayed, the monk knew that his body would not have far to travel after he breathed his last. Even more important to this monk, I suspect, was his trust that the Psalms and prayers in the sanctuary would carry on, even without his voice.

Walking through the woods and back to the chapel, I realize that these Psalms and praises are being prayed as I live my busy life back home, whether or not my voice is joining in. Tightened muscles in my back loosen and release as I consider how this doxology will continue, even when my voice is silenced. In the meantime, however, I want to join the birds and the trees and the rest of creation in the grand melody of adoration to the everlasting Lord. I live in hope that the frailty and decay of my body will not be the final measure of my life, but that on the final day my renewed body will lift up a voice to join the multitude in the song of praise. I sing now as one whose life is "hidden with Christ in God." From that place of hiddenness, I look forward to the end. "When Christ who is your life is revealed, then you also will be revealed with him in glory" (Col. 3:3–4).

*Glory be to the Father, and to the Son, and to the Holy Spirit. As it was in the beginning, is now, and ever shall be, world without end. Amen.*

# *Acknowledgments*

Each breath is a gift, and I am indebted to the insights and labor of many mortals who helped breathe life into this book. I thank God for them.

Early in my research process, the invitation to lecture on death and dying at Trinity Evangelical Divinity School gave me an opportunity to probe the topic both sociologically and theologically. Then in 2016 I received a generous grant from the Louisville Institute to fund a series of colloquies entitled "Congregational Life and the Dying: Cultivating Resurrection Hope in a Medicalized Age," which put pastors and scholars in conversation. The contributions of a wide range of scholars were invaluable in these colloquies, but the core group of pastors involved especially helped shape my thoughts: Ann Conklin, Katlyn DeVries, Travis Else, Tyler Johnson, Phil Letizia, and Noah and Kristen Livingston. Your insights into the issues that are central for congregations today helped guide my reflections, and many of you later gave input on drafts of this book. I am grateful!

After several years of exploring death and dying in a broader way, I developed a strategy for pursuing the topic in this book, which focuses not only on medical care and the end of life but also on the mortality of all Christians as a reality that God uses in the Christian life. This strategy required moving beyond the usual academic approach of describing and analyzing the concepts in the relevant literature. Instead, my goal has been to weave together the narrative, sociological, and theological aspects of death and dying in a more organic way. For this process, Brazos Press provided invaluable help through the work of Arika Theule-VanDam and Tim West as well as Bob Hosack and Jim Kinney. I would have made little progress on this path apart from the astute feedback of students and pastors who read multiple drafts of each chapter. My thanks to Jake Chipka, Anne Elzinga, Anna Erickson, Ross Hoekstra, Katy Johnson, Nathan Longfield, Cassie Nelson-Rogalski, Sara Sanchez-Timmer, James Schetelich, and Brandon and Stephanie Smith. A special thanks to Katlyn DeVries and Emily Holehan, who not only provided incredibly valuable feedback but also gave vital administrative support for the colloquies.

I have many fellow scholars and writers to thank as well. Thank you to Matthew Levering and David Luy for inviting me to the 2016 colloquy of the Chicago Theological Initiative, which focused on Christian approaches to death and dying. The stellar group of historians and theologians at the colloquy pushed my own reflections to deeper levels, and I am in their debt. I am also indebted to Michael Allen, Sarah Arthur, Suzanne McDonald, and Deanna Thompson for helpful feedback on drafts of various chapters. Psychology professor Daryl van Tongeren gave me an orientation to the work of terror management theory and was my companion in admiring Ernest Becker's astonishing book *The Denial of Death*. I'm grateful to two biblical scholars, my wife, Rachel Billings, and Jon Levenson, who was her PhD adviser at Harvard, for providing crucial insights that led to the overall movement of the book from Sheol to the temple.

Finally, I am grateful for the countless conversations with other cancer patients and their caretakers, which provided wisdom and insight throughout my research and writing. I thank God for all of you.

This book is dedicated to my parents, Tom and Nancy Billings. Thank you for your durable love, extending to both my body and my soul. This helped prepare me not only for life but for death as well. I love you.

# *Notes*

## Introduction

1. Benedict, *The Rule of Saint Benedict*, trans. Leonard Doyle (Collegeville, MN: Liturgical Press, 2001), 35.

2. "SENS Research Foundation: Our Research," https://www.sens.org/our-research/.

3. Aubrey de Grey, "Aubrey de Grey, Fully Aubrey David Nicholas Jasper de Grey: Great Thoughts Treasury," accessed April 9, 2020, http://www.greatthoughtstreasury .com/author/aubrey-de-grey-fully-aubrey-david-nicholas-jasper-de-grey.

4. Jonathan Edwards, *Letters and Personal Writings*, vol. 16 of *The Works of Jonathan Edwards*, ed. George S. Claghorn (New Haven: Yale University Press, 1998), 753.

5. By "terminal" cancer, I mean an incurable cancer that leads to death, if death does not come by some other means. I have a terminal cancer in this sense. Sometimes "terminal" is used to refer to illnesses in the final months before death. But thankfully, recent treatments have helped to slow the progression of my cancer.

6. Nabih Bulos, "For Former U.S. Special Forces Operative Turned Aid Worker, a Dramatic Rescue in Mosul," *Los Angeles Times*, June 16, 2017, https://www.latimes .com/world/la-fg-iraq-mosul-eubank-20170616-story.html.

7. J. Todd Billings, *Rejoicing in Lament: Wrestling with Incurable Cancer and Life in Christ* (Grand Rapids: Brazos, 2015).

8. For an illuminating description of this mutual haunting within a cross-pressured identity, see James K. A. Smith, *How (Not) to Be Secular: Reading Charles Taylor* (Grand Rapids: Eerdmans, 2014), 3–17.

9. Charles Taylor, *A Secular Age* (Cambridge, MA: Belknap, 2007), 302.

10. Augustine, *Sermon 52*, in *The Cambridge Edition of Early Christian Writings*, vol. 1, *God*, ed. Andrew Radde-Gallwitz, trans. Mark DelCogliano (Cambridge: Cambridge University Press, 2017), 321.

11. Franciscus Junius, *A Treatise on True Theology with the Life of Franciscus Junius*, trans. David C. Noe (Grand Rapids: Reformation Heritage Books, 2014), 119–20.

12. *The 1979 Book of Common Prayer* (Oxford: Oxford University Press, 2005), 184.

13. Joel Osteen, *Your Best Life Now: 7 Steps to Living at Your Full Potential*, rev. and exp. ed. (New York: FaithWords, 2015).

## Chapter 1: Welcome to Sheol

1. See Jon D. Levenson, *Resurrection and the Restoration of Israel: The Ultimate Victory of the God of Life* (New Haven: Yale University Press, 2008), 94–97.

2. Levenson, *Resurrection and the Restoration of Israel*, 95.

3. Sheryl Sandberg and Adam Grant, *Option B: Facing Adversity, Building Resilience, and Finding Joy* (New York: Knopf, 2017), 6.

4. Heidelberg Catechism, Question and Answer 44, in *Our Faith: Ecumenical Creeds, Reformed Confessions, and Other Resources* (Grand Rapids: Faith Alive Christian Resources, 2013), 83. The Heidelberg Catechism uses this as a gloss for the "descent into hell" in the Apostles' Creed. Whether or not one receives it in that sense, I take it as a profound reflection on the significance of Christ's cross-shaped suffering. For an illuminating account of the Apostles' Creed's "descent into hell" as a "descent to the dead," I recommend Matthew Y. Emerson, *"He Descended to the Dead": An Evangelical Theology of Holy Saturday* (Downers Grove, IL: IVP Academic, 2019).

5. Thomas Lynch, *The Undertaking: Life Studies from the Dismal Trade* (New York: Norton, 2009), 36.

6. Atul Gawande, *Being Mortal: Medicine and What Matters in the End* (New York: Picador, 2017), 6.

7. Ludwig Wittgenstein, *Tractatus Logico-Philosophicus*, trans. D. F. Pears and B. F. McGuinness (London: Routledge, 1961), 72.

8. Douglas J. Moo and Jonathan A. Moo, *Creation Care: A Biblical Theology of the Natural World* (Grand Rapids: Zondervan Academic, 2018), 73–76.

9. Charles Duhigg, *Smarter Faster Better: The Transformative Power of Real Productivity* (New York: Random House, 2017), 24.

10. Duhigg, *Smarter Faster Better*, 20.

11. C. S. Lewis, *A Grief Observed* (San Francisco: HarperOne, 2001), 3.

12. Joan Didion, *The Year of Magical Thinking* (New York: Vintage, 2007), 28.

13. Didion, *Year of Magical Thinking*, 30.

14. Geoffrey Gorer, *Death, Grief, and Mourning* (Garden City, NY: Doubleday, 1965), xiii.

15. Gorer, *Death, Grief, and Mourning*, quoted in Didion, *Year of Magical Thinking*, 60.

16. Emily Post, *Etiquette in Society, in Business, in Politics and at Home* (New York: Funk & Wagnalls, 1922), 388.

17. Christian Wiman, *My Bright Abyss: Meditation of a Modern Believer* (New York: Farrar, Straus & Giroux, 2014), 56.

18. Jonathan Haidt, *The Happiness Hypothesis: Finding Modern Truth in Ancient Wisdom* (New York: Basic Books, 2005), 82.

19. Gawande, *Being Mortal*, 8.

## Chapter 2: Two Views of Mortality

1. J. R. R. Tolkien, *The Silmarillion* (Boston: Houghton Mifflin Harcourt, 2012), xiv–xv.

2. Ephraim Radner, *A Time to Keep: Theology, Mortality, and the Shape of a Human Life* (Waco: Baylor University Press, 2017), 128.

3. Radner, *Time to Keep*, 128.

4. Irenaeus, *Against Heresies* 2.22.4, in *The Ante-Nicene Fathers*, ed. and trans. A. Roberts, J. Donaldson, and A. C. Coxe (Grand Rapids: Eerdmans, 1956), 1:391.

5. John C. Cavadini, "Two Ancient Christian Views on Suffering and Death," in *Christian Dying: Witnesses from the Tradition*, ed. George Kalantzis and Matthew Levering (Eugene, OR: Cascade Books, 2018), 99. I am indebted to Cavadini for this metaphor, as well as for his illuminating comparison of Irenaeus and Augustine on death, which informs my account.

6. Irenaeus, *Against Heresies* 3.19.3, quoted in Kalantzis and Levering, *Christian Dying*, 102.

7. Irenaeus, *Against Heresies* 4.38.1, quoted in Kalantzis and Levering, *Christian Dying*, 100.

8. According to *The Martyrdom of Polycarp*, in *The Ante-Nicene Fathers: Translations of the Writings of the Fathers down to A.D. 325*, ed. Alexander Roberts and James Donaldson (Buffalo, 1887), 1:39–44.

9. Augustine, *Augustine: Earlier Writings*, ed. and trans. J. H. S. Burleigh (Louisville: Westminster John Knox, 1953), 58.

10. Augustine, *City of God* 13.15, trans. Henry Bettenson (New York: Penguin, 2004), 524.

11. Helmut Thielicke, *Death and Life* (Philadelphia: Fortress, 1970), 105 (emphasis added).

12. Augustine, *City of God* 13.11 (trans. Bettenson, 520).

13. Augustine, *Confessions* 2.4, trans. R. S. Pine-Coffin (Harmondsworth, UK: Penguin, 1961), 47.

14. Augustine, *City of God* 13.15 (trans. Bettenson, 524).

15. Augustine, *Homilies on the Gospel of St. John* 36.4, in *The Nicene and Post-Nicene Fathers*, ed. Philip Schaff, trans. John Gibb and James Innes (Grand Rapids: Eerdmans, 1978), 7:209.

16. Augustine, *Homilies on the Gospel of St. John* 36.4, in *The Nicene and Post-Nicene Fathers*, 7:209.

17. Augustine, *Sermon* 317, quoted in Arthur A. Just Jr., ed., *Luke*, Ancient Christian Commentary on Scripture: New Testament 3 (Downers Grove, IL: InterVarsity, 2003), 361.

18. P. D. James, *A Certain Justice* (New York: Knopf, 1997), 247–48.

## Chapter 3: Mortals in Denial

1. Quoted in Thomas Dekker, *Four Birds of Noah's Ark: A Prayer Book from the Time of Shakespeare*, ed. Robert Hudson (Grand Rapids: Eerdmans, 2017), 150.

2. Sander L. Koole, Tom Pyszczynski, and Sheldon Solomon, "The Cultural Animal: Twenty Years of Terror Management Theory and Research," in *Handbook of Experimental Existential Psychology*, ed. Jeff Greenberg, Sander L. Koole, and Tom Pyszczynski (New York: Guilford, 2004), 16.

3. Peter Brown, *Augustine of Hippo: A Biography* (Berkeley: University of California Press, 2013), 39.

4. John Calvin, *Commentary on the Psalms, 1845–49*, trans. James Anderson (Edinburgh: Calvin Translation Society, 1847), 464.

5. Ernest Becker, *The Denial of Death* (New York: Free Press, 1997), 16.

6. Becker, *Denial of Death*, 17.

7. Becker, *Denial of Death*, xvii.

8. Becker, *Denial of Death*, 86.

9. Michael S. Roth, "Why Freud Still Haunts Us," World.edu, September 23, 2014, https://world.edu/why-freud-still-haunts-us/.

10. Becker, *Denial of Death*, 99.

11. Otto Rank, *"Will Therapy" and "Truth and Reality"* (New York: Knopf, 1968), 121–22, 155, quoted in Becker, *Denial of Death*, 100.

12. Gregory Zilboorg, *Psychoanalysis and Religion* (New York: Farrar, Straus and Cudahy, 1962), 255, quoted in Becker, *Denial of Death*, 122–23.

13. Koole, Pyszczynski, and Solomon, "Cultural Animal," 23.

14. See Leonard L. Martin, W. Keith Campbell, and Christopher D. Henry, "The Road of Awakening: Mortality Acknowledgment as a Call to Authentic Living," in *Handbook of Experimental Existential Psychology*, ed. Jeff Greenberg, Sander L. Koole, and Tom Pyszczynski (New York: The Guilford Press, 2004), 436.

15. Becker, *Denial of Death*, 159.

16. Becker, *Denial of Death*, 182–88.

17. Becker, *Denial of Death*, 177–78.

18. Paul Kalanithi, *When Breath Becomes Air* (New York: Random House, 2016), 161–62.

19. Becker, *Denial of Death*, 166.

20. For a development of this theme in light of the work of Becker, see Richard Beck, *The Slavery of Death* (Eugene, OR: Cascade Books, 2013), 44–58.

## Chapter 4: Interplanetary Exploration

1. Kate Bowler, "What to Say When You Meet the Angel of Death at a Party," *New York Times*, January 26, 2018, https://www.nytimes.com/2018/01/26/opinion/sunday/cancer-what-to-say.html.

2. See National Center for Health Statistics, *Vital Statistics of the United States, 1994*, preprint of vol. 2, *Mortality*, part A, § 6 life tables, Centers for Disease Control and Prevention, March 1998, https://www.cdc.gov/nchs/data/lifetables/life94_2.pdf; "Uganda—Life Expectancy at Birth [1994]," Countryeconomy.com, https://country economy.com/demography/life-expectancy/uganda?year=1994.

3. This section draws from my unpublished 1995 manuscript "A Stumbling Block," a nonfiction essay written shortly after my time in Uganda. As with other personal stories in this book, names have been altered.

4. Ephraim Radner, "Whistling Past the Grave," *First Things*, November 2016, 39–44, https://www.firstthings.com/article/2016/11/whistling-past-the-grave. I borrow the phrase "the great health transition" from Radner. I am indebted to his analysis both in this article and in his fine book *A Time to Keep: Theology, Mortality, and the Shape of a Human Life* (Waco: Baylor University Press, 2017).

5. Data taken from the US Department of Health and Human Services; see *2017 Profile of Older Americans* (Administration for Community Living and Administration on Aging, April 2018), 3, https://acl.gov/sites/default/files/Aging%20and%20Disability %20in%20America/2017OlderAmericansProfile.pdf.

6. John Calvin, *Treatises against the Anabaptists and against the Libertines*, trans. and ed. Benjamin Wirt Farley (Grand Rapids: Baker Academic, 2001), 322.

7. Mark Scarlata, *The Abiding Presence: A Theological Commentary on Exodus* (London: SCM, 2018), 190. As Scarlata points out, a fundamental difference between the tabernacle and the idol of the golden calf is that the calf is a self-initiated, self-made way to attempt to approach the Lord.

8. Radner, *Time to Keep*, 25.

9. James K. A. Smith, *You Are What You Love: The Spiritual Power of Habit* (Grand Rapids: Brazos, 2016), 46.

10. Smith, *You Are What You Love*, 44, emphasis in original.

11. Smith, *You Are What You Love*, 46.

12. Radner, *Time to Keep*, 25.

13. On this point: many hospices provide a very helpful counterliturgy, in that medical interventions in hospice are sufficiently minimal so that loved ones can be present with the dying. After death, they are allowed to touch and spend time with the body of the deceased, rather than treating the body as a contagion.

14. James K. A. Smith, "The Cultural Liturgy of Dying" (lecture given at "Congregational Life and the Dying: Renewing Resurrection Hope in a Medical Age," a colloquy sponsored by the Louisville Institute at Western Theological Seminary, Holland, MI, October 13, 2016).

15. My thought on this point has been influenced by the probing analysis of Thomas G. Long in *Accompany Them with Singing: The Christian Funeral* (Louisville: Westminster John Knox, 2009).

16. Caitlin Doughty, *Smoke Gets in Your Eyes: And Other Lessons from the Crematory* (New York: Norton, 2015), 234.

17. Atul Gawande, *Being Mortal: Medicine and What Matters in the End* (New York: Picador, 2017), 156.

18. Gawande, *Being Mortal*, 9.

19. Gawande, *Being Mortal*, 9.

20. Martin Luther, *Luther's Works*, vol. 42, *Devotional Writings I*, ed. Helmut T. Lehmann and Martin O. Dietrich (Philadelphia: Fortress, 1969), 101–2.

21. Luther, *Luther's Works*, 42:99.

22. Martin Luther, "The Holy and Blessed Sacrament of Baptism, 1519," in *The Annotated Luther*, vol. 1, *The Roots of Reform*, ed. Timothy J. Wengert, trans. Dirk G. Lange (Minneapolis: Fortress, 2015), 209, quoted in David Luy, "Dying for the Last Time: Martin Luther on Christian Death," in *Christian Dying: Witnesses from the Tradition*, ed. George Kalantzis and Matthew Levering (Eugene, OR: Cascade Books, 2018), 158. I am indebted to Luy's insightful essay in my account of Luther on this point.

23. Quoted in Luy, "Dying for the Last Time," 142.

24. Martin Luther, *Treatise on Good Works, 1520*, ed. Timothy J. Wengert, The Annotated Luther Study Edition (Minneapolis: Fortress, 2016), 156.

25. "If you want to be cured of your sin, you must not pull back from God but run to him with more confidence than ever, entreating him as if you had suddenly been struck with some physical malady" (Luther, *Treatise on Good Works*, 313).

26. Luther, *Treatise on Good Works*, 328.

27. Kelly M. Kapic, "Faith, Hope and Love: A Theological Meditation on Suffering and Sanctification," in *Sanctification: Explorations in Theology and Practice*,

ed. Kelly M. Kapic (Downers Grove, IL: IVP Academic, 2014), 220. My account of Luther on this point draws upon Kapic's excellent essay.

28. Quoted from Luther's "Fourteen Consolations," in Kapic, "Faith, Hope and Love," 228.

## Chapter 5: The Way of Prosperity and the Christian Way

1. Jim Bakker, *Eight Keys to Success* (Charlotte: PTL Television Network, 1980), 30.

2. I adapt here from the thesis of the excellent book by Rankin Wilbourne and Brian Gregor, *The Cross before Me: Reimagining the Way to the Good Life* (Colorado Springs: David C. Cook, 2019), 28.

3. Gerard A. Silvestri et al., "Importance of Faith on Medical Decisions regarding Cancer Care," *Journal of Clinical Oncology* 21, no. 7 (April 1, 2003): 1379–82.

4. Tracy A. Balboni et al., "Religiousness and Spiritual Support among Advanced Cancer Patients and Associations with End-of-Life Treatment Preferences and Quality of Life," *Journal of Clinical Oncology* 25, no. 5 (February 10, 2007): 555–60.

5. See Lee Caplan et al., "Religiosity after a Diagnosis of Cancer among Older Adults," *Journal of Religion, Spirituality and Aging* 26, no. 4 (January 1, 2014): 357–69.

6. Clay Routledge, *Supernatural: Death, Meaning, and the Power of the Invisible World* (New York: Oxford University Press, 2018), 123–46.

7. Quoted in Christian Wiman, *My Bright Abyss: Meditation of a Modern Believer* (New York: Farrar, Straus & Giroux, 2014), 143.

8. Atul Gawande, *Being Mortal: Medicine and What Matters in the End* (New York: Picador, 2017), 174.

9. Gawande, *Being Mortal*, 171–72.

10. Holly Prigerson et al., "Religious Coping and Use of Intensive Life-Prolonging Care Near Death in Patients with Advanced Cancer," *Journal of the American Medical Association* 301, no. 11 (March 18, 2009): 1140–47. "Our study sample was predominantly Christian" (1146).

11. See Balboni et al., "Religiousness and Spiritual Support among Advanced Cancer Patients."

12. Joseph Brownstein, "Finding Religion at the End of Life: Patients of Faith Seek Lifesaving Care," ABC News, March 17, 2009, https://abcnews.go.com/Health/Mind MoodNews/story?id=7105959&page=1.

13. Atul Gawande, "What Should Medicine Do When It Can't Save You?," *The New Yorker*, July 26, 2010, https://www.newyorker.com/magazine/2010/08/02/letting-go-2.

14. "Spirit and Power—A 10-Country Survey of Pentecostals," Pew Research Center's Religion and Public Life Project, October 5, 2006, https://www.pewresearch.org /wp-content/uploads/sites/7/2006/10/pentecostals-08.pdf, p. 30.

15. "Spirit and Power—A 10-Country Survey of Pentecostals."

16. Joseph Prince, "God's Promises," Joseph Prince Ministries, https://www.joseph prince.org/blog/gods-promises.

17. Prince, "God's Promises."

18. Ralph P. Martin, *2 Corinthians*, Word Biblical Commentary 40 (Waco: Nelson, 1985), 412.

19. Martin, *2 Corinthians*, 412. For an exploration of the broader biblical and theological issues raised by the notion of a "divine passive" and evil, see J. Todd Billings,

*Rejoicing in Lament: Wrestling with Incurable Cancer and Life in Christ* (Grand Rapids: Brazos, 2015), chaps. 3–4.

20. Prince, "God's Promises."

21. Victor Paul Furnish, *II Corinthians* (Garden City, NY: Doubleday, 1984), 550.

22. Martin Luther, *Luther's Works*, ed. Jaroslav Pelikan (St. Louis: Concordia, 1955), 30:126.

23. "The gospel writers carefully insist that faith itself is not the cause of miracles," Crump argues. Often Jesus performs miracles "in spite of the disciples' lack of faith," and he performs others "quite independently of any apparent faith." See Crump, *Knocking on Heaven's Door: A New Testament Theology of Petitionary Prayer* (Grand Rapids: Baker Academic, 2006), 42–45.

24. As shown by Kate Bowler, who makes this link. See Bowler, *Blessed: A History of the American Prosperity Gospel* (New York: Oxford University Press, 2018), 18–20.

25. Bowler, *Blessed*, 329.

26. Bowler, *Blessed*, 18.

27. Marianne Meye Thompson, *Colossians and Philemon*, The Two Horizons New Testament Commentary (Grand Rapids: Eerdmans, 2005), 73.

28. Heidelberg Catechism, Question and Answer 1, in *Our Faith: Ecumenical Creeds, Reformed Confessions, and Other Resources* (Grand Rapids: Faith Alive Christian Resources, 2013), 69.

## Chapter 6: The Fracturing of Our Stories, and Life after Death

1. Jeremy Begbie makes this point eloquently in *Resounding Truth: Christian Wisdom in the World of Music* (Grand Rapids: Baker Academic, 2007), 277–94.

2. James L. Kugel, *In the Valley of the Shadow: On the Foundations of Religious Belief* (New York: Free Press, 2011), 2.

3. New Testament scholars are not sure what Hebrew or Greek version of Isa. 25:8 Paul is quoting when he says, "Death has been swallowed up in victory." But his Greek tense makes it clear that this accomplished victory will be received in the future at the coming resurrection.

4. Gerald L. Bray, ed., *1–2 Corinthians*, Ancient Christian Commentary on Scripture: New Testament 7, 2nd ed. (Downers Grove, IL: IVP Academic, 2006), 182.

5. The Apostles' Creed, in *Our Faith: Ecumenical Creeds, Reformed Confessions, and Other Resources* (Grand Rapids: Faith Alive Christian Resources, 2013), 13.

6. For an insightful account of how cancer patients, in particular, experience a traumatic rupture in their life stories, and how Christians can relate this ongoing trauma to their faith, I highly recommend Deanna Thompson, *Glimpsing Resurrection: Cancer, Trauma, and Ministry* (Louisville: Westminster John Knox, 2018).

7. Maggie Fox, "Fewer Americans Believe in God—Yet They Still Believe in Afterlife," NBC News, March 21, 2016, https://www.nbcnews.com/better/wellness/fewer-americans-believe-god-yet-they-still-believe-afterlife-n542966.

8. Fox, "Fewer Americans Believe in God."

9. Robert Green, *George Bush: Business Executive and U.S. President* (Chicago: Ferguson, 2000), 39.

10. Michael Brice-Saddler and Steve Hendrix, "George and Barbara Bush Never Stopped Agonizing over the Death of Their 3-Year-Old, Robin," *Washington Post*,

December 6, 2018, https://www.washingtonpost.com/history/2018/12/06/george-barbara
-bush-never-stopped-agonizing-over-death-their-year-old-robin/.

11. Brice-Saddler and Hendrix, "George and Barbara Bush."

12. For a helpful account of the way in which 1 Thess. 4–5 looks toward the "day of the Lord" as one, great cosmic event involving the return of Christ in glory and the resurrection of the dead, see Anthony Hoekema, *The Bible and the Future* (Grand Rapids: Eerdmans, 1979), 164–72.

13. Some Christian scholars call into question the mode and possibility of the intermediate state because they embrace an anthropology in which the person's identity is completely inseparable from a physical body (physicalism). While this raises a set of theological issues that I cannot address here, Princeton Seminary's Dale Allison provides an important judgment on how the New Testament material relates to this question, observing that "the New Testament doesn't anticipate physicalism. Matthew, Mark, the author of Luke-Acts, John, and Paul as well as the authors of Hebrews, James, 1 Peter, 2 Peter, and Revelation all believed that the self or some part of it could leave the body and even survive without it." Dale Allison Jr., *Night Comes: Death, Imagination, and the Last Things* (Grand Rapids: Eerdmans, 2016), 33.

14. Sigmund Freud, *Reflections on War and Death* (New York: Moffat, Yard and Co., 1918), 41.

15. Anthony C. Thiselton, *Life after Death: A New Approach to the Last Things* (Grand Rapids: Eerdmans, 2011), 20.

16. Thiselton, *Life after Death*, 21.

17. Karl Barth, *Church Dogmatics* (Edinburgh: T&T Clark, 1956), III/2, 589. Barth gives a probing exploration of these Old Testament themes about death in *Church Dogmatics* III/2, 587–95.

18. Carol Zaleski, *The Life of the World to Come: Near-Death Experience and Christian Hope* (New York: Oxford University Press, 1996), 14.

19. Joshua J. Mark, "Ramesses II," *Ancient History Encyclopedia*, September 2, 2009, https://www.ancient.eu/Ramesses_II/.

20. For an overview of the biblical material suggesting that the intermediate state involves an entry into the conscious presence of Christ, see Hoekema, *The Bible and the Future*, 94–108.

21. "Give Me Jesus (First Version)," NegroSpirituals.com, https://www.negrospiri
tuals.com/songs/give_me_jesus1.htm.

22. Raymond Moody, *Life after Life: The Bestselling Original Investigation That Revealed "Near-Death Experiences,"* special anniversary ed. (New York: HarperOne, 2015), 17, 19.

23. Moody, *Life after Life*, 21–26.

24. Moody, *Life after Life*, 47.

25. Moody, *Life after Life*, 52–53.

26. Moody, *Life after Life*, 58.

27. Moody, *Life after Life*, 72–73.

28. Moody, *Life after Life*, 8.

29. Moody, *Life after Life*, 7.

30. Moody, *Life after Life*, 176.

31. Moody, *Life after Life*, xix.

32. "*Heaven Is for Real* among Amazon's All-Time Best Sellers," Alive Literary Agency (blog), October 8, 2015, https://aliveliterary.com/heaven-is-for-real-among -amazons-all-time-best-sellers/.

33. Indeed, the intrigue of these stories in our "scientific age" underlies the popularity of Dr. Neal's book, as well as of Eben Alexander's 2012 book, *Proof of Heaven: A Neurosurgeon's Journey into the Afterlife* (New York: Simon & Schuster, 2012).

34. Maud Newton, "My Son Went to Heaven, and All I Got Was a No. 1 Best Seller," *New York Times*, April 27, 2012, https://www.nytimes.com/2012/04/29/magazine/my -son-went-to-heaven-and-all-i-got-was-a-no-1-best-seller.html.

35. Todd Burpo with Lynn Vincent, *Heaven Is for Real: A Little Boy's Astounding Story of His Trip to Heaven and Back* (Nashville: Nelson, 2010), 63.

36. See, e.g., Karlis Osis and Erlendur Haraldsson, *At the Hour of Death: A New Look at Evidence for Life after Death*, 3rd ed. (Norwalk, CT: Hastings House, 1997), 40, 69, 73.

37. Eben Alexander, "My Experience in Coma," http://ebenalexander.com/about /my-experience-in-coma/.

38. See Carol Zaleski, *Otherworld Journeys: Accounts of Near-Death Experience in Medieval and Modern Times* (New York: Oxford University Press, 1988); and Zaleski, *The Life of the World to Come: Near-Death Experience and Christian Hope* (New York: Oxford University Press, 1996).

39. Zaleski, *Otherworld Journeys*, 89.

40. Gregory I, *Dialogues*, as quoted in Zaleski, *Otherworld Journeys*, 89.

41. Zaleski, *Otherworld Journeys*, 88–89.

42. Jonathan Merritt, "Heaven and Near-Death Experiences: Separating Fact from Fiction," Religion News Service, January 1, 2016, https://religionnews.com/2016/01/01 /heaven-and-near-death-experiences-separating-fact-from-fiction/.

43. On this point see Alvin Plantinga, *Warrant and Proper Function* (New York: Oxford University Press, 1993), especially chap. 1.

44. See John Calvin, *Institutes of the Christian Religion*, ed. John T. McNeill, trans. Ford Lewis Battles (Philadelphia: Westminster John Knox, 1960), 1.4.1, 1.5.8.

45. Clay Routledge, *Supernatural: Death, Meaning, and the Power of the Invisible World* (New York: Oxford University Press, 2018), 36.

46. Routledge, *Supernatural*, 37.

47. Routledge, *Supernatural*, 40.

48. Routledge, *Supernatural*, 171.

49. Routledge, *Supernatural*, 122.

50. Routledge, *Supernatural*, 29.

51. C. S. Lewis, *God in the Dock* (Grand Rapids: Eerdmans, 2014), 58.

52. Lewis, *God in the Dock*, 59.

53. Lewis, *God in the Dock*, 60.

## Chapter 7: Hoping for the End as Mortals

1. See "Crown Him with Many Crowns," lyrics by Matthew Bridges (1851); see Hymnary.org, https://hymnary.org/text/crown_him_with_many_crowns.

2. David Foster Wallace, "This Is Water" (commencement address, Kenyon College, May 21, 2005). This quotation is from an adapted version in "David Foster Wallace

on Life and Work," *Wall Street Journal*, September 19, 2008, https://www.wsj.com /articles/SB122178211966454607.

3. My thanks to Emily Holehan for this point. On the Modeh Ani, see Tzvi Freeman, "Modeh Ani," Chabad.org, https://www.chabad.org/library/article_cdo/aid/1466224 /jewish/Modeh-Ani.htm.

4. Martin Luther, *D. Martin Luthers Werke: Kritische Gesamtausgabe*, 3:276.26–27 (no. 3339), quoted in Hans Schwarz, *Eschatology* (Grand Rapids: Eerdmans, 2000), 403.

5. Kevin J. Madigan and Jon D. Levenson, *Resurrection: The Power of God for Christians and Jews* (New Haven: Yale University Press, 2009), 146.

6. Jon D. Levenson, *Resurrection and the Restoration of Israel: The Ultimate Victory of the God of Life* (New Haven: Yale University Press, 2006), 110, 124–27.

7. Levenson, *Resurrection and the Restoration of Israel*, 180.

8. C. S. Lewis, *Miracles* (San Francisco: HarperOne, 2015), 157.

9. This is eloquently unpacked in Adrio König, *The Eclipse of Christ in Eschatology: Toward a Christ-Centered Approach* (Grand Rapids: Eerdmans, 1989).

10. Here I draw upon the terminology and description of Sandra L. Richter, *The Epic of Eden: A Christian Entry into the Old Testament* (Downers Grove, IL: IVP Academic, 2008), 120–21.

11. Richter, *Epic of Eden*, 181.

12. Richter, *Epic of Eden*, 181.

13. Richter, *Epic of Eden*, 255.

14. Jon D. Levenson, *Sinai and Zion* (New York: HarperSanFrancisco, 1987), 168.

15. On Christ's judgment on the abuses of the temple of his day and his claim to embody the temple in his person, see Nicholas Perrin, *Jesus the Temple* (Grand Rapids: Baker Academic, 2010), 80–113.

16. Donald A. Hagner, *Matthew 14–28*, Word Biblical Commentary 33B (Nashville: Nelson, 1995). See also Heb. 10:19–20.

17. In this reading of the Lord's Prayer I am indebted to the work of Nicholas Perrin, who gives an insightful and much more extensive account of the temple context and implications for the Lord's Prayer in *Jesus the Priest* (Grand Rapids: Baker Academic, 2018), 28–53.

18. Christian Smith with Melinda Lundquist Denton, *Soul Searching: The Religious and Spiritual Lives of American Teenagers* (New York: Oxford University Press, 2009), 162–63.

19. My thanks to Emily Holehan for this illustration.

20. L. K. Crocker, "Temple, Solomon's," in *The Lexham Bible Dictionary*, ed. John D. Barry et al. (Bellingham, WA: Lexham, 2016).

21. John Calvin, *Commentary on the Epistles of Paul the Apostle to the Corinthians*, trans. John Pringle (Edinburgh: Calvin Translation Society, 1849), 2:205–6.

22. For a helpful exploration of the significance of the relevant Old Testament texts, and then of how the apostle Paul takes them up in his theology, see Matthew D. Aernie and Donald E. Hartley, *The Righteous and Merciful Judge: The Day of the Lord in the Life and Theology of Paul* (Bellingham, WA: Lexham, 2018), 25–54, 104–205.

23. P. D. James, *Original Sin* (New York: Knopf, 1995), 232.

24. Fleming Rutledge, *The Crucifixion: Understanding the Death of Jesus Christ* (Grand Rapids: Eerdmans, 2017), 322.

25. "Paul takes his reevaluation of his advantages in the flesh another radical step further by declaring, *I consider them garbage.* The word *garbage* denotes 'excrement, manure, . . . kitchen scraps.'" G. Walter Hansen, *The Letter to the Philippians* (Grand Rapids: Eerdmans, 2009), 236.

26. For a concise account of how union with Christ, in justification and sanctification, is central to Paul's theology of the Christian life and hope, see Grant Macaskill, *Living in Union with Christ: Paul's Gospel and Christian Moral Identity* (Grand Rapids: Baker Academic, 2019).

27. Jonathan Edwards, *Sermons and Discourses, 1720–1723*, ed. Wilson H. Kimnach, The Works of Jonathan Edwards (New Haven: Yale University Press, 1992), 10:313.

28. Edwards, *Sermons and Discourses*, 10:313–16.

29. Philip Roth, *Everyman* (New York: Vintage, 2007), 32.

30. Roth, *Everyman*, 51.

31. Roth, *Everyman*, 52.

32. Roth, *Everyman*, 169.

33. Roth, *Everyman*, 161.

## Conclusion

1. Peter C. Craigie, *Psalms 1–50*, Word Biblical Commentary 19 (Waco: Word, 1983), 310–11.

2. David Brooks, *The Second Mountain: The Quest for a Moral Life* (New York: Random House, 2019), xxii.

# Scripture Index

## Old Testament

### Genesis
1  199
1:26  35
3:19  180
3:22  51
3:24  193
12:2  184
15:5  184
15:6  184
17:10–11  77
18:14  184
25:8  53, 140

### Exodus
6:7  154
25:8  192
26:30  192

### Leviticus
12:3  77
17–26  50

### 1 Samuel
2:6  186

### 2 Samuel
14:14  158
15:14  36

### 2 Kings
4:34  186

### Job
1:21  61
9:22–23  61
10:8–9  63
12:10  61
12:14  63
19:7–9  65
21:13  162
38–39  70
38:4–7  70
42:16  70
42:17  50, 70

### Psalms
3  36, 37, 38
3:7  37, 40
6:2–3  135
8:4  155
22  29
22:1  30
24:3–4  26, 200
27:4  25, 131
33:8  89
39  216
39:2  16
39:4–5  79, 115, 214

40:2  37
62:1–2a  93
84:2  47, 191
84:10  191
86:1  22
86:13  22
88  22
88:3  22
88:4–5  40
88:12  22
90:1  86
90:2  86
90:4–6  85–86
90:10  86, 115
90:12  85
95  89
95:1–7  88
96:10–13  204
102:3  93
102:7–9  27
102:12  93
102:24  28
107:10  210
107:19–20  23
115:3–4  192
115:17  160
135:15–17  192
137:1  37, 40
137:3  37–38
137:7–9  38

139:8  47, 64
139:11–12  64
139:15  133
149:3  197

### Proverbs
1:12  41
10:4–6  140
27:20  41

### Ecclesiastes
2:11  46
5:15  131
6:7  69
9:4  69
9:6–7  69
9:10  160

### Isaiah
5:14  40–41
6:3  194
25:8  229n3
40:5  201
40:8  182
53:5  135
55:12  119

### Ezekiel
47:1–12  197

**Jonah**
1–2  24–26
1:3  24
2:2  24, 162
2:3–4  24
2:6  26
2:7  25

**Haggai**
2:6–7  201
2:6–9  201

**New Testament**
**Matthew**
3:4  78
5:1–12  147
5:3–5  139
5:8  139
5:44  197
6:10  196
6:19–34  147
6:25–28  143
6:32  143
6:33–34  143
12:40  75
19:16–30  139
21:12–13  195
25:1–13  139
27:46  30, 75
27:51  195

**Mark**
15:34  30, 75

**Luke**
1:7  209
1:68–69  210
1:78–79  210
6:46–49  139
23:43  157

**John**
1:14  30
2:18–22  30

2:19  195
10:10  134

**Romans**
1:20  171
5:12  50
6:3  164
6:5  164
8:17  139
8:22  11
8:23  11
8:23–25  19
8:26  12
8:34  205
8:38–39  157
14:8  14

**1 Corinthians**
1:22–23  135
1:25  135
3:16  198
6:17  200
6:19  198
6:19–20  200
13:12  17, 159, 168,
  180
15:25–28  209
15:26  50
15:42–58  176
15:54  150
16:22  196

**2 Corinthians**
4:7  199
4:10  137
4:11  199, 217
4:16  131
4:16–5:10  176
4:17  131
4:18  131
5:8  156
12:7  136
12:8  136

12:9  56, 135, 136,
  183
12:9b–10  137
12:10  135
13:12  159

**Galatians**
3:26–27  206
6:14  65

**Ephesians**
2:6–22  142
2:15  142

**Philippians**
1:10  206
1:20–21  206
1:20–26  176
1:21–23  156
2:7–8  57
3:8  206
3:8–9  206
3:21  206

**Colossians**
1:19–20  195, 205
1:20  205
1:27  19
3:1–4  142
3:3–4  220

**1 Thessalonians**
4–5  230n12
4:13–14  175
4:13–16  155
4:14  145
4:15  154
5:2  154, 155

**2 Thessalonians**
2:16–17  211

**1 Timothy**
6:15–16  71

**2 Timothy**
4:1  200

**Hebrews**
1:2–3  75
1:3  64
2:9  69, 92, 163
2:10–11  74
2:14–15  75, 93
2:15  84
5:7  64
5:8–9  57
8:5  192
9:12  64
11:1  159
11:13  213

**1 Peter**
1:3–5  140
1:6  139

**1 John**
1:5  66

**Revelation**
1:17–18  175
1:18  164
3:5  207
6:9–11  157
14:13  163
18:2  202
18:2–3  202
21:3  154, 155
21:3–4  196
21:4  155
21:22  209
21:23  19
21:27  202
22:1–2  215
22:13  171
22:20  196

# Subject Index

Alexander, Eben, 168
Apostles' Creed, 157, 171, 200, 224n4
*ars moriendi* (art of dying), 113–19
Augustine, 17, 59–66, 78

Bakker, Jim, 121–23, 130–31, 144
Bakker, Tammy Faye, 121–23, 144
Barth, Karl, 160
Becker, Ernest, 79–92
*Being Mortal* (Gawande), 114
Benedict of Nursia, 10–11, 83
Bonhoeffer, Dietrich, 81
Book of Common Prayer, 18
Bowler, Kate, 99, 229n24
Bush, Barbara, 152–53, 169
Bush, George H. W., 152–53, 169
Bush, George W., 152
Bush, Robin, 152–53, 157, 169, 174

Calvin, John, 79, 104, 199, 231n44
*Confessions* (Augustine), 62
Craigie, Peter, 216–17
cross, theology of the, 18–19, 64, 123–24, 134–46
"Crown Him with Many Crowns," 177–78
Crump, David, 138
cultural liturgies, 106–9, 216

Davidman, Joy, 38
day of the Lord, the, 18, 150–56, 171, 180, 193, 196, 201–7, 218–19, 232n22
death
 denial of. *See* Becker, Ernest
 as divine pedagogy, 55–59
 and embracing mortality, 11–14, 50, 54–59, 68–69, 86–93, 113–19, 129, 213–17
 as enemy, 30, 49–52, 59–66, 67–71
 fear of, 9–12, 30–34, 72–85, 105–13, 161
 as gift, 11–16, 49–59, 67–71, 116
 medicalization of, 31–34, 105–13
 as mystery, 62–63, 67–68, 158–62
 remembrance of, 10–11. See also *ars moriendi*
 as rest, 162–64
 stories of, 31–34, 52–59, 60–67, 101–3, 113, 161–62
 victory over, 92, 149–50, 158–60, 183–87, 195–96, 209
*Death, Grief, and Mourning* (Gorer), 39
de Grey, Aubrey, 9–10, 161
*Denial of Death, The* (Becker), 79–80, 90
Didion, Joan, 39, 44
Doughty, Caitlin, 114
Duhigg, Charles, 35–36
dwelling place. *See* temple

Edwards, Jonathan, 10–11, 207
Eubank, David, 13
Eubank, Karin, 13
*Everyman* (Roth), 208

freedom
  from slavery to fear of death, 69–71,
    74–76, 92–93. *See also* death: and
    embracing mortality
  to live small/in the moment/as creatures,
    76–79, 87–89, 118, 175, 179–81, 213–20
Freud, Sigmund, 80, 82, 159
funerals, 31–34, 55, 60–67, 109

Gawande, Atul, 47, 114, 127–28
"Give Me Jesus," 164
*God in the Dock* (Lewis), 174
*Good Place, The* (TV show), 197
Gorer, Geoffrey, 39
Gregory I (pope), 168

"Hallelujah" chorus (Handel), 182–83,
  187
healing, theology of, 131, 136–46
heaven, 16, 181–82, 190–209
  as family reunion, 151–54, 169–70
  as theophany, 154–57, 170–71
  *See also* temple; union with Christ
*Heaven Is for Real* (Burpo), 166–68
*Heaven Promise, The* (McKnight), 168
Heidelberg Catechism
  Q & A 1  145–47
  Q & A 44  30
hope, theology of
  Christian, 11, 34, 61, 68, 73, 86, 92, 97,
    132, 190–95, 213–15, 219
  and infertility, 183–90
  *See also* kingdom prosperity; prosperity
    gospel; resurrection; union with
    Christ
Hopkins, Gerard Manley, 213

intermediate state, 149–57, 162–64, 230n13,
  230n20
Irenaeus, 55–59

James, P. D., 67, 203
Jesus Christ
  cry of dereliction, 29–30, 52, 75
  as King, 16, 19, 35, 71, 76, 92–93, 97, 119,
    124, 139, 144–46, 150–51, 177, 182–86,
    196, 199–211
  as pioneer in suffering and death, 30, 52,
    57, 63–76, 92, 164, 214
  as priest, 63–65, 146, 163–64, 186, 193–95,
    206
  and Sheol, 30, 52, 57, 63–65, 75, 224n4
  as temple. *See* temple: Christ as
  *See also New Testament citations in the
    Scripture index*; union with Christ
Job, 141, 207
Jordan, Michael, 122–23
judgment, divine, 157, 170–71, 180, 200–
  209. *See also* day of the Lord, the
Junius, Franciscus, 17

Kalanithi, Paul, 85
Kapic, Kelly, 117
Kenyon, E. W., 141–42
Kierkegaard, Søren, 81–82
King, Martin Luther, Jr., 81, 205
kingdom prosperity, 144–47
Kugel, James, 149

lament, 22–30, 61–66, 135, 141, 160, 215
Levenson, Jon, 27, 184–85, 194
Lewis, C. S., 38, 174, 186
*Life after Life* (Moody), 165
Lindbeck, George, 126
Lord's Prayer, 16, 124, 128, 195–96
Luther, Martin, 115–17, 119, 137, 182

Madigan, Kevin, 184
Manichees, 78, 80

McKnight, Scot, 168–69
medicine, modern, 98–113
  and aging prevention, 9–10
  "alternative medicine," 42–43
  and extreme measures, 127–45
memorial services. *See* funerals
*Messiah* (Handel), 201. *See also* "Hallelujah" chorus
"Mighty Fortress Is Our God, A" (Luther), 119
*Miracles* (Lewis), 186
Modeh Ani (prayer), 181
Moody, Raymond, 165–66

near death experiences (NDEs), 164–71, 174
*90 Minutes in Heaven* (Piper), 166
Newton, Maud, 167

Paul (apostle). *See individual Pauline letters in the Scripture index*
Pelagius, 59
Pit, the. *See* Sheol
Plantinga, Alvin, 170
Polycarp, 58
Post, Emily, 39–40
Prince, Joseph, 134–36
prosperity gospel, 121–46
  and flourishing and health, 131–35
  and healing miracles, 128–31, 134–38, 141
  as realized new creation, 141
  as opposed to true kingdom prosperity/shalom, 123–24, 142–46
  medical. *See* medicine, modern: and extreme measures

Radner, Ephraim, 54, 105–8
Ramesses II, 160–61
Rank, Otto, 82
*Rejoicing in Lament* (Billings), 14, 51
resurrection, 15–19, 30, 109, 116–19, 140–43, 149–64, 169–75, 177–83, 190–97, 204–11

Richter, Sandra, 193
Roth, Philip, 208
Routledge, Clay, 172
Rutledge, Fleming, 203

Sandberg, Sheryl, 29
Sheol, 18, 21–47, 137, 162
  as consuming, 40–45
  and control, loss of, 34–40
  and idols, 190
  land of dead, 22, 162
*Smarter Faster Better* (Duhigg), 35
Smith, James K. A., 106–7, 109, 118. *See also* cultural liturgies
*Smoke Gets in Your Eyes* (Doughty), 114
*Supernatural* (Routledge), 172

Taylor, Charles, 15
temple, 18, 24–26, 66, 163, 190–96, 218
  as body of believers/the church, 65, 198–99
  Christ as, 16, 30, 65, 154, 191–99, 206, 218. *See also* union with Christ
  purity, 77–78
  tabernacle, 25, 192, 193, 197
terror management theory (TMT), 72–75, 171–76
Thielicke, Helmut, 62
Thiselton, Anthony, 159
*To Heaven and Back* (Neal), 166
Tolkien, J. R. R., 51
Tutu, Desmond, 205

union with Christ, 74–76, 142–43, 154–64, 182, 196–209

Wallace, David Foster, 178–79, 205
Wiman, Christian, 41
Wisdom literature, 140–41

Zaleski, Carol, 160, 168

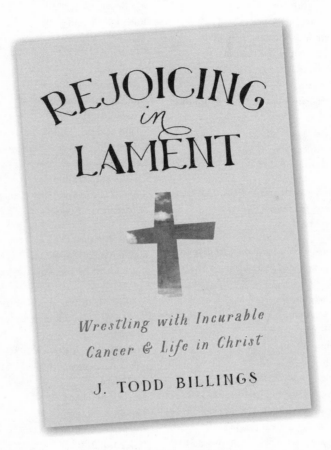
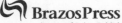